Living in

ROME

Bruno Racine

Photographs by Alain Fleischer

Translated from the French by Deke Dusinberre

Flammarion

Editorial Direction
Ghislaine Bavoillot

Editorial Management
Sandrine Balihaut Martin

Translation
Deke Dusinberre
Bernard Wooding (Connoisseur's Guide)

Copyediting
Bernard Wooding

Graphic design (English edition)
Laurent Calot and Emmanuel Laparra
for GUDUL prod.

Graphic Design (French edition)
Marc Walter / Bela Vista

Production
Murielle Vaux

© Flammarion, Paris 1999
ISBN: 2-0801-3675-5
Numéro d'édition: FA 3675-02
Dépot légal: December 1999

Printed in Italy by Canale

Contents

The Charm of Rome

"Rome is a major capital and a minor town," commented Stendhal in 1828. Since that time, the ancient city of the popes has become the capital of unified Italy (1870) and changed in scale. It has reclaimed the fallow land within the walls begun in 271 c.e. by Emperor Aurelian, and has spread into the once deserted, melancholy parts of "rural Rome" so dear to many generations of artists and writers. Yet Rome still retains the uniqueness which lent it so much charm in the early nineteenth century. No other city anywhere, even in Italy, is quite like it. Venice is a magnificent, moving tribute to its past glory, defending relics inch by inch; Florence, with all its masterpieces, must constantly live down the fact that it has been stripped of its former rank of capital, as must the sublimely chaotic Naples. Rome, meanwhile, enjoys a unique privilege—time has its own special quality there, whether considered from the standpoint of history or from that of everyday life. To a degree unmatched anywhere else, the passing of thirty centuries has intimately wedded grandeur on the one hand to familiarity on the other.

If Rome is the city par excellence where life is sweet—can you imagine Fellini shooting *La Dolce Vita* in London, New York or Paris?—that is due to a paradox: no other place in the world is so steeped in time, deposited in layers like some geological phenomenon, lending a patina to marble and a sheen to surfaces; yet no other place displays so much detachment toward time, as though eternity were its birthright. The constant sense of urgency that characterizes the planet's great metropolises is much weaker in Rome, although not unknown. Or rather, it only appears in spurts, in the feverish preparations for a given festivity such as the grand jubilee year 2000. Long-time residents, of course, will inevitably mention (with a pang of nostalgia) the days when you could still find a parking space in front of your bank on Via del Corso, as American writer Milton Gendel wittily put it. Outside events barely affected the pace of daily life back then, when a long midday siesta still divided the day in two—a custom that is steadily losing ground.

Preceding pages:
Late-nineteenth-century photographs of Rome—the Colosseum, the Arch of Constantine, Castel Sant'Angelo across the Tiber and Piazza Navona.
Left: The Forum.
(Marc Walter Collection)

Above: No other city affirms the grandeur of the past as forcefully as Rome, where ancient sculpture dots gardens, adorns courtyards and graces facades. Rome cannot escape its past, yet also knows that time is fleeting.

Left: Despite its seven hills, Rome is a horizontal, compact city. Although only a few large squares provide gaps for light to penetrate, the holy city is a place where heaven and earth seem drawn together. This upward thrust is symbolized by the domes of Christian Rome, whether squat or tall.

Rome suffers from the same problems as all major cities, namely pollution, inadequate housing, transportation and town planning. They are all the more difficult to resolve since maneuvering room has been greatly restricted by the weight of historic heritage and by successive delays. With a certain fatalism,

The charm of Rome comes from the pleasure of strolling through the city at random, say in the maze of narrow streets around Campo Marzio, cluttered by the tables of an unpretentious *trattoria* or by the gilded frames spilling from a restorer's excessively tiny workshop. It means thrilling to the sudden, haphazard emergence of all those squares, some of them theatrical and majestic, others mere breathing spaces placed under a Madonna's watchful gaze. Everybody can relive, in their own way, the amazement of Anita Ekberg in *La Dolce Vita* when she suddenly comes upon the Fontana di Trevi after wandering lost through deserted alleyways. The charm of Rome stems from all those fountains scattered everywhere, traces of antiquity's obsession with channeling water into the city, both above and below ground. Although Rome is certainly a big city—noisy and sometimes stifling—it has not lost completely the rural feel pictured in those eighteenth- and nineteenth-century landscape paintings called *vedute*. Both within and without the old Roman walls, vast green spaces are reminders that the papal city occupied only a fraction of the former imperial capital, the *caput mundi*. And for anyone viewing the city from a height, the neighborhoods built after unification are topped with a multitude of terrace gardens, as though nature has risen off the ground in order to get nearer to the sun (the resurgence of a timeless aspiration which even during imperial days had girded the roofs of Rome with greenery).

The eye is constantly drawn to Rome's countless architectural details. It can be fun to identify the emblems of popes or spot the whimsical carvings that decorate even utilitarian structures such as fountains. The city has a truly inexhaustible repertoire of forms.

Rome may love grandeur, but it detests affectation—there is nothing haughty about its elegance. Antique dealers or cabinet makers will casually spill into the street if their premises are too small. Aloofness is not part of Rome's sense of hierarchy.

Romans endlessly discuss the inefficiency of a *burocrazia* which does its best to complicate life.

Yet for outsiders, the city's tradition of urbanity seems to soften the harsh edges of modern life. Travelers arriving in Rome are nearly always struck by the politeness and spontaneous kindness of initial encounters— neither the grumbling mask adopted by so many Parisian waiters and taxi drivers (perhaps out of shyness), nor the impeccable but sometimes disdainful decorum of London.

Founded as the city of seven hills, Rome has always hosted a constant dialogue between the heavens and the earth. The most visible signs of its thrust toward light are the columns and obelisks inherited from antiquity, and the campaniles and domes of Christian Rome. Bernini's celebrated glory of angels in the apse of Saint Peter's is the most famous—and probably most lavish—depiction of this communion of the heavenly and the earthly, but there are thousands of others, no less touching if very modest, scattered throughout the city. Visitors are inevitably struck by the multitude of churches, chapels and oratories, yet holy awe is uncommon in Rome. Even the great basilicas, set in imposing squares, do not create a feeling of distance or remove; they are humanized by the statues crowning them, such as those on San Giovanni in Laterano, enlivened by a compelling sense of movement. Most churches are intimate in feeling—sometimes spare, sometimes glittery like a reception room. They flow easily into the street, becoming a part of everyday life, a place of passage as much as a place of prayer. They host all major family events, and for weddings will be hung in red velvet and bedecked with flowers.

A Roman park, street or square would be unthinkable without a fountain. The city's ancient obsession with water prompted French author Julien Gracq to describe it as an "aquatic coven." This picture, though a treat for the eyes, cannot convey the peaceful sound of splashing water or its cooling effect.

In the end, Rome's charm must be experienced rather than merely described. This may not occur immediately, as Stendhal had already noted in his day. It may not happen at all to many overly eager tourists who allot just three days to get through Saint Peter's, the Vatican museums, the Forum, the Colosseum, the Pantheon and the Spanish Steps. A hurried visitor might just be stricken by love at first sight, but he or she is equally likely to gag on the heavy diet of artistic riches.

The city's charm is more likely to be felt by people who discover it step by step, without a stopwatch, far from paths trodden by the flood of tourists. Appreciating the good life in Rome also means joining the good-humored lines that form in front of the delightfully old-fashioned movie theaters in Testaccio on spring and summer evenings,

Although its narrow streets traditionally shade it from the sun, Rome has blossomed with rooftop terraces in the twentieth century, providing new and unusual views not only of major landmarks but also of other roofs. Life in Rome alternates pleasantly between sun and shade, close-up views and distant vistas.

With its hundreds of churches, some fifteen centuries old, Rome is punctuated by religious celebrations both public and private. For weddings and formal occasions, churches are often draped in richly colored velvet (right), a lavishness that may seem unrefined next to the mysterious shimmer of mosaics

in the half-light of old basilicas (above).

later moving on to a nearby bar for a drink with friends. It means taking the time every morning in the café to chat about everything and nothing with the waiter who, should you lack the cash needed for a taxi to the airport, will lend you the money until the next time you drop by. Outsiders must take the time to let themselves be seduced, becoming slowly—and permanently—impregnated. Such grace can befall anyone. As Montaigne wrote over four centuries ago, "It is the commonest city in the world, where foreignness and national differences count the least . . . ; everyone feels at home."

Over the centuries, Rome has always aroused grand emotions, whether triggered by the grandeur of classical antiquity or by the effervescence of baroque days, whether seeking the twilight of poetic ruins or the sunshine of shimmering fountains.

Whereas French writer Chateaubriand, on hearing the bells of Saint Peter's while standing beneath the arches of the Colosseum, was moved by the correspondence between Christian Rome and pagan Rome, the likes of Edward Gibbon and Gustave Flaubert resented seeing the most grandiose vestige of the Roman Empire spoiled by "processions of monks." Hippolyte Taine, on seeing the Pantheon, felt transported back to the triumph of Augustus, imagining he heard "the solemn chant of verses when Virgil celebrated the glory of that great day"; but he only felt that thrill if he willfully overlooked the "dirty, baroque square where wretched hackneys park, on the lookout for foreigners." To modern eyes this same square, with its faded colors and careless invasion of cafés, has become emblematic of Rome's pleasant lifestyle.

Every period (and every individual) sees the city through its own infatuations and prejudices, its own obsessions and phobias. Whence inevitable contradictions. Pier Paolo Pasolini, who knew every aspect of Rome— including the most sordid—could only say: "Rome is certainly the most beautiful city in Italy, if not the world. But it is also the ugliest. And the most welcoming, the most overwrought, the richest, the poorest . . ." Love of Rome is an ongoing miracle that reconciles believers and atheists, classical rigor and baroque exuberance, attachment to the past and passion for life.

May this book, the fruit of a passion born thirty-five years ago, deliver all that feeling intact.

Right: The church of San Giovanni a Porta Latina stands on its own, not far from the spot where Saint John allegedly emerged unscathed from boiling oil. By adopting the gound plan and columns of ancient Rome's basilicas, Christian Rome established an architectural bridge across a religious break.

Stone
and Color

ROME'S STONE, BRICK AND PLASTER SHIMMER IN COUNTLESS HUES, DEPENDING ON TIME OF DAY AND SEASON. THE CITY'S INCOMPARABLE LIGHT, EXTOLLED BY GOETHE AND STENDHAL, IS ENDLESSLY SEDUCTIVE—ESPECIALLY AT SUNSET, WHEN ALL OF ROME SEEMS ABLAZE.

Every city is associated with a vital feature that conveys the depths of its soul. Memories of Paris are inseparable from its sky (a special gray which echoes the color of rooftops and reflects the surface of the Seine), just as Venice seems to express itself completely in the poetic qualities of water. Rome is first of all a city of stone, founded on rock by a landed people: *Tu es Petrus, et super hanc petram aedificabo ecclesiam meam* ("Thou art Peter [rock], and upon this rock I will build my church"). The scriptural pun on *Petrus* and *petram*, written in giant gold letters inside Saint Peter's, implies a unified reality, one that is simultaneously physical and spiritual: divinity is incarnate on earth, and faith is a rock. Christianity lent a new dimension to pagan Rome's pretensions to universality, but the materials it used to express its mission were the same. Thus despite the religious rupture provoked by Peter and Paul, the eye receives an impression of continuity in Rome. This is due to stone in all its variations—precious marble or modest brick—but also to light. Rome's poetic qualities are not built on an opaque substance, but on one that glows.

THE PINK BRICK OF OSTIA

Anyone wanting to appreciate the link between the ancient city and the modern one will not be wasting time by going first to Ostia. Rome's port during the republican and imperial eras, Ostia eventually silted up and was abandoned. Unjustly—if luckily—it does not enjoy the same tourist reputation as Pompeii and Herculaneum. Nor does the slow decline of this merchant, working-class town have the same tragic dimension as the cities wiped from the map by the eruption of Vesuvius. And yet the ruins of Ostia produce the same lasting impression. The absence of crowds make a visit all the more worthwhile; even during the high season, only a handful

Below: Brilliant white against the deep blue winter sky, this antique mask adorns a rooftop along the Tiber, perpetuating the tradition of ornaments called acroteria. Rome's ubiquitous relics of the past, even when simple or worn, lend everyday life a grandeur unmatched elsewhere.

Preceding pages: The tiled floor of the church of Santa Maria in Trastevere.

Right: Marble, peperino and brick—three materials used extensively in antiquity—are still emblematic of Rome. Peperino, a volcanic rock found abundantly in Latium, was both easy to carve and remarkably robust. Brick, even more economical, was more or less indestructible. Such austere masonry was adorned in marble ranging from the commonest to the rarest varieties, a symbol of luxury for which ancient Romans acquired a taste as their conquests grew.

Left: Many sculptures from the ruins of Ostia recall the affluence of imperial Rome's port city. The play of light and shadow on the highly worked drapery of this statue enhances the beauty of the marble, set against a masonry wall long since stripped of its embellishments.

Ostia has been intelligently reconstructed using fragments found at the site. The shaft of this column is of cipollino, a variety of marble highly prized by Romans but no longer found today. The skill of ancient stone carvers can be seen in the acanthus leaves on the capital and the delicate patterns on the cornice. Such highly refined decoration covered robust brick masonry, whose ease of use encouraged architectural boldness.

of strollers or passersby get beyond the famous Piazzale delle Corporazioni where merchants set up shop in ancient times. Yet there are rewards for anyone who wanders down the maze of streets and buildings in surrounding neighborhoods, making a way through the high, fragrant grass. Ostia's main streets have retained their basalt paving stones, imposing slabs whose surfaces are worn and gouged by the wheels of chariots. This dark gray basalt can still be found in modern Rome, usually in the form of small square or irregular cobbles called *sanpietrini*.

Once you lift your eyes in Ostia, however, brick is king. It should be seen at sunset to appreciate its warm glow, even if that means playing hide-and-seek with the whistle-blowing guards who try to drive visitors toward the exit. Roman bricks do not have the dark red color typical of England and the Netherlands. Pale, tending toward pink or yellow ocher, they supplied the Romans with an ideal, inexpensive, uniform building material. Brick was as indestructible as peperino (the dark volcanic rock bequeathed by Etruscan builders) and less subject to erosion than travertine (a white stone whose surface is pitted with countless small holes), two materials nevertheless employed extensively both then and now; and nothing was simpler than masking the modesty of brick with magnificent facings. In Ostia, brick's coppery backdrop enhances the traces of marble and mosaic found more or less everywhere. Here, a bar still seems ready to receive customers seeking refreshment; there, a column-maker's warehouse still has

shafts lying amid wild mint; further on, a dwelling has a series of small salons decorated in marble of every color. Everything points to a lifestyle that has vanished, yet was not unlike our own. A perfectly simple Christian basilica is very moving—it is almost as though you can still hear Saint Augustine chatting with his mother, Saint Monica. That was roughly when Ostia's story came to an end, just as Christian Rome's was about to take off.

The road from Ostia to Rome passes through the site chosen by Mussolini for the Universal Exposition of Rome (EUR). Despite the bombastic inscription engraved on the main building—visible even from the highway—the architecture conveys distinct power and sobriety, its coldness tempered by travertine. With its arched bays, the

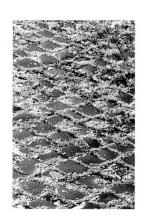

Ancient Romans paved their roads with large blocks of basalt that still display the ruts made by the wheels of chariots. The same stone, cut into smaller, irregular cubes, is still used to cobble many streets in Rome (despite the increasing use of asphalt). Grass grows abundantly between such cobblestones, which are charmingly called *sanpietrini*.

Left: The ruins of Ostia offer visitors many clues to life in ancient Rome. All that remains of this portico is a granite column, a few brick niches separated by fine marble columns, and the fragrant weeds growing in every crack.

Above: Roman engineers invented roof vaulting. Thanks to extensive use of brick, they could erect buildings several stories high, some of which were forerunners of the modern apartment block. Long vaulted passageways ringed the ground floor of these buildings, often built around garden-courtyards.

This lion mask (below), a common emblem in antiquity that has never gone out of fashion, contrasts with the austere rigor of the Pyramid of Caius Cestius, a rich Roman who died two thousand years ago. His strange funeral memorial (right), inspired by the conquest of Egypt, is

27 meters high and overlooks graves in the Protestant Cemetery, which contains the remains of two great English poets, Keats and Shelley.

building seems to come straight from a painting by Giorgio de Chirico, yet at the same time evokes the pure forms of some predella by a Sienese or Florentine old master. Rome is re-entered via the Porta San Paolo, which sums up the city in its own way: Aurelian's ancient wall has been largely gutted, leaving just two fine brick towers flanking the antique passageway; opposite is a modern subway entrance, ennobled by a portico and pediment in pure classical style; meanwhile, the strange Pyramid of Caius Cestius, with its fine silhouette and white marble facing, adds a touch of phoney Egyptian exoticism. The pyramid reflects the Romans' attraction for the Orient shortly after their conquest of Egypt. All around reigns a pleasant—and equally Roman— disorder, but traffic, despite a certain casualness concerning the rules of right-of-way, manages to avoid gridlock.

TANGLES OF STONE

It is tempting to assert that nothing is ever destroyed in Rome, that everything new is made from the old. Ancient buildings, when not simply converted, served as quarries for nearly twelve centuries. Pagan Rome turned into Christian Rome with the greatest of ease, if at the cost of irreplaceable losses (the Pantheon's bronzes, for example, melted down to make the baldachin for Saint Peter's). The church of Santa Maria in Cosmedin, famous for its *bocca della verità* (a mask with a "mouth of truth" that serves as the oldest known lie detector), was thus set between the columns of an ancient grain depot dating from the empire. More or less everywhere across town, churches founded in the first centuries of the Christian era display the traces of the multiple additions, transformations and renovations executed through the ages: ancient columns (more or less mismatched), mosaics from the Carolingian period, thirteenth-century tiling (magnificent inlays of medieval colored marble, executed by the Cosmati dynasty of artists), carved and gilded ceilings from the Renaissance, and chapels and decoration

Right: The Markets of Trajan at the foot of the Quirinal Hill are a perfect illustration of Roman genius: a sense of practicality combined with the ability to improve models inherited from classical Greece. These brick arcades still seem ready to welcome merchants' stalls and throngs of customers. In the foreground are the ruins of the imperial Forum, whose excavation required the demolition of very old neighborhoods. The street behind the Markets of Trajan, meanwhile, retains its medieval appearance. The palaces and towers were built right into the antique remains. Here the Casa dei Cavalieri di Roma, with its fine arcade, overlooks Trajan's Forum, adding to Rome's timeless tangle of stone.

Left: Whereas life came to a sudden halt in Pompeii and Herculaneum, Ostia died a slow death. Thus the warehouse of a column merchant was never completely emptied; shafts of white marble, stacked like cannons, still lie among the weeds.

A fountain flows into a tub-like basin through an antique mask, whose human face seems to be changing into a shell. This fine composition decorates the forecourt of the basilica of Santa Sabina.

Right: The Romans invented modern town planning. To prevent construction on riverbanks subject to flooding, the government established "no building zones" (*non aedificandi*). One of the boundary markers, still in place, can be seen in the basement of Palazzo Farnese.

which date from from the Counter-Reformation and baroque days.

Many churches incorporated vestiges of earlier buildings above or below ground. Few, in short, seem to have survived the centuries with little alteration, and these remain special places where the early days of Christianity can be felt with particular impact. Yet on top of the Aventine Hill sits Santa Sabina, founded in the fifth century and restored in 1936 to its medieval state, when Pope Honorius III allocated the church to Saint Dominic. Boasting twenty-four ancient columns of flawless Greek marble, all in the finest Corinthian order—not mismatched, as in so many other churches built of bric-a-brac—Santa Sabina is a hymn to light, which is filtered by high alabaster

windows. Rather than the anguish of damnation distilled by so many dark churches in other climes, here there radiates the certainty of salvation. The mosaic on the inner wall shows Christ uniting the faithful descended from Judaism and paganism. The church itself is a moving demonstration of a perfect synthesis of ancient art and early Christianity, of Greece and the Gospels, of stone and light—the white marble columns, the floor paved in red porphyry and green serpentine, and the mosaic in gold and blue all form a most harmonious symphony.

Whereas Santa Sabina creates a feeling of unity, elsewhere there are amazing tangles and layers, notably on the Caelian Hill, as seen in the basilica of Santi Giovanni e Paolo and especially the basilica of San Clemente. The latter incorporates two ancient houses, a temple dedicated to Mithra (a brief rival of Christ), an initial church burned by the Normans in the ninth century (still covered with magnificent, if half-vanished, mosaics) and finally the "modern" church with its thirteenth-century mosaic (perhaps the most magnificent in Rome), its Renaissance frescoes and its wonderful coffered ceiling. Other surprises are to be found in the basements of palaces and more modest residences: the cellars of the Palazzo Farnese contain major antique relics such as a boundary marker that has stood unmoved for two thousand years and a mosaic known as "the acrobat"; the Villa Medici encroaches on an imperial palace and a large, late-empire cistern (whose dark red color has survived). The convent of

Right: Magnificent effects of light play on spiraling columns in the vestibule of Santa Sabina on the Aventine Hill. This fifth-century basilica is one of the most charming in Rome. The many antique remains, such as columns, sarcophagi and Christian inscriptions, help to create a serene, meditative atmosphere. A sense of human frailty yet also of immortality is etched into Rome's stones, whose smooth surfaces reflect light in such a way that they seem to glow from within.

Trinità dei Monti was built on a network of cellars that contain numerous earthen jars of oil which still seem ready for use. It no longer seems surprising that today you can dine underground in the Roman vaults of Pompey's Theater, or that the basement of a bar on Via di Campo Marzio, near the parliament, contains vestiges of a gigantic sundial dating from the Augustan age (the dial's shadow was cast by the Egyptian obelisk now standing in Piazza del Popolo).

Rome stubbornly seeks to demonstrate, through its very stones, that life triumphs over death. The occasionally incongruous use of remnants from the past is not designed to spark romantic reveries at the sight of poignant ruins of bygone eras, nor is it a moralizing reminder of the disasters that have befallen the city throughout its long history. The most recent catastrophe was the sadly notorious sack of Rome by the Connétable de Bourbon's imperial army in 1527; since then, there has been the flowering of the late Renaissance and Counter-Reformation, then that of baroque art, which effaced earlier destructions a hundred times over. The army dispatched by France in 1849 to restore Pius IX to the papal throne produced no damage (the French cannonball lodged in the outer wall of San Pietro in Montorio, on the Janiculum Hill, seems more like a droll curiosity, whatever the commemorative inscription may say). And thanks to the intercession of Pius XII, the bombs of World War II largely spared the city, notwithstanding civilian victims and the damage caused to the fine

basilica of San Lorenzo Fuori le Mura. More or less everywhere, a trained eye will note antique souvenirs in the walls of houses of both rich and poor—for example, a mask set in a corner, or columns poking out from thick masonry. This practice—which might be called natural—reflects an optimistic view of existence and contributes to Rome's unique sense of lifestyle.

The famous painter Ingres was first a resident and later director of the French Academy in Rome, where he followed an age-old custom by having antique sculptures set right into the walls of the Academy's headquarters in the Villa Medici. Perhaps the sight of this studious character was designed to remind artists of the virtues of meditation.

Left: Although mutilated, this small replica of some Greek masterpiece set into the walls of the Villa Medici retains unique power. The faded color of the wall brings out the modeling of the figure, which still bears traces of red paint. The very simple setting felicitously combines classical ideals with a romantic vision.

Right: This composition in the grounds of the Villa Medici, at the end of a lane that must have been trod by the likes of Berlioz and Carpeaux, is quintessentially Roman. It displays a sense of architecture in which power is combined with gracefulness, while vestiges of the past—statues which may be copies or casts, a fountain flowing into an antique sarcophagus—are always placed at the service of the present. It is easy to imagine generations of artists coming to this cooling fountain. The ocher sheen evoking sunset, although not as ancient as it might seem, remains Rome's color par excellence.

HERALDRY IN STONE

That lifestyle exudes a certain atmosphere of nobility and grandeur—another legacy of antiquity—also reflected in the local enthusiasm for (some might say obsession with) commemorative inscriptions, usually in Latin (a lapidary language if ever there was one). At every turn, plaques of marble or travertine boast of construction—modest or grandiose—undertaken by popes. The trained eye will immediately recognize the coats of arms of grand families that produced popes and cardinals—the Farnese fleur-de-lis (sometimes confused with that of French kings), the Medici "pills" (as Stendhal called them), the della Rovere oak, the Barberini bees, the Borghese dragon and

eagle, and the Doria Pamphili dove and olive branch. The proliferation of these emblems, combined with Saint Peter's keys and tiara, is one of Rome's distinctive signs. It is not surprising that they grace church pediments and palace balconies, but they can even be found on modest utilitarian projects, urban improvements and all kinds of repairs executed down through the centuries. The city thus begins to look like a book of heraldry. But that does not mean it wallows in nostalgia for the past; Rome never underwent an upheaval as radical and violent as the revolution that shook France, and it was only in the 1960s, during Paul VI's papacy, that the grand families of papal Rome (some of them nearly a thousand years old, such as the Colonnas, Orsinis and Massimos) lost the honorific offices at the Holy See that had traditionally been their prerogative. To the extent that the constraints of modern life permit, they continue to maintain a living presence in many old palaces and grace society circles, such as the hunting and chess clubs.

Rome manages to lend grandeur to everything. The most everyday object can thus find itself magnified. Sewer spouts, for example, are marked with four letters that once made the ancient world tremble: SPQR (*Senatus Populusque Romanus*). Or take the plaques supposedly enjoining residents from "fouling" (*fare immondezze*) the streets: most of them were very finely engraved in the eighteenth century and almost never repeat the same wording, as though they were an exercise in rhetorical virtuosity. Irony can be

Papal Rome, with a court unlike any other, was a city where the art of appearances was not to be disdained. Churches and palaces bear the escutcheons of the grand prelates and aristocrats who built or embellished them. These blazons were simple and somewhat stiff in the fifteenth century, but as the baroque period approached they became animated by an increasingly extravagant sense of movement, as illustrated by this example.

Two unusually fanciful mermaids hold the papal coat of arms belonging to Pius IX, whose long reign coincided with Italian unification. At the outset he had been a darling of liberals, but after calling on the French army to crush the 1848 Roman Republic he became a tireless castigator of "modern errors."

Right: Pope Paul V Borghese encouraged the rise of baroque art, as this powerful architecture testifies. The rules of classicism were broken by its bold indentations and the figure reclining on a curved pediment. The Borghese eagle perches on a capital like a bird of prey, making the emblem of Savoy—added later to the balcony—seem petty.

PAVLVS · V · PONT · MAX

AN · SAL · MDCXV · PONTIF · X

Travertine is perhaps the Roman stone par excellence. More common than marble yet more noble than brick, over time it acquires a sheen that tempers its pitted surface. Rome abhors uniformity, which is why no facade or wall is completely devoid of ornamental relief. The Borghese eagle (top, right) discreetly enhances a lintel, while the Farnese fleur-de-lis emerges from a perfect sphere *(bottom, center)*. The coat of arms of Pius IV, one of the four Medici popes (bottom, right), still seems restrained compared to the extravagances of the baroque era—an escutcheon dripping with curves like some freakish shell (bottom, left), or the garlands and angels springing from the church of Santi Vincenzo e Anastasio, built by Cardinal Mazarin (top, left).

read into both the solemnity of the injunction and the gravity of the punishment. Does that mean the wording of the law was more an object of aesthetic contemplation than an order to be taken seriously?

That question might still be asked today, prompted for example by the sight of a *vigile urbano*, a white-gloved traffic cop choreographing the flow of cars into Piazza Venezia at the foot of Via del Corso with all the flair of a ballet master. A Roman friend told me about a policeman who stopped him one day when he was riding his Vespa with his girlfriend behind him, heading the wrong way up a one-way street. The officer of the law never opened his mouth, but pointed his forefinger to the one-way sign, then used the forefinger and middle finger to indicate the illegality of two persons astride the scooter, only to wave them off with the back of the hand, not even obliging them to turn around! And in what other city in the world would you see a garage crowned by the inscription E*st omnium vicissitudo* ("All is change")? Or a greeting placed above an otherwise ordinary doorway: *Laeta patet amicis* ("Opens joyfully to friends")? Or this piece of publicity, worthy of a real estate ad targeting classical scholars, on a building in Piazza della Trinità dei Monti, high above the city: H*ic purior aer, late hic prospectus in Urbem* ("Unpolluted air, great view of city")?

ROME'S TRUE COLORS

For a long time now, Rome has stretched beyond the original seven hills—Capitoline, Palatine, Aventine, Caelian, Quirinal, Esquiline, and Viminal. It has incorporated Pincio and Janiculum Hills, not to mention more recent extensions. Those vantage points are the best places to appreciate the beauty of the light in Rome, which is constantly changing. You have to see the white, painful light of summer (suddenly extinguished, on occasion, by the approach of an extraordinarily powerful storm); you have to experience the warm tones of spring and fall (and of sunset) which make ocher walls vibrate and turn white marble or travertine golden; you should also see how

Below: Reportedly introduced by Piedmontese victors after 1870, the red-ocher wash covering walls has become Rome's favorite color. Fortunately, it is unlikely to be completely eliminated by the recent concern for historical accuracy which favors the paler colors of earlier centuries.

Left: Depicted in mid-action, this angel above Piazza di Trevi is carrying the "glory," or halo of golden beams, that baroque artists bestowed upon images of God and saints. In contrast to the stunning glory in the apse of Saint Peter's, this one is a wonderful demonstration of Rome's special familiarity with everything divine.

Rome's signature is obvious in such ordinary yet special details as a window with a fine carved architrave, green shutters that stand out against a warm-hued wall, and a climbing plant that clings to every protuberance. Seen on Piazza Campitelli at the foot of the Capitoline Hill.

Left: Vicolo del Divino Amore, in the heart of Rome's historic center, is typical of the old neighborhoods. The strong architecture of the church underscores the verticality of this group of buildings, combined with a diversity of horizontal planes. The street provides an opening for light without totally eliminating the shade which is so vital in summer.

the winter sun peaks, so to speak, at rooftop level, driving its warmth deep into rooms that are so carefully shuttered from its rays in summer. Thus from high on hills or rooftops, the gaze can take in the overall color of the city and its infinite shades, dominated by ocher hues—or maybe I should say "once dominated" by ocher. The fact is that two opposing camps now differ over Rome's "true" colors. Everyone was accustomed to the warm tones of the ocher washes that were assumed to be the city's eternal color. So much so that the immaculate white of the notorious Vittoriano (a monument to the glory of national unity whose great mass overwhelms the church of Santa Maria in Aracoeli and the Capitoline Hill) was perceived as bad taste. So much so that the absence of those colors in old depictions of the city went unnoticed; of course, everyone recognized the Palazzo del Quirinale in the background of Ingres' admirable portrait of the painter F. M. Granet, but for a long time its whiteness seemed to be a question of poetic license or artistic whim rather than accurate observation. Only specialists knew that prior to the second half of the nineteenth century Rome dressed only in pale colors—ivory white or "heavenly" blue.

As the jubilee year 2000 approached, the city decided to transform itself. With remarkable energy and determination, almost all public buildings were restored, while private owners were encouraged to refurbish their property. In a matter of months, the city was covered in scaffolding.

Not a week went by without the launch of a major new work site. Even Parisians had not experienced such frenzy when André Malraux decided to rid the city of the blackish coating that had covered it since the days of coal heating. And in Paris, at least, things were straightforward: dressed stone was to be returned to the original golden white color

of local sandstone, and plaster would recover its whiteness. Things were infinitely more complicated in Rome: should the Villa Borghese be restored to the state in which the previous century had left it, or to its original state of an almost total whiteness? And what about the Palazzo del Quirinale, whose severely simple facade, overlooking the square, was painted a few years ago in the brightest of oranges? No one quibbled, of course, over the cleaning of brick, marble and travertine, for the removal of grime

A sense of architecture is apparent even in relatively simple buildings. These facades near the Pantheon show how sunshine emphasizes the lines of architraves and cornices. The fine sense of movement illustrates Rome's hatred of flatness.

Left: For over fifteen centuries, devotion to Mary has never wavered in Rome, as demonstrated by the great number of churches and basilicas dedicated to her. The city is also dotted with more modest images, often placed on the corner of a house or palazzo, protected by a canopy of stone or metal. At Mary's feet are often found lighted lamps or bouquets of flowers, symbolizing popular belief that she will intercede with her son, expressed by the three Latin words *ora pro nobis* ("pray for us").

Right: Palazzo del Quirinale, the official residence of the president of Italy, has three long facades built in the strict spirit of the Counter-Reformation. Although old paintings show a white mass perched above the city, certain sections were restored a few years ago to the ocher, almost orange color it was given in the nineteenth century. This color certainly generates an extraordinary shimmer when struck by the sun, but facades restored more recently have opted for the sixteenth century's ivory tones, which harmonize more closely with the sober travertine moldings.

restored them to their initial beauty, as was the case for a building as emblematic as Saint Peter's. But when it came to coats of paint or plaster, long discussion was required before deciding to return certain buildings to the former color of marmorino, a costly mixture of chalk and marble dust whose ivory whiteness breaks with the ochers of the past century. That decision was applied to the remaining facades of the Palazzo del Quirinale, as well as to the Villa Borghese and the Villa Medici.

Having closely witnessed the restoration of the facades of the Villa Medici—one of the most remarkable edifices of the late sixteenth century—I can testify to the seriousness of the research undertaken to re-create the quality of the original surface and the restorers' enthusiasm as they constantly sought the right tone, the finest sheen. As with the Villa Borghese, the results are incontrovertibly beautiful. The garden facade of the Villa Medici was originally an open-air sculpture museum: it had niches containing antique masterpieces, while Roman bas-reliefs were set right into the masonry itself. The niches were emptied in the eighteenth century to decorate palaces in Florence, but the bas-reliefs remained in place. Formerly covered in grime, the whole thing now shimmers in every shade of marble and travertine. Similarly, it is impossible to remain unmoved by the charm of the pale blue wash of the pavilion crowning the Farnese Gardens, on the Palatine Hill, whose aerial lightness is best admired from the Aventine.

One question remains unresolved: in the eighteenth century, all of Rome was a harmony of pale colors; in the following century, it was united in stronger, warmer tones. Today's return to paler facades, meanwhile, can only be partial—although perfectly justifiable when it comes to older edifices, it would be pointless for later buildings whose "historic" color is ocher. Doesn't that mean that Rome, so attractive for its overall harmony, runs the risk of appearing somewhat discordant in the future? Most important of all, the special efforts undertaken for the jubilee year 2000 should not mask the fact that maintenance is as important as restoration—will the ivory white and pastel tones so delightful today stand up to the ravages of pollution? The ochers of yore had the advantage of acquiring special charm as they aged. Can the new hues be prevented from becoming lifeless? The necessary measures will have to be taken if the stone and colors of Rome are to remain one of the wonders of the world.

Left: Devout believers invoke the Virgin in a wide variety of touching names. This Madonna del Buon Consiglio (Madonna of Good Advice) in the center of Trastevere has a stream of bouquets and plants placed at her feet by people with a prayer to be answered or gratitude to express.

Lower Right: The ocher washes daubed on walls everywhere in Rome in the nineteenth century lose none of their beauty and charm as they age. The neglect they suffer reveals a certain conception of time and life, a wariness of everything new and shiny, and an acceptance of the countless gradations that time imparts to the surface of things—a metaphor for human wisdom.

The heraldic tradition is perpetuated by popes and cardinals. The latter have long been granted nominal title to a parish in Rome, as indicated by a coat of arms on the church. Sant'Apollinare near Piazza Navona, for example, features an umbrella pine with the Latin motto, *Radicatus in caritate* ("Rooted in charity").

Strolling
in Rome

ROME IS MADE FOR STROLLING. NARROW, WINDING STREETS SUDDENLY OPEN ONTO SQUARES—BOTH TINY AND MAJESTIC—WHERE FOUNTAINS GLITTER IN THE SUN. MARVELOUS DISCOVERIES AND NEW SURPRISES CONSTANTLY AWAIT UNHURRIED PEDESTRIANS.

Hard to believe, perhaps, but these ancient vestiges now house Rome's stock exchange. Rome is not a financial capital nowadays, as indicated by this mask of stone overlooking a quiet square where nuns stroll. And yet the peperino walls and magnificent colonnade of the original temple, built in the second century in honor of the deified emperor Hadrian, provide convincing proof of former imperial power.

It is impossible to describe the charm of Rome without mentioning the ubiquitousness of reminders of the past. If one mythological figure were to be chosen as the patron god of Rome, a strong claim could be made for Mnemosyne, goddess of memory. The course of history has not been much more pacific here than elsewhere, yet even in the city's darkest hours when it could offer only the rubble of earlier grandeur, Rome never forgot its sense of historic dignity; rivals that sought to supplant it—Constantinople and Moscow, the "second" and "third" Romes—eventually curbed their ambitions. Nor should Mnemosyne, "memory," be confused with Clio, "history." Memory is always poetic, embellished, based on freedom and reverie, so a concern for archaeological accuracy can deal it a fatal blow by stultifying the imagination.

THE EVER-PRESENT PAST

Although recent urban improvement has been done intelligently, visitors walking down Via dei Fori Imperiali may almost feel pain at the sight of this gash that cuts through the heart of the city like a wound. In order to understand what such urban thoroughfares have eliminated, the visitor need merely walk behind Trajan's Markets (whose perfect semicircle can be seen from Via dei Fori Imperiali) to Salita del Grillo and Via Tor dei Conti, which offer a nearly intact vision of medieval Rome—*Roma turrita*, the turreted town that juxtaposed defensive towers and ancient walls.

Are today's tourists who traipse down the Forum's Via Sacra under a grueling sun truly moved by the image of the horses of Castor and Pollux who came to drink at the fountain of Juturna on the eve of the battle of Lake Regillus? Are they aware that, not far from there, they can stand on the exact spot of Caesar's funeral pyre? Is Cicero more than just a name when they pass by the rostrum, now razed, where the orator first stirred crowds and where his severed head was later displayed on the orders of Mark Antony? Perhaps, but the grandeur of Rome may in fact have been felt with greater force when the scattered remnants of the Forum were still covered by pastures. Grazing herds were joined by the few columns and triumphal arches poking above the ground, silent witnesses to the past whose enigmatic presence possessed an incomparable power of suggestion.

With its tall columns and domed churches, Rome is a city where visitors must always look skywards. That message is repeated by this bearded atlas, whose muscles strain as he holds up a celestial musician. The sound of the trumpet perhaps announces the Judgment Day, yet conveys an irresistible feeling of jubilation.

Right: The church of Santissimo Nome di Maria was built to commemorate Jan Sobieski's 1683 victory over the Turks outside Vienna. It faces Trajan's Column, a monument depicting the second-century deeds of Emperor Trajan. Pope Gregory the Great, who reigned from 590 to 604, saved the column for posterity following a revelation that the pagan emperor's virtues had earned him a place in heaven. The statue of Saint Peter on top only replaced Trajan in the late sixteenth century.

Preceding pages: The Fontana di Trevi.

After having lived in Trastevere for a long time, in the Middle Ages the Jewish community in Rome regrouped across the river. Then, during the activist climate of the Counter-Reformation, Pope Paul IV decided to restrict Jews to a special neighborhood. Once a week, they were obliged to attend a sermon at which a preacher demonstrated the alleged superiority of the Christian faith. The system survived for three centuries, and was only abolished in 1848

under Pius IX. The streets of the Ghetto—or what remains of it—retain a melancholy atmosphere.

This enchanting impression, as described by travelers of yore, can still be had, but only by night. Subtle lighting picks out the most remarkable monuments—large masses loom in the darkness, giving a striking impression of grandeur, while secondary vestiges remain in the shadows. Thanks to the magic of electricity, the Palatine recovers imperial magnificence: a strange marriage of modernity and antiquity.

The city boasts only a small number of major Roman buildings in a good state of preservation. The famous—perhaps too famous—Colosseum, invaded by swarms of tourists and souvenir shops, suffers in comparison with the Pantheon, saved by its transformation into a church and by the charm of its neighborhood. At first sight, Castel Sant'Angelo hardly looks like Hadrian's mausoleum, and visitors who enter Santa Maria degli Angeli are more conscious of Michelangelo's church than of the Baths of Diocletian.

In certain cases, the presence of the past is almost virtual. The Circus Maximus originally stood in the hollow dividing the Aventine and Palatine Hills. But here there are no walls, no raked seating, no racks of postcards. The obelisks which once marked the path of chariot races have been taken elsewhere, now replaced by a solitary old cypress as magnificent as it is minuscule in such a vast space. Strollers, a few pairs of lovers, and joggers visit the site, which, thanks to the dimensions, retains a feeling of solitude, almost abandonment—an abandonment so respectful of the vanished

edifice, however, that it strictly retains its shape. Here, perhaps more than at the Forum, modern visitors can get an idea of the poignant feeling that gripped travelers in centuries past. What remains of the stands where the roar of the crowd used to echo? It is not even an empty shell, just an imprint on the ground. Far off, meanwhile, the dome of Saint Peter's—almost lightweight in the distance—magnifies another kind of triumph.

More charming are the countless, often modest vestiges that blend into the overall ambiance so felicitously, reviving the glamor of the ancient world suddenly and almost magically, at a bend in a street. Start, for example, from Michelangelo's Piazza del Campidoglio on the Capitoline Hill, but instead of heading toward the Forum and Colosseum, walk in the opposite direction, toward the recently cleaned Teatro di Marcello. It represents a wonderful example of continuity and inventiveness, since tucked inside it is the feudal fortress of the powerful Savelli family, transformed in the Renaissance into a pleasant dwelling by the no less illustrious Orsini family. From there, carry on to the Portico of Octavia. You are now approaching the Ghetto, a neighborhood steeped in mystery and melancholy, a reminder of the days when Pope Paul IV began harassing and humiliating Rome's Jewish community in 1555. Yet the juxtaposition of antique remains with more or less well-maintained dwellings produces one of Rome's most evocative sectors. Via del Portico d'Ottavia, in

Pasquino is an antique statue discovered near Piazza Navona in the Renaissance. Placed at the corner of a palazzo, it soon acquired the name of a neighborhood craftsman known for his rebellious temperament since, despite a strict ban, the statue would be covered with satirical messages and gibes at night. This custom slowly died out when freedom of the press was obtained, but it resurfaces from time to time.

Right: A typical glimpse of sky at the end of a narrow street, with a view of the Forum of Augustus. Three gigantic columns of white marble are the most visible remains of a temple to Mars the Avenger, erected by Augustus to commemorate his victory over the assassins of his adoptive father, Julius Caesar.

Due to its meandering path, the Tiber sometimes offers surprising vistas, such as this angle which strikingly foreshortens the long avenue leading to Saint Peter's. Unlike Paris or Florence, Rome was never organized around its river, whose shores were long ignored. They were somewhat

particular, has often inspired artists, its charm remaining unaltered. The house of Lorenzo Manilio, a Renaissance humanist, has survived in its almost original state, its facade decorated with several ancient relics, including the front of a sarcophagus featuring three busts carved in high relief.

THE TIBER RIVER AND ISLAND

From there, by heading back toward the river, you can cross over to the Isola Tiberina (Tiber Island) on Ponte Fabricio, the oldest bridge in Rome, known in the Middle Ages as "the Jewish bridge." It had better luck than the Ponte Rotto nearby, swept away by a flood in the sixteenth century except for a single span which now stands alone in the middle of the river. Towering over the island is the Romanesque bell tower of the church of San Bartolomeo, alongside a former Franciscan monastery. The latter, disbanded in the nineteenth century, was built from a very ancient fortified dwelling. Indeed, the island long remained in the hands of two powerful feudal families—the Pierleoni, followed by the Caetani, who left it in the sixteenth century.

The island has also had a medical vocation for the past two thousand years. The current hospital of Fatebenefratelli was built on the site of a temple to Aesculapius, Roman god of medicine, erected in the third century B.C.E. (It was in memory of a cure that occurred here that Rahere, chancellor to Henry I of England, founded Saint Bartholomew's, one of the most important hospitals in London.)

The Isola Tiberina illustrates one of the key differences between Rome and, say, Paris. Ever since the founding of the French monarchy, the Ile de la Cité in the Seine has always hosted the major symbols of spiritual and temporal power, the banks of the river providing a fine backdrop for the grandeur of governance, whereas the island in the middle

Ponte Sant'Angelo dates back to Emperor Hadrian, who wanted to connect his future mausoleum (now called Castel Sant'Angelo) to the city. In 1669, Pope Clement IX commissioned Bernini to supply statues of angels holding instruments of the Passion. The two statues done by the master himself were thought so beautiful that they were placed in the church of Sant'Andrea delle Fratte near Piazza di Spagna. The statues on the bridge, throbbing with life, were the work of Bernini's students.

improved by the banks built in the nineteenth century, but have never lost their charming air of neglect, as seen here above Ponte Sant'Angelo.

A little further on, Palazzo Cenci evokes one of the most tragic episodes in sixteenth-century Rome: young Beatrice Cenci, accused of witchcraft and parricide, was sentenced to death by the pope, who wanted to lay his hands on her family property (see Shelley's tragic poem *The Cenci*). The Ghetto's own traditions, meanwhile, have survived into the present, for several restaurants still propose dishes such as the famous "Jewish-style artichokes," fried crisply on the outside but tender inside.

of the Tiber, long in the hands of families quick to challenge papal authority, has been more a place of relegation, like some medieval leper house kept a good distance from the rest of the city.

Piazza San Bartolomeo is endearing rather than majestic; it features a small central monument dedicated to the island's patron saint and, opposite the church, the hospital pharmacy, which is one of the oldest in Rome. A stroll along the quays ringing the island produces a strange feeling: the modern world is right there, given the continuous flow of automobiles on the far banks of the river, and yet the dominant impression is one of separation. Near the tip of the island, pointed like the prow of a ship, the Tiber goes over a waterfall where its ordinarily sullen waters boil. The enchanting atmosphere persists even during fine weather, when the island's perimeter becomes busier, and it is sometimes difficult to tear yourself away from this open-air cloister and rejoin the city.

Plans are now afoot to "improve" the banks of the Tiber. It is true that they seem abandoned, prey to chaotic vegetation more or less everywhere. Ancient Rome turned its back on the river, into which its sewers flowed. The Tiber was glorified only in the form of allegorical statues, depicted as an old man with majestic beard. Roman indifference has persisted into the present day, even though the Tiber flows right through the center of town. Such negligence, in every other respect deplorable, at least provides a perspective on the city that is highly typical of the Rome of yore.

A Tour Through Trastevere

Thanks to another Roman bridge—the Ponte Cestio—the Isola Tiberina leads to one of the most famous of those typically Roman neighborhoods: Trastevere ("Trans-Tiber"). In ancient days, this suburb of Rome was inhabited above all by foreigners, which is why Christianity, a little-practiced religion imported from the East, seems to have had its first acknowledged site of worship there. That was in the third century C.E., during the papacy of Saint Calixtus, right where the basilica of Santa Maria in Trastevere now stands, which is still the heart of the neighborhood. Losing oneself in the maze of alleyways and squares, full of craft shops and

During the empire Trastevere was populated by foreigners, notably from Syria and Palestine, and has been a world apart ever since. Incorporated into the city by Aurelian's walls, it remained a working-class neighborhood down through the centuries. In 1849 Trastevere offered fierce resistance to French troops sent to restore Pope Pius IX. It was made fashionable by Americans in the 1950s, when artists and intellectuals moved there. Even

if the number of traditional workshops is declining inexorably, the neighborhood has retained its character and still rings with the accents of the local dialect.

trattorie, is one of Rome's great delights. Here, by way of example, is a brief tour: the Ponte Cestio gives onto a strange, substantially restored medieval dwelling whose brick facade incorporates a number of antique fragments. Behind the house is Piazza in Piscinula, featuring the chapel of San Benedetto with Rome's tiniest, and perhaps most charming, medieval bell tower. Via della Lungaretta runs from the piazza straight down to Santa Maria in Trastevere. On the way, it passes the ancient basilica of San Crisogono, notable for its twelfth-century mosaic flooring (a veritable catalogue of precious marble), its twenty ancient columns in red granite, and its handsome blue and gold ceiling with the coat of arms of Scipione Borghese.

Far left: Across the river from Trastevere, a fine baroque fountain stands in the middle of Piazza Bocca della Verità. Behind it a robust twelfth-century campanile rises above the very old basilica of Santa Maria in Cosmedin. The most famous, if not most interesting, feature of the church is the Bocca della Verità, an ancient sewer spout in the form of a mask with a mouth (*bocca*) that allegedly closes on the hand of anyone not telling the truth (*verità*). This entire part of Rome was still semi-rural in the nineteenth century.

This witty and delightful composition is a tribute to Trilussa, a poet who wrote exclusively in Roman dialect. He was the finest twentieth-century representative of Trastevere's willfully satirical, working-class spirit. Piazza Trilussa, on the banks of the Tiber, is highly typical of the neighborhood.

At night, Piazza Sant'Ignazio looks even more like a stage set than during the day. The small building in the middle, now housing a police station, could function as a backdrop for the church whose ceiling is a masterpiece of baroque trompe l'oeil. As skillful as this composition is, Rome is not a city where visual order reigns.

Lower right: Ponte Vittorio Emmanuele II bears the name of the king who brought the popes' temporal power to an end. In a forward-looking compromise, the bridge is not aligned with the long perspective from Saint Peter's. This subtle discontinuity reflects the complex nature of relations between Rome's spiritual and political authorities—a situation not simply resolved by the legal convenience of making the Vatican a foreign entity. This nighttime view illustrates the city's basic unity.

Further along, at No. 97, a plaque and carved bust of a woman recall the sacrifice of Giuditta Tavani Arquati and her companions, who rebelled against papal power and who, for three hours, held out in the house against the attack of *vili e feroci mercenari*, a rather unkind way of referring to the French troops charged with defending Pius IX (although a good reminder of the turbulent past of this working-class neighborhood). Via della Lungaretta crosses several small squares such as Piazza San Rufina, whose chapel is also capped by another tiny campanile. None of these squares, however, rivals Piazza di Santa Maria in Trastevere. Square in shape, flanked by palaces and simpler buildings, graced in the middle with the famous shell fountain, it is characterized by delightful details that disturb overly orderly minds. The mosaic on the outside facade of Santa Maria

curves inward to shield itself from the rain, while the church itself, with its fine campanile, is not centered on the square but stuck in a corner. The small streets leading into the square (Via della Paglia and Via della Fonte dell'Olio) seem more like corridors leading behind the stage of some theater.

Taking Via della Paglia, turn right down Via della Scala as far as the fine baroque church of Santa Maria della Scala and the old pharmacy of the same name. Backtracking, you can return to the starting point not by taking Via della Lungaretta but instead, for example, winding along Via della Cisterna, Via dei Fienaroli and Via delle Fratte. This route leads past Piazza Mastai, named after the family of Pope Pius IX, who in 1863 built a majestic tobacco factory of a kind to be seen only in Rome. It bears the Latin inscription *officinam nicotaniis foliis elaborandis*.

Behind the factory is one of Trastevere's most private sectors. Less crowded than the Santa Maria area, it focuses on the church of Santa Cecilia with its fine, flowery forecourt. In summer, this oasis of peace and serenity offers a welcome halt to the few strollers who pass this way before heading off again in

Right: The basilica of Santa Maria in Trastevere allegedly stands on the first permanent site of Christian worship in Rome, founded here about 220 by Pope Calixtus. The area was marked by a miracle even before the Christian era, when oil poured from a natural spring. The event, recorded in the name of nearby Via Fonte dell'Olio, was interpreted by Christians as a harbinger of Christ. The current church dates primarily from the twelfth century, with a fine campanile of brick and a facade of gold mosaics showing the Virgin enthroned. The portico, crowned by baroque statues, was renovated in the eighteenth century. Behind the cast-iron gates can be seen many stone fragments set into the wall, several of them belonging to edifices predating the current church. Piazza Santa Maria in Trastevere is still the heart of the neighborhood. Although touristy on summer evenings, at other times it retains a peaceful, small-town atmosphere that has withstood the march of time.

Left: The magnificent dome of the church of Sant'Andrea della Valle, second in size only to Saint Peter's, is glimpsed from a narrow street on the former site of Pompey's Theater. At ground level, nothing survives of that theater—the first in ancient Rome to be built of stone—but the curved shape of the street, the slope of the terrain and various underground remnants attest to its presence not far from Campo de' Fiori. The charm of strolling through the center of Rome comes from this layering of history, from the play of light and shadow in narrow streets and the sudden emergence of wonderful views.

Right: Every morning, market farmers bring their fruit and vegetables to Campo de' Fiori. The transportation, display and weighing of produce are all done very simply in this vast open-air market. Roman markets eschew artifice, which explains their warm atmosphere.

search of the church of San Francesco a Ripa, a place of pilgrimage for all admirers of Bernini. Piazza Santa Cecilia, the nearby Piazza dei Mendicanti, and Via San Michele together comprise a tableau which should be seen "in the raw" before restorations make it look too slick. It is difficult to avoid a sense of nostalgia in this part of Rome, with the worn, cracking plaster everywhere, the greenery tumbling down the walls, an ancient restaurant called Da Meo Pattaca, and a pizzeria with the evocative name of Roma Sparita ("Vanished Rome"). Via di Santa Cecilia heads back toward the Tiber, not far from the Ponte Cestio, which leads back to our earlier route in the Ghetto.

TOWARD CAMPO DE' FIORI

Via del Portico d'Ottavia is quite near one of Rome's most charming squares, Piazza Mattei, which takes it name from a powerful family that owned much of the neighborhood prior to the eighteenth century. The most remarkable feature is not so much Palazzo Costaguti (whose fine doorway of travertine seems somewhat squeezed into a corner) as the famous Fontana delle Tartarughe. The fountain was commissioned in the late sixteenth century from Giacomo della Porta, one of the main architects of the new Saint Peter's. Originally, the fountain comprised only the bowl held by four bronze adolescents, each with one foot on the head of a dolphin. During the baroque period, four incongruous if natural turtles were added to this elegant, graceful composition, lending it originality and a touch of whimsy.

A stone's throw away, set somewhat back from the square on Via dei Funari, is the gate to the Palazzo Mattei di Giove. Now the headquarters of Italy's Institute of History and of the National Record Library, the palazzo's main courtyard is worth a peek. With its collection of antique statues and bas-reliefs set in the walls, it bears witness to the collecting mania of the Mattei family, otherwise primarily known for their simple and pious lifestyle. The great poet Giacomo Leopardi spent several months there in 1823, in the family of his uncle, who succeeded the Matteis. Given his stern judgment on this

Not far from Campo de' Fiori, a former chapel on Largo del Pallaro now houses the "Academy of the Superfluous," whose very name indicates its agenda. The techniques taught here, which include trompe l'oeil and imitation marbling, are so closely linked to baroque

illusionism that "superfluity" certainly constitutes a key artistic school in Rome.

This startling collection of antique busts and bas-reliefs fills the inner courtyard of Palazzo Mattei di Giove, built in the early seventeenth century. Known for their piety, the Matteis were also great collectors. The considerable quantity of ancient statues that came to light during the Renaissance explains the packed display, bordering on saturation. Although questionable, the theatrical effect retains all its impact.

"horrible jumble," it would seem that his romantic view was fairly removed from our own.

At the end of Via dei Giubbonari, just before Campo de' Fiori, the city retains the mark of Pompey's Theater, the first in Rome not built of wood. Although nothing exists above ground, the placement of the raked seating can be detected in the slope of the ground, while the semicircular shape of the theater can be seen in the curve of the houses, like a plaster model from which the mold has been removed (Largo del Pallaro and Via di Grotta Pinta are the most evocative in this respect). Below ground, however, many vestiges of the theater have been preserved.

A former little chapel on Largo del Pallaro, meanwhile, houses the "Academy of the Superfluous" which offers courses on, among other things, the eminently Roman arts of trompe l'oeil and imitation marbling. To the

right of the chapel is a dark, covered passage that some people find squalid, but which is certainly picturesque. A little lamp burns constantly at the foot of a statue of the Madonna. This passage opens onto Piazza del Biscione, a pretty urban setting just off Campo de' Fiori. One day I saw the following announcement posted there: "A priest will come to this address on Thursday, from 4:30 to 7:00 P.M., to give families an Easter blessing" (*Presso questo numero civico passerà il sacerdote per la benedizione alle famiglie*).

Campo de' Fiori, which is in the shape of a long rectangle, acts as a veritable light trap, illuminating the countless colors of the non-stop market held there. Florists alternate with fruit-and-vegetable stalls and cheap clothing merchants. The fragrant smells and gleaming colors make this one of the best places to appreciate a key element in Roman cooking:

the use of simple, fresh, local produce as the basis of regional cuisine. The houses flanking the campo are of no particular interest, apart from typical touches like the colors of the walls and details such as a papal escutcheon or a mosaic madonna. One side of the square, in fact, was never truly completed.

Seen from Campo de' Fiori, Palazzo Pio Righetti over on Piazza del Biscione looks like a stage set, a facade with nothing behind it. This slice of palace rises up above lower, less noble buildings, one of which houses the Farnese movie theater. A statue of Giordano Bruno stands in the center of the campo, testifying to a period when the kingdom of Italy was asserting itself against the papacy. This bronze monument to one of the most famous victims of the Inquisition is regularly decked with flowers by advocates of free thought. Ringed by pleasant terraces of cafés and restaurants, the square is the theater of a constantly shifting crowd.

Below: An old-fashioned barber shop, of which fewer and fewer exist, on Piazza Mattei. The pleasure of a morning shave before breakfast, while reading a newspaper, belongs to a vanished lifestyle. The very term *salone* (salon) evokes a quality of human relations that Rome, despite everything, has managed to preserve more than other major capitals.

The late-sixteenth-century Fontana delle Tartarughe on Piazza Mattei combines the sinewy elegance of the early Renaissance with the baroque impulsion toward movement. According to legend, a Mattei duke had the fountain built in one night after having gambled away enormous sums, to demonstrate what he was still capable of doing.

Left: Pumpkins worthy of a fairy tale, garlic in tresses, artichokes in colorful varieties, watermelons cooling in a public fountain: these images recorded in Campo de' Fiori illustrate the importance played by local produce in the Roman concept of good living.

Right: Over the centuries, Campo de' Fiori has been the scene of executions as well as festivities. The most famous victim was the heretical monk Giordano Bruno, sentenced by the Inquisition and burned alive in 1600. A bronze statue in the square commemorates Bruno. The only bonfires in the piazza today occur after the market closes. With its surrounding cafés and restaurants, the square is a favorite meeting place for Romans.

AROUND PALAZZO FARNESE

Many streets in the old center of Rome are named after trades once practiced there and long-vanished crafts now live on in such names. Via dei Baullari, for instance, refers to the guild of trunk-makers. Connecting Campo de' Fiori to Piazza Farnese, this street is today lined with bustling cafés. This view offers a glimpse of Palazzo Farnese, recently restored to its original pale color.

From the Campo de' Fiori, Via dei Baullari leads to Palazzo Farnese. This palace, perhaps the finest in Rome, has long served as the French Embassy and was bought by the French government in 1911. In 1936, however, Mussolini exercised Italy's repurchase option which became effective after twenty-five years. Since that time, Italy has rented the palazzo to France for a symbolic fee. France recently restored the building's admirable facade—a product of the genius of Sangallo and Michelangelo—freeing it from a thick layer of dust and revealing strange decoration in brick, with geometric patterns in different colors and irregular shapes. Are we to assume that brilliant architects allowed bricklayers free

reign with their fancy? The piazza itself affords a striking contrast with Campo de' Fiori. It is less lively and more geometric, although its solemnity is not marked by coldness—despite the imposing symmetry of two immense antique granite basins, topped by the Farnese fleur-de-lis, the structures are highly disparate, and the paving in the square has pronounced undulations that would be unthinkable in Paris or London.

Less then 100 meters away, Palazzo Spada in Piazza Capo di Ferro, although built at the same time as Palazzo Farnese, projects an entirely different spirit. Its facade is a joyful collection of stucco decoration and statues, but the main attraction is a gem of baroque art: Borromini's "perspective," a short passageway made to seem much longer thanks to an optical illusion. Today the palace houses Italy's Consiglio di Stato (supreme administrative court) and a museum.

By skirting around Palazzo Spada you arrive at the foot of Via Giulia. A bridge straddles the street, linking the Palazzo Farnese to its outbuildings. A little further up is Santa Maria della Morte. This small church was assigned to a very old confraternity charged with providing a Christian burial to corpses abandoned in the countryside. The crypt is an amazing place, because some of its furnishings—notably the lamps—are composed of bones; this is not a common sight in Rome, where religion rarely exploits a fear of death. Via Giulia, a long, perfectly straight street, is one of the finest examples of Renaissance town planning. Laid out by

With its grotesque mask and granite basin, the Fontana del Mascherone on Via Giulia is one of the finest examples of the countless fountains dotting the city. Ancient Rome's engineers devised an amazing system for supplying the city with potable water, and some of today's fountains still use the ancient network.

Right: Two magnificent Roman basins decorate the square in the front of Palazzo Farnese. The heraldic fleur-de-lis reaching toward the sky has never seemed more apt, with the bending petals mimicking the spray of water tumbling back into the basin.

Left: A perfect contrast to the Palazzo Farnese can be seen nearby in Palazzo Spada, built in 1540 for Cardinal Capo di Ferro and acquired a century later by Cardinal Spada. The palace courtyard is a model of fanciful refinement, even though the ornamentation may seem excessive. Delicate stucco garlands lend a touch of gracefulness to the more virile statues of ancient heroes housed in the niches. Home to Italy's Consiglio di Stato, the recently restored Palazzo Spada once again sparkles in its original colors.

the great Julius II (Michelangelo's pope), the street is flanked by palaces whose austere facades often mask delightful interiors.

Thus a random stroll down Via Giulia can offer glimpses—since it is still possible in Rome to broach entrances without being halted by an electronically locked door—of courtyards decorated with antique steles or bathtubs transformed into fountains, walls decorated with graffiti, and private gardens (at No. 146, for example). Via Giulia is also the realm of antique dealers—furniture and gilt frames glow softly in window displays, maintained in a half-light thanks to subtle lighting. The part of the street I find most charming begins at the former papal prison and continues to San Giovanni dei Fiorentini (the church of the Florentine community, dedicated to Saint John the Baptist). The architecture of the prison, built in 1655 on the order of Innocent X, is amazingly modern and almost seems to date from the 1930s. The Latin inscription at the top, unthinkable anywhere other than Rome, is worth deciphering since it refers to justice and mercy, to safer yet gentler imprisonment: *securiori ac mitiori reorum custodiae*. Today the prison is headquarters for the country's anti-mafia squad.

An alley leads to the oratory of Sant'Eligio degli Orefici (Saint Eloy of the Goldsmiths), whose very pure design is allegedly the work of Raphael himself. On a street corner a little further along, at No. 66, rises the imposing, austere Palazzo Sacchetti, built for Cardinal Ricci di Montepulciano, the very man who undertook

Palazzo Spada presents several faces. After the decorative exuberance of its facade and main courtyard, the rear displays a more sober elegance (left). The most famous and surprising feature, however, is Borromini's trompe-l'oeil perspective (above): a shaft of sunlight illuminates a small statue at the end of a passage that appears much longer than it actually is, thanks to skillful optical effects.

Right: "Babuino" is an antique statue found near Piazza di Spagna. Set on a fountain, it later gave its name to an entire street. Babuino is one of Rome's best-known "talking" statues (along with Pasquino and a few others), although the satirical broadsides formerly affixed to it have today been replaced by less sophisticated graffiti.

Below: The ends of Piazza Navona follow the original curve of Domitian's Stadium. But the occasionally bloody spectacles staged there in ancient times—such as the martyrdom of Saint Agnes—have given way to a more peaceful show. The piazza is now a favorite spot for Romans and tourists alike, who crowd the cafés and ice-cream parlors.

to build the Villa Medici. The palace, having been acquired by the Sacchettis, is still inhabited by descendants of that very old family; they have preserved the remarkable interior decoration, notably a set of frescoes painted in the mid sixteenth century by Francesco Salviati. Here, every detail counts: on the opposite corner from the palazzo, at No. 99, a house was recently restored to pale blue, giving a good idea of the city's former visage; at the base of the palace itself, a round-cheeked child astride two dolphins is all that remains of a fountain; next door, when the carriage gate is open, you can see beyond the courtyard into the greenery of an indoor garden crowned by an enormous antique head.

PIAZZA NAVONA

Although already famous, it is hard to avoid mentioning Piazza Navona, which is rather like the heart of papal Rome. Anyone arriving from Campo de' Fiori should stop and greet Pasquino, an antique statue that remains one of Rome's leading figures despite its poor condition. In papal times, when free speech was subject to severe restrictions, the people's voice could be heard through this and several other stone characters (such as the one on Via del Babuino). In a city teeming with miracles, what could be more normal than "talking" statues? At night, Pasquino and his colleagues would be covered with broadsides that showed little respect for the government of His Holiness—a fine example of the subtle compromises by which the Italian mentality reconciles the absolute authority of infallible government with an awareness of human imperfection. These days, insolent statues have lost their monopoly on criticism, and graffiti has unfortunately replaced the broadsides of the past, but the tradition of satire is still alive and well in Rome.

Piazza Navona represents a wonderful example of continuity and metamorphosis. Its shape faithfully reflects the outline of Domitian's Stadium, site of the martyrdom of Saint Agnes, one of the city's most venerated saints. Almost no vestiges of the antique stadium survive in the square itself. The foundations of a 1930s building, in contrast, turned up the remains of an arch with impressive travertine facing. But archaeology has no place in Piazza Navona. Triumphant

Right: Piazza Navona draws crowds in all seasons. There are hordes of children during Christmas and Epiphany, when the square is dense with stalls selling nativity scenes, candy and gifts. The piazza's oblong shape ensures that it receives sunlight all day long and gives it a certain intimacy. The nonstop show is so varied you can spend hours sitting on a travertine bench or at the edge of a fountain. The play of light on the ocher facades and the statues populating the fountains is enchanting in its own right.

Commissioned from Bernini in 1640 by Pope Urban VIII (the pride of the Barberini family, whose heraldic bees can be seen everywhere in Rome), the Fontana del Tritone stands in the center of Piazza Barberini. Somewhat dulled by modern buildings, the piazza, which opens onto Via Vittorio Veneto, is one of Rome's familiar landmarks. Bernini's spirited art is brilliantly exemplified by the triton blowing heartily into a conch shell.

seventeenth-century Rome dissolved the antique shell, so to speak, the better to adopt its shape. Since that time, the square has become one of the centers of festive Roman life. Overrun with tourists during the high season, Piazza Navona can be delightfully animated at the approach of Christmas and Epiphany (two holidays that entail treating children to gifts) when the square hosts outdoor nativity scenes and itinerant merchants. That is perhaps the time of year when the delicious hot chocolate served by various cafés around the square tastes best. As at Piazza San Marco in Venice, you can choose a café according to the position of the sun: Tre Scalini in the morning, for example (order a *tartufo*, their wonderful chocolate cake), and the Caffè di Colombia in the afternoon. Despite its scale, Piazza Navona is not overwhelming. Buildings close it off on all sides, some of them majestic (such as Palazzo Pamphili and the church of Sant'Agnese, which owes its swirling architecture to the genius of Borromini), others surprisingly modest. Since the piazza is linked to the exterior only through a few narrow streets, it generates a warm feeling of intimacy; the heterogeneity of the facades, meanwhile, forestalls any sense of pomposity or solemnity—a natural majesty wins out.

The three large fountains along the main axis are all different but felicitously share the reassuring laws of symmetry and baroque whimsy. The Fontana dei Quattro Fiumi, in the middle, is the most spectacular. Persistent legends surround this magnificent composition by Bernini, notably concerning

the meaning he intended to give the allegorical figures representing four rivers. The old man symbolizing the Rio de la Plata thus seems to be extending a disapproving hand toward the facade of the church by Bernini's great rival Borromini, while the neighboring figure, symbolizing the Nile, shields his face. Such a tendentious interpretation is chronologically impossible, since the church was built after the fountain, yet it reflects the Romans' undying delight in satire and controversy.

It is possible to spend hours contemplating the ever-changing spectacle of Piazza Navona—the flow of the crowd, the shifting play of sunlight around the square, or the wit of outdoor artists who produce caricatures for courageous tourists. The piazza also serves as a point of departure—or landmark—for anyone who wants to wander through the maze of surrounding streets. The street over by Tre Scalini leads to one of Rome's most evocative sites: passing under a brick arch, you come to the church of Santa Maria della Pace with its fine, curving facade and cloister by Bramante, which often hosts exhibitions of twentieth-century art. Thus you suddenly find yourself transported, a few paces from one of the city's liveliest squares, to an atmosphere of meditation and silence (or the closest you can get to silence in Rome). Opposite the church is the aptly named Via della Pace, where a table at the café of the same name will offer a peaceful view of the large, ocher houses trailing ivy, a welcome touch of greenery in a neighborhood where trees are rare.

The Fontana di Nettuno, located at the north end of Piazza Navona, dates from the nineteenth century. Although this fountain cannot rival Bernini's admirable Fontana dei Quattro Fiumi in the center of the square, the powerful figure of Neptune and the indisputable grace of the sea nymphs have their merits.

THE PANTHEON DISTRICT

The church of Santa Maria sopra Minerva stands near the ancient site of several Egyptian temples, one of which was dedicated to Isis and Serapis. An obelisk from that complex now graces a fountain in front of the church, although the elephant at its base is more interesting. This

charming piece of baroque whimsy by Bernini is also a symbol of wisdom.

Leaving Piazza Navona from the opposite side, you enter a neighborhood which has its own charm. It does not matter if you get lost in this series of small, irregularly shaped squares (such as Piazza della Minerva, Piazza della Maddelena and Piazza dei Rondanini), because you will still wind up in Piazza della Rotonda where the Pantheon stands. These squares offer

delightful places to dine on summer evenings. For people who love Rome, the Pantheon is perhaps the true heart of the city. This emblematic building seems somewhat sunken, minimizing its intimidating presence, because the level of the ground has risen continually since antiquity. Stripped of its exterior decoration over the centuries, time has lent the Pantheon an austerity that it certainly did not display originally.

Piazza della Rotonda with its fountain surmounted by an obelisk of Rameses the Great is smaller and therefore more intimate than Piazza Navona. It is one of those places where you suddenly forget all your cares. You can find a seat on the terraces of the cafés that flank it in summer as well as winter (under an umbrella outfitted, if necessary, with a heater). The square and surrounding streets are busy both in the evening and during working hours, without ever being oppressively crowded. Many business and financial people can be seen there, since Via dei Pastini leads straight to the Piazza di Pietra, where the stock exchange (Borsa) is located. The latter is lodged in a temple to the deified Hadrian, dating from the second century C.E., which still boasts a wall of peperino—the volcanic stone used in antiquity—and a colonnade.

Past the stock exchange, turn down Via de' Burrò into Piazza Sant'Ignazio. There stands the church of the same name, famous for an amazing trompe-l'oeil ceiling by Andrea Pozzo and magnificently lavish altars below which are buried two leading Jesuit figures, Saints Aloysius Gonzaga and John Berchmans. The church and square form a single ensemble so successful that it seems natural at first glance, although in fact it represents a skillful composition steeped in the theatrical aesthetics dear to the seventeenth and eighteenth centuries: the houses seem more like stage sets than dwellings, and the building opposite the church seems designed primarily to mask the exit of actors—as though passersby, like all human beings, do nothing more than play a role all their lives.

Right: Also featuring an Egyptian obelisk from the temples on Campo Marzio, the imposing fountain opposite the Pantheon in Piazza della Rotonda is a lively late-sixteenth-century composition. Since the dawn of time, water—the symbol of life—has always been associated with monsters. Here contorted figures, leering or cackling (not unlike gargoyles on Gothic cathedrals), oversee the wholesome play of water sparkling in the sun.

AROUND THE FONTANA DI TREVI

The Fontana di Trevi is another of those legendary places that it would be impossible—and unfair—to overlook. The decoration of the fountain itself, all in travertine, is thoroughly intertwined with the architecture of the palazzo against which it is set—you might even say into which it is set, as it is a perfect example of the baroque disdain for sharp, rational distinctions. Statues of Neptune and other pagan gods attest to the openmindedness of the two eighteenth-century popes responsible for this amazing creation. In another attack on the classical sense of proportion, the square itself affords almost no distance from the fountain, as if spattering were the rule. The small church of Santi Vincenzo e Anastasio, at an angle to the fountain, offers a fine baroque facade full of cherubs and garlands; it was commissioned by Cardinal Mazarin, Louis XIV's famous prime minister, whose name is immodestly displayed on the frieze. Inside the church, placed just to the side of the entrance, is a touching funerary monument that reflects a very Roman sense of compassion. It is dedicated to a six-year-old girl (*virguncula* in Latin) beloved by everyone in the neighborhood, who died during one Christmas mass—she was so modest that it was against her wish (*contra votum*) that her parents installed the inscription. In the crypt of the church are preserved the hearts and lungs of nearly all the popes from Sixtus V to Leo XIII.

The ground floor of the building opposite the fountain is marked by a series of antique columns; anywhere else, such relics would be highlighted, but here they simply frame the windows of fashion boutiques. On the right side of the piazza, meanwhile, is one of the oldest pharmacies not only in Rome but all of Europe; founded in 1522, it still boasts a fine interior of woodwork and porcelain jars.

Not far from the Fontana di Trevi is the neighborhood of Piazza di Spagna and, a little further on, Piazza del Popolo. This is the part of Rome that has been sought out by foreigners and artists since the seventeenth century. Goethe, Keats, Ingres, Corot, Thorwaldsen, Stendhal, Wagner, Andersen, Henry James, Gogol and many others lived here or frequented the area. It is organized around long, straight streets that radiate from the two main squares. One typical street is Via Sistina, which offers a long perspective from the Trinità dei Monti down to Santa Maria Maggiore, a perfect example of the determination of Renaissance town planning to put some order into the chaos bequeathed by the Middle Ages, while etching the names of great popes into the urban fabric (in this case Sixtus V, a man of the people and a firm pope). In the 1950s, Via Sistina, like nearby Via Gregoriana, became a high street of fashion, featuring famous names such as Valentino, Balestra and Cappuci. It has retained this role today, with a reputation for elegance and grand hotels such as the Hassler (famous for its panoramic view of Rome) and the Hotel de la Ville (remarkable for its interwar architecture and decoration by Hungarian architect Josef Vago).

Right: It was in 19 B.C.E. that Agrippa, son-in-law of Augustus, decided to bring water to Rome via an aqueduct some 20 kilometers long. Called Acqua Vergine (because the spring was found by a young virgin), it still runs beneath the city and feeds several fountains, the most famous and spectacular being the Fontana di Trevi. Built in 1762, the fountain is attached to the facade of a palazzo. Neptune, god of the sea, bursts forth on a chariot as his tritons try to control the spirited team of horses. Although it may appear excessively theatrical, and although the superstitious behavior of thousands of tourists may annoy, this final demonstration of dazzle by papal Rome should be seen as a paean to life.

A restorer repairs the Fontana del Facchino, located on the corner of Via Lata and Via del Corso. Water pours into the basin from a small wine cask held by a porter (*facchino*), thereby reversing the miracle of the Marriage of Cana. The sculptor allegedly used the features of a notorious drunk for the porter.

Two lovers, all alone on the Spanish Steps in the early morning light. When Rome is seen from rooftop level, the city's domes rise up on the horizon (here, San Carlo al Corso, which many tourists initially mistake for Saint Peter's).

FROM TRINITÀ DEI MONTI TO PIAZZA DI SPAGNA

From the lofty church of Trinità dei Monti, the eye can take in the city in all its scope. Two domes stand out—in the foreground is San Carlo al Corso, the parish church of the Milanese, which seems almost as high as Saint Peter's, visible in the background. The horizon is trimmed with the green mass of the Janiculum Hill, forming a dark railing around the large ocher patch of city. The high platform of the Trinità dei Monti offers a unique view of the white marble stairway—the famous Spanish Steps— running down to Piazza di Spagna. Built by the architect Francesco de Sanctis, the Spanish Steps resulted from the munificence of Cardinal Melchior de Polignac, ambassador of French king Louis XV, and were a felicitous outcome to the neighborhood rivalry that long pitted the French (on top of the hill) against the Spanish (at the bottom). This rivalry was a distant memory by the eighteenth century, when Bourbons reigned in both Paris and Madrid.

The staircase, bedecked in fine weather by a multitude of azaleas and oleanders planted by the city, is one of the preferred meeting spots for young Romans, who arrive via the nearby subway stop. They gather on the steps as soon as weather permits, and in the thirty years I have been watching this spectacle, the ritual of making acquaintance, never aggressive, has remained unchanged. Only sartorial fashion has evolved, while the

Right: After interminable negotiations between the Holy See and Louis XIV (who wanted to place his own equestrian statue there), the stairway linking the French convent of Trinità dei Monti to Piazza di Spagna was finally built under Louis XV. With their curving paths and multiple landings, the Spanish Steps create a remarkably fluid effect. Tourists and young Romans have made the steps a favorite meeting place, especially since a subway station opened on Piazza di Spagna. Conceived in the baroque spirit of grand festive occasions, the steps are not the place to come for solitude, except in the early morning.

use of cellphones by teenagers has added a touch of modernity to the poetry of making a date. At times it can be hard to forge a path up the steps, but any sense of being smothered is diminished by the good-natured atmosphere, shared by the piazza itself and surrounding streets.

Those streets, notably the famous Via di Condotti, are the realm of luxury boutiques. Although some stores have retained a fairly conventional appearance, others play the card of contemporary design, introducing modernity into an otherwise immutable environment. To my eyes, the most interesting example of this phenomenon is Ruffo, a shop located a little further along, on the corner of Vicolo d'Alibert and Via del Babuino. On Saturday afternoons, all

Via Gregoriana has been a chic fashion district since the 1950s. But it is also a rendezvous for art historians, who come to consult the extensive collection at the Biblioteca Hertziana, a German institution housed in the strange Palazzo Zuccari, where doors and windows look like the gaping mouths of monsters.

Left: Via Margutta, just off Via del Babuino, seems provincially quiet. In the nineteenth century artists' quarters were built here, of which vast studios have survived. Several scenes from *Roman Holiday* were shot in one of the courtyards, near Fellini's house. Antique stores and art galleries now line the street, but the painters who exhibit outdoors primarily target the tourist trade.

these streets are invaded by a dense crowd.

Piazza di Spagna itself has a strange shape, like two irregular triangles joined at their tips. On the smaller side is the Spanish Embassy, which has occupied the same site for three hundred years. The charm of its interior courtyard can be glimpsed through a fine wrought-iron gate. Facing the embassy is a large statue of the Immaculate Virgin set atop a column. The adjacent Piazza Mignanelli offers a kind of hidden passage up to the Trinità dei Monti. At the foot of the Spanish Steps, the standard fountain—here, in the form of a ship—tempts tourists to take a cool dip when the weather is scorching, despite official prohibitions. The larger part of the Piazza di Spagna is used as a parking zone for horse-drawn cabs, and leads to the subway station. Tall palm trees give it the feel of a resort on the Riviera. The buildings flanking the square, almost all topped by terraces, offer the eye a variety of colors— recent restorations have not imposed a false unity. I could never imagine the Keats memorial in any color other than the strong yet time-worn pink it is today.

A passerby drinks from the fountain on Via Margutta. This is a somewhat disconcerting adaptation of traditional models, in which grimacing masks are set in a rigid, modern structure. Every stroll through Rome includes a refreshing halt at one of the countless street fountains dotting the city.

TOWARD PIAZZA DEL POPOLO

Piazza di Spagna is linked to Piazza del Popolo by Via del Babuino. Here antique shops rival fashion boutiques for top billing. Thus the latest sartorial trends alternate with paintings set in magnificently worked frames, furniture in gilded wood, sculptures and objets d'art. At No. 185, the Ritz Saddler clothing store provides an idea of the celebrities who frequented this street in its heyday, since the shop window displays several pages of autographs. The lion's share belong to the movie industry—Richard Burton, Liz Taylor, Sophia Loren, Monica Vitti, Antonioni, Virna Lisi, Ugo Tognazzi, Vittorio Gassman, Brigitte Bardot, Anthony Quinn, Alfred Hitchcock and Roman Polanski. But others come from literature (Moravia and Arbasino), theater (Strehler), the fine arts and politics. Another famous street, Via Margutta, which joins Via del Babuino at two different junctions, was the special realm of artists, notably those from northern Europe. All along the street you can still see the tall arched windows typical of a traditional artist's studio. At No. 53, the English founded the British Academy of Arts in 1821; the Patrizi family long retained ownership of this artists' residence. Set in a forecourt full of greenery, its imposing mass maintains a majestic distance from the street. The courtyard of the neighboring building, meanwhile, served as a set for several scenes of William Wyler's *Roman Holiday*.

This sea monster—more cute than terrifying—decorates one of the monumental fountains that architect Giuseppe Valadier placed around Piazza del Popolo, which was entirely refurbished in the early nineteenth century.

In the background is the baroque church of Santa Maria di Montesanto, completed in 1675 by Bernini, which stands at the head of Via del Corso along with its false twin, Santa Maria dei Miracoli.

The morning light plays on Piazza del Popolo. In the middle rises an Egyptian obelisk originally set in the Circus Maximus; transporting and erecting it here in the sixteenth century was a technical feat.

Right: From the ramps built on the slopes of the Pincio by Valadier you can see the star crowning Porta del Popolo, decorated by Bernini with the arms of the Chigis (the family of Pope Alexander VII). The very simple bell tower of Santa Maria del Popolo hardly hints at the treasures within.

On either side of the street are antique stores and art galleries. On Saturdays and Sundays, artists exhibit their paintings on the street in an atmosphere similar to Montmartre in Paris. Fans of comic-book character Corto Maltese will find a spot devoted to their hero, not far from the house where Giulietta Masina and Federico Fellini lived (No. 110). Two small marble plaques are engraved with their names, the sole, discreet testimony of their long residence in this red, one-story house whose terrace can be glimpsed from the street. Fellini's day always began in exactly the same way: after having a shave at a barbershop on Via del Babuino between 8 and 9 A.M., he would go to Feltrinelli's bookstore, where he liked to browse among the shelves—"Leafing through a book," Fellini would say, "is better than traveling." Then he would buy the morning papers and take a seat at Canova's on Piazza del Popolo, which he preferred to Caffè Rosati across the way because the latter was too exposed to the sun for his liking. He always took this stroll alone, and the best way to talk to him was to accost him along the way, because he delighted in such apparently chance encounters.

Via del Babuino ends at Piazza del Popolo, which has just been totally restored. Its current state dates from the early nineteenth century and bears the mark of the neoclassical approach of its architect, Giuseppe Valadier. The square gives an idea of the transformations Napoleon would have brought to Rome had his empire survived longer. Now a pedestrian district, the piazza

Uniformed police ride up and down the lanes of the Pincio, probably more for the health of their steeds than from a need to maintain order. Few major cities have police as human and tolerant as they are in Rome—which is not to suggest they cannot be firm on occasion.

Left: Casina Valadier, a charming neoclassical building on the edge of the Pincio, can be glimpsed through the trees in the fine light of a winter's day. Already appreciated in antiquity for its beautiful gardens, the Pincio Hill remains one of the most pleasant promenades in Rome. Laid out during the Napoleonic period, it offers fine views of the city all the while providing delightful shade and fountains.

has the charm of a promenade. Because the space constantly plays on effects of symmetry and contrast, there are different vistas with almost every step. Thus the two churches flanking Via del Corso seem identical at first glance, yet their bell towers are different and even their ground plans vary, having been built on dissimilar plots. Across the piazza, Santa Maria del Popolo, one of the richest "museum-churches" in Rome thanks notably to its Caravaggios, is topped by a little bell tower almost medieval in spirit. These details temper, without completely destroying, the impression of coldness that Valadier's highly rational design might give. With the first rays of light, however, when the sun rises above the Pincio Hill and plays on the myriad *sanpietrini* (those rectangular, typically Roman cobblestones), this great and nearly empty space of stone, enlivened by the play of fountains, pigeons and a few passersby, acquires singular beauty. Where Via del Corso joins the square—narrow but imperceptibly widening as it enters—the crowds flock for the simple pleasure of walking or sitting for a moment on the edge of the central fountain, beneath the Egyptian obelisk. The square then becomes every bit as lively as Piazza di Spagna.

The ramp that loops up toward the Pincio makes it possible to take in Piazza del Popolo from various heights—as the stroller climbs, the vista broadens to include the background of the city and the dome of Saint Peter's as it slowly emerges over the horizon. The road leads back to the Trinità dei Monti, passing Casina Valadier, a graceful

eighteenth-building that long housed one of Rome's most elegant restaurants but is now awaiting new employment.

A stone's throw away is the pavilion of San Gaetano, marking the boundary of the Villa Medici. In 1804, the villa became the seat of the French Academy in Rome, previously housed in a palazzo on Via del Corso. This fortunate initiative by Napoleon has provided a wonderful setting for generations of major French artists in all fields, such as Ingres, Carpeaux, Berlioz, Bizet and Debussy. It was in this pavilion that Ingres had his studio when he lodged at the Academy. On the city side, the imposing facade of the Villa Medici has been restored to its original whiteness for the jubilee year 2000. The little antique fountain placed in the middle of the balcony on the third floor has been plumbed with water again, lending a touch of softness and whimsy to an otherwise austere facade that gives no hint of the building's inner exuberance. Below, a wooded garden extends almost as far as Via del Babuino. On this property, which still belongs to the French Academy, Cardinal Ferdinando de' Medici had hoped to erect a monumental fountain; all that exists of this grandiose plan is a fresco in one of the villa's pavilions. The promenade, formerly a dirt path, has always been a favorite of artists, and Roman antique dealers still offer a large number of drawings and sketches done near the Villa Medici, notably of the famous basin in front of the entrance (which Corot immortalized, at the expense of taking several liberties with the landscape).

The fanciful rear facade of the Villa Medici comes as a surprise after its austere front. It has recently been restored to its sixteenth-century color, a handsome ivory tone designed to harmonize with the travertine moldings and antique marble sculptures placed in niches or set into the wall.

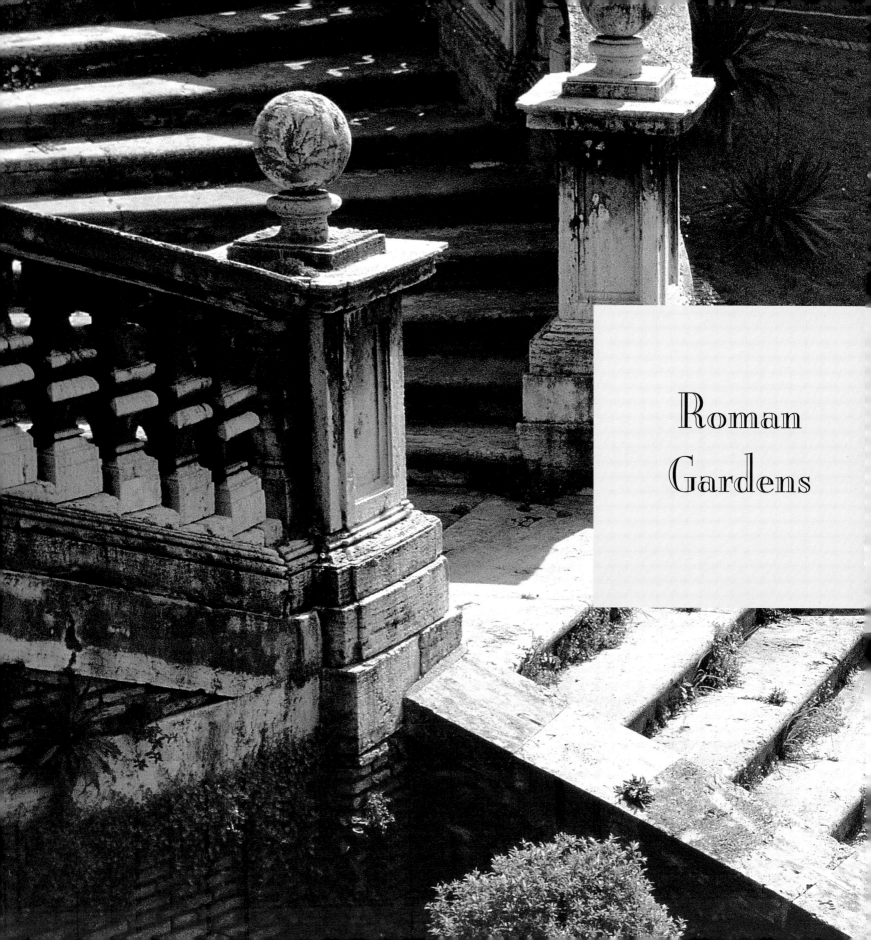

Roman
Gardens

ENTIRE HILLS HAVE RETAINED THEIR CLOAK OF GREENERY, RECALLING THE RURAL ROME OF THE PAST. A DIFFERENT VIEW OF THE CITY EMERGES FROM THE PUBLIC AND PRIVATE GARDENS OF PRINCELY VILLAS, IN THE SCENTED SHADE OF ORANGE TREES AND UMBRELLA PINES.

Clivo di Rocca Savelli, seen here on a fine winter's day, is one of Rome's most mysterious streets. It runs along the garden of Santa Sabina before heading down to the Tiber. Vegetation cascades down the walls and slopes of the Aventine, one of the hills that has best preserved the green spaces which covered it in the Middle Ages.

Preceding pages: The gardens of Villa Aldobrandini on the Quirinal Hill.

U nlike London and Paris, which have steadily grow outward from a constant historic center, the heart of Rome has shifted from the legendary citadel of Romulus. Although city hall is still located on Capitoline Hill, this steadfastness owes more to an "archaeological" and quasi-symbolic loyalty—in the face of the vicissitudes of the past—rather than to any real link with the city's historical existence. After a period of extraordinary expansion during the imperial period, urbanized space slowly shrank as the population dwindled to tens of thousands of inhabitants, down from one million in the first century c.e. Like the rim of froth left on a beach by an ebbing tide, the Aurelian Wall, built when foreign threats began weighing on the empire, marked the limits of a city that was largely virtual by the sixth century.

A fragile and exposed papacy picked up the torch, but within this fortress that had lost nine-tenths of its population and contained buildings of no use to a defeated power, the countryside reclaimed its rights. Crops, fallow land and pastures remained present throughout the Middle Ages, and it was not until the Renaissance that the large estates that had been the pride of ancient Rome, such as the famous gardens of Lucullus, were resurrected alongside the enthusiastic exhumation of antique statues. It was not uncommon to see a powerful prelate or his family establish both a "town residence" and a "country home," the latter sometimes situated within—rather than without—the third-century walls. Thus the Farneses' gardens crowned the Palatine Hill not far from their magnificent urban *palazzo*, while Ferdinando de' Medici's Pincio villa was close to the Florentine family's mansion.

Despite mutilation—due perhaps to modern thieves—this sculpture in the garden of the Villa Aldobrandini has lost none of its suggestive power. A couple stretched out on a banqueting bed with a young child sitting at the feet of the woman shows how Etruscans commemorated their dead. Roman parks are not only places to relax or play, they also offer food for thought.

Unlike its counterpart in Frascati, the Villa Aldobrandini on the Quirinal Hill has a garden that remains fairly private thanks to its inconspicuous entrance. Seen from the street, it looks like a hanging garden. Inside, it is dotted with statues such as this highly expressive baroque figure.

FROM THE VIA APPIA TO PALACE GARDENS

The entire area running from the Colosseum to the Aurelian Wall remains a sea of greenery today, providing a highly suggestive picture of Rome prior to 1870. This vast expanse is dotted with ruins both imposing (the Baths of Caracalla) and discreet (the Tomb of the Scipios), together with isolated churches such as San Cesareo. Even now, Via di Porta San Sebastiano and Via di Porta Latina, at the head of the Via Appia Antica, flanked on both sides by time-worn walls, resemble more country roads than modern city streets.

Near the old gate called Porta Latina, French Renaissance priest Benoît Adam decided to erect an oratory to the memory of the apostle John cheerfully emerging straight from a bath of boiling oil: San Giovanni in Oleo (St. John in Oil). The motto etched over the entrance ("At God's discretion") and the elegance of the architecture (to which Borromini would add a crowning pine cone in the seventeenth century), conjure up an image of a prelate who was refined and doubtless pious enough to want to meditate during his promenades.

Another haven of peace is the little courtyard in front of the church of San Giovanni a Porta Latina, with its centuries-old cedar tree and medieval well. Not far away begins the Via Appia Antica, a key sight which is best visited on a weekday, when solitude makes reverie possible. A seedy place at night—as it must already have been two thousand years ago—the "Appian Way" still boasts its original cobbles and its rows of tombs, both famous and modest, between cypress trees and umbrella pines. This evocative image has lost none of its power, to my mind, yet the ancient road can also be enjoyed for its liveliness on Saturdays and Sundays, when it is closed to traffic and becomes thronged with strolling and picnicking Romans.

The repopulation and growth of the city since the late nineteenth century have obviously diminished its rustic side, but reminders survive more or less everywhere. Even where the city has apparently gained the upper hand, the countryside has not said its last word. Grass grows fairly uninhibitedly between the paving stones of sidewalks (and sometimes in the streets), between gaps in walls, and on the roofs and domes of churches. In the heart of the old city it is not uncommon to see veritable screens of

The fame of the Via Appia Antica in no way dulls the emotion of strolling down it today. Lined with ruined tombs and monuments, it is beautiful both when deserted and when crowded with promenading Romans on weekends. Like all ancient ruins, however, its special poetic quality is best experienced at sunset.

Below: Somewhat unexpected here, this statue of a tailor is set in a niche of vegetation in the gardens of Palazzo del Quirinale. The palm in the foreground is indicative of the

variety of trees found in the park. In the nineteenth century, all kinds of exotic trees—some of them extremely rare in Europe—were planted alongside the standard Mediterranean varieties.

greenery tumbling from terraces and balconies, combining with the ocher walls to create a fresco of autumnal colors imbued with a certain melancholy. Where else but Rome could you see a quirky palazzo with cascades of ivy drawing together a columned portico, a tiny barber shop and—in memory of some miracle that occurred there—a star-studded madonna?

As it grew, the city dismembered the immense Ludovisi estate, which once rivaled Versailles, in order to create a neighborhood along Via Vittorio Veneto. In Fellini's day the area became the center of Roman life; although still elegant, it has since lost its role as a meeting place for intellectuals and film-makers. The sole vestige from the magnificent Ludovisi estate is the Casino dell'Aurora, set among later buildings, which gives just a

partial idea of the lifestyle of a family famous for its extraordinary collection of antiques. Other estates in the center of town were lucky enough to survive, such as those on the Quirinal Hill, namely Villa Aldobrandini and the Palazzo del Quirinale. The latter has been the residence of the president of the Republic of Italy ever since the fall of the Savoy monarchy in 1946. This enormous dwelling was once the main papal residence. Napoleon planned magnificent renovations for it, calling in particular on the talent of Ingres, but did not have the time to carry them out (any more than his son, styled the king of Rome). On its nearly ten acres of land, Mediterranean trees mingle with more exotic varieties, including a surprising selection of palm trees. A stroll in the admirably maintained gardens, open to the public one day per year, gives an idea of what the papal lifestyle must once have been like. A sense of grandeur did not exclude all whimsy and humor, as is evident from the hidden spouts that spurt water on surprised strollers who venture too close to the Fontana della Civetta. Then there is the coffee house built by Ferdinando Fuga at the request of Benedict XIV, reflecting all the elegance and refinement of the eighteenth century. The Quirinal gardens once descended lower than they do today, and it is well worth going to admire the grotto that was dug beneath the terrace of the palace. Now separated from the rest of the park, it includes a hydraulic organ whose music was seemingly played by angels of stone.

Left: This elegant fountain once adorned the gardens at Caserta (the "Versailles" of the Neapolitan branch of the Bourbon family). After the unification of Italy, King Umberto I had it moved to Palazzo del Quirinale. Perhaps art-loving popes would have been open-minded enough to accept these charming bathers for whom it is hard to find any edifying meaning. The white marble contrasts handsomely with the greenery and flower beds of what is probably the best-kept garden in Rome.

Right: This amazing boxwood maze is seen from a delightful edifice called the House of Urban VIII, tucked away amid the gardens on the Quirinal Hill. Wisteria hanging from the house adds a touch of bright color to this mysterious composition.

Right: When tourists look through the keyhole in the gate of the Priorata di Malta to espy Saint Peter's, they have no idea of the beauty of the garden within. The skillfully designed flower beds provide a counterpoint to Piranesi's remarkable architecture, notably the order's chapel, where he is buried. As suggested by these rose bushes set in boxwood hedges, the pattern of the Maltese cross is present everywhere.

Left and below: The Knights of Malta have the privilege of owning one of the most secret gardens in Rome, on top of the Aventine Hill. A cast-iron bench offers a place of rest or meditation along a fine alley ending in the bust of a philosopher set in a rocaille niche. The Italian-style garden is dotted with sculptures that serve as landmarks, breaking the monotony of certain stretches of greenery and discreetly affirming the superiority of humankind over nature.

Two Verdant Hills: Celio and Aventino

The Quirinal Hill is further evidence of the Roman tendency to seek the heights when laying out their gardens. Among the seven hills of ancient Rome, two have miraculously preserved this tradition. Such is the case with the Caelian Hill (Celio), one of Rome's most secret wonders. The easiest way to approach it is to start from Piazza delle Navicella (thus named for its fountain in the shape of a *navicella*, or small ship) and head up Clivo di Scauro, passing in front of the basilica of Santi Giovanni e Paolo, built on the ruins of an ancient house. Then you reach Villa Celimontana, the former estate of the dukes of Mattei, which has its own special charm. Situated right in the city yet some distance from the center and all main thoroughfares, it forms an island of absolute calm. "We became absorbed for two full hours," wrote Stendhal, "at the end of one of those lanes in the Villa Mattei—a sublime view of the Roman countryside which no one had told us about." The description still holds true, except for the fact that the Mattei family has been replaced by the Italian Geographical Society. The layout of the grounds has remained unchanged, and the foliage is particularly exuberant. Pines, cedars, palm trees and green oaks provide shade for the crowds of statues, columns and other antique marbles that were once part of the famous Mattei collection. Not far away, heading back toward the Colosseum, you come upon the church of San Gregorio, whose

restrained baroque facade rises majestically above a fine staircase. The place to pause, however, is the little enclosure next door. At the end of a garden closed by a gate, three chapels evoke the lives of Saint Andrew, Saint Gregory and Saint Gregory's mother. In addition to frescoes by Guido Reni and Domenichino, the site is known for a moving legend: Saint Gregory was giving food to the poor when an angel came and sat among them—an old, worn marble table still found there is allegedly the one where the miracle occurred. For visitors touched mainly by the poetic aspect of that tale, today's miracle resides in the timeless serenity that the place generates.

Another historic hill which is worth a leisurely stroll is the Aventine (Aventino), located along the edge of the Tiber somewhat outside the center of town. It has made only grudging concessions to urbanization, and must therefore be attacked on foot, starting from the church of Santa Maria in Cosmedin. This part of Rome was still countryside until the early twentieth century. Many old drawings and paintings show, in addition to ancient monuments that still stand today, cattle drinking at the baroque fountain in the middle

Top: The basilica of Santa Sabina is probably the most striking building on the Aventine Hill and one of the most unforgettable sights of Rome. The church and monastery belong to the Dominicans, who perpetuate the memory of their founder. It is easy to imagine Saint Dominic meditating in the cloisters, which create an introspective atmosphere as intense today as it must have been seven hundred years ago.

Left: Such sobriety contrasts with the elegance of motifs devised by Piranesi for the Knights of Malta, whose military vocation was becoming a thing of the past by the eighteenth century.

of what is now Piazza Bocca della Verità.

If you turn left on leaving the church, shortly after crossing Via della Greca you come to the foot of one of the oddest streets in Rome. Clivo di Rocca Savelli, which climbs to the top of the Aventine Hill, is a kind of enclave of the past that seems to defy modernity. The street, if you can call it that, rises in steps between two roughly rendered walls overflowing with vegetation. This passage lined with street lights from another era is inaccessible to cars and little used. By looking back every now and then as you climb, the city begins to appear below you, yet the sound of traffic remains muffled. I know of few places in Rome that make such a strong impression. The *clivo* leads to a public park which has replaced the medieval fortress of the powerful Savelli family. Planted with orange trees, the edge of this garden offers one of the finest views of Rome on one side and a good view of the apse of the church of Santa Sabina on the other. I once heard Cardinal Poupard call the Aventine "the hill that prays." Indeed, it hosts a large number of monasteries and cloisters, each a spiritual garden, such as the one in Santa Sabina where Dominicans meditate.

A little further on, the monastic garden of Sant'Alessio evokes one of the most touching of Christian Rome's many legends. Highly popular in the Middle Ages, the tale of "the poor boy under the stairs" recounts how Alexis (Alessio), son of a patrician, returned to Rome after a long voyage to Syria where he converted to Christianity. His family no longer recognized him, and he died years later after having worked for them as a servant, sleeping at the foot of the

staircase. Although the interior of the church was rather badly restored during the nineteenth century, it is hard to remain unmoved at the sight of the ancient well belonging to the house of Alexis, strangely planted in the middle of the nave, and at the wooden staircase allegedly from the same house, glorified by a baroque setting.

Still further down the street is Piazza dei Cavalieri di Malta, masterfully designed by Piranesi, where the residence of the Grand Prior of the Italian Knights of Malta stands. A peephole in the gate of the residence, now well known to tourists, provides a spyglass-view of the dome of Saint Peter's. During the high season, an ice-cream seller takes advantage of the windfall. Special permission is required, however, to visit the garden, with its orange trees, boxwood and cypresses—another marvel of design by Piranesi, who is buried there.

Villa Celimontana does not have one of the better-known parks in Rome, although it covers much of the Caelian Hill. Tourists tend to overlook it, but its charm is no secret to Romans. The estate once belonged to the Mattei family, and its preservation has helped make the Caelian one of the city's greener hills, along with the Palatine. The park boasts handsome exotic trees and vestiges of antiquity that include an Egyptian obelisk dedicated to Rameses II.

On the Heights of Pincio and Gianicolo

Two other hills, although not among the original seven, are still covered in gardens. The Pincio includes the gardens of the Trinità dei Monti and the Villa Medici, and a large part of the grounds of the Villa Borghese, which extends over 200 acres. The Borghese estate boasts nearly four centuries of history. It began with Cardinal Scipione Borghese, nephew of Pope Paul V, who wanted to build himself a pleasant residence that could house his precious collection of artworks and also serve as a setting for his magnificent festivities, including hunting parties. As a refined prelate and enlightened patron, the cardinal assembled an extraordinary collection of sculptures, paintings and objets d'art by such glittering names as Raphael, Caravaggio and Bernini. The family continued to add to the collection until Prince Camillo Borghese, husband of Pauline Bonaparte, was obliged to sell a large number of antique pieces to France (where they are now proudly displayed in the Louvre). That loss was perhaps more than made up by Canova's famous statue of Pauline as Venus, in the pose of a goddess confident of her powers of seduction. The grounds themselves were organized in three sections. The first two were laid out in a highly rational way, with lanes of elm and cypress dividing spaces that harbored a theater, fountains, a hidden garden and countless other follies. The third park was left wild until late-eighteenth-century modifications added an artificial lake and the island containing the temple to Aesculapius, now one of the ground's more attractive spots. The park hosts not only the Galleria Borghese, but also institutions as prestigious as the Museo Nazionale Etrusco di Villa Giulia and the Galleria Nazionale d'Arte Moderna, not to mention several foreign academies.

The edge of the Pincio affords a unique view of Rome, especially in the morning when, on clear days, the dome of Saint Peter's appears in all its whiteness and at sunset, when its gray-blue silhouette stands out sharply against the reddening backdrop. Rome's municipal and national governments have undertaken a vast renovation of the magnificent Pincio site. The most spectacular and long-awaited refurbishment concerned the Galleria Borghese, which has just

In the grounds of his villa, Cardinal Ferdinando de' Medici built an artificial mount—Parnassus—which provides a magnificent view of Rome. This vantage point, now surrounded by laurel, also offers a unique view of the villa's twin towers, whose whiteness stands out spectacularly against the sea of green and, further off, the city of Rome.

Right: The grounds of the Villa Medici are like an open-air museum. Most of the famous statues once there were shipped to Florence by Medici heirs in the eighteenth century. Faithful copies (here, of the captive kings in porphyry) re-create the original atmosphere in the shade of large umbrella pines planted in the nineteenth century.

Below: The Villa Medici's lanes are dotted with terms—tapered pedestals topped by a carved head—in the antique manner. Although a few in the garden have been replaced by copies for reasons of preservation, the villa is lucky to possess almost all its original terms, which acted as benevolent spirits.

Right: This statue with its melancholy grace adorns a fountain at the Villa Medici. Probably placed here in the nineteenth century, it exemplifies a certain romantic vision of Rome: a poignant sense of beauty and of passing time. Stendhal, who fell in love with Milan at age eighteen, gained affection for Rome only slowly; whereas Milan was youthful love-at-first-sight, Rome was like an "elder sister" whose gravity suited the mature man. Several scenes from *La Dolce Vita* suggest that this feeling survives in the modern view of the city, which some people mask with frivolity.

Left: The legend of Niobe is one of the most tragic in classical mythology. Having been the object of Jupiter's attentions, Niobe made the mistake of arousing Juno's ire through her boastfulness. Juno turned Niobe's children, of whom she was so proud, into stone. The Niobid group was the largest sculpture unearthed during the Renaissance, and became the pride of Ferdinando de' Medici's collection at the Villa Medici. The original pieces are now in the Uffizi in Florence, but Balthus had casts made so that the group could be reconstituted in the garden of the villa, where their tortured figures are set among acanthus.

Top: Lying among the acanthus at the Villa Medici, one of Niobe's children, turned to stone, resembles a piece of sculpture from archaic Greece.

Lower right: A mascaron in stone keeps watch over the gate between villa and park. This gate is no longer used since Balthus blocked it with a colossal statue of Dea Roma (originally a cumbersome gift from Pope Gregory XIII to Cardinal Ferdinando).

Far right: At the end of a garden lane at the Villa Medici, a goddess watches over a fountain flowing into an antique sarcophagus. The layout of the garden has not changed since it was created over four hundred years ago, but the vegetation is a product of the nineteenth century—denser and darker than that of earlier periods. This impression is accentuated by the natural growth of the hedges, which, seeking light, have slowly narrowed the width of the lanes.

In the nineteenth century it was a custom—an obsession even—to fill public parks in Rome with figures of famous (or now-forgotten) people. Some are grandiose, not to say pompous, such as the equestrian statues of Garibaldi and his wife on the Janiculum Hill. Others are more discreet, such as this tribute to Byron hidden in the greenery of the Villa Borghese. In a city which pays relatively little homage to foreigners, Byron shares the privilege of a statue with Victor Hugo and Goethe (who lived near Piazza del Popolo from 1786 to 1788, and was profoundly marked by his stay in the Eternal City).

reopened in all the splendor of its 1798 remodeling. The focus has now shifted to the gardens. These are dotted with edifices which bear poetic-sounding names, such as the Casino della Meridiana with its aviary (*uccelliera*), and which have been left in a state of semi-abandon for decades. When this ambitious undertaking is finally complete, Rome will have a "museum park" probably unmatched anywhere. It already represents one of the wonders of the city.

Directly opposite the Pincio, overlooking Trastevere, is the Janiculum (Gianicolo), another hill that has remained verdant. The large terrace dominated by the equestrian statue of Garibaldi is well known to tourists, but the gardens and cloister of Sant'Onofrio are among the city's most evocative sites, particularly popular with lovers. Sant'Onofrio is located at the foot of Passeggiata del Gianicolo when arriving from the Vatican. The spot should be famous, because it houses the tomb of Torquato Tasso, a celebrated Italian poet whose influence extended across Europe in the seventeenth century. Yet it seems to be little known, and you will almost always find yourself alone, regardless of season. The Franciscan monastery has a cloister with an upper gallery that sports brilliantly colored geraniums. Perfectly maintained, it is a wonderful place to meditate, with its recently restored frescoes recounting the legendary life of Saint Onophrius, son of a king of Persia. The garden in front of the church, with its fountain and palm trees, is another haven of peace with a vista that encompasses a large part of the city. A plaque on the church points

out that Chateaubriand felt special affection for this spot. "If I have the luck to end my days here, I have arranged to have a small room in Sant'Onofrio, next to the bedroom where Tasso died. In one of the most beautiful spots on earth, among orange trees and green oaks, with all of Rome before my eyes every morning as I get down to work, between the poet's deathbed and his tomb, I will invoke the muse of fame and misfortune." Modern visitors will easily succumb to the charm of this little garden even if their reveries do not accord with the melancholy overtones of Chateaubriand's romantic vision. At the other end of the hill, on the winding loops of Via Garibaldi, stands the monastery—formerly Spanish—of San Pietro in Montorio, famous for its circular Tempietto by Bramante, next to the Spanish Academy, whose artists enjoy one of the finest views of Rome.

On that same end of the Janiculum, but on the slope facing away from the city, the grounds of Villa Doria Pamphili are even more extensive and hillier than those of the Villa Borghese. Stands of pine and vast stretches of grass give it a more rustic feel. It is particularly worth visiting in the springtime, when the lawn is invaded by daisy-like flowers called *margheritini dei prati*, "little meadow marguerites." A cascading fountain tumbles into a pond of fine dimensions. The water is somewhat invaded by vegetation, much to the satisfaction of the frogs and the children trying to spot them through the camouflage. Although much of the park is inspired by the English landscape style, the monumental theater at the foot of the villa and the

The seventeenth-century grounds of the Villa Borghese were radically altered by Camillo Borghese, who married Pauline Bonaparte. Its lanes are dotted with many statues, monuments and pavilions. Details like this fountain mask and fine vase add charm (below), as does a reflecting pond before a simple loggia guarded by four lions (right).

The view of the city from the Janiculum Hill is perhaps more beautiful than from the Pincio opposite. The buildings and churches of old Rome seem closer and the light at dusk is unmatched. Trees descend almost down to Trastevere, ringing the city's ocher volumes in green. The view is conducive to meditation, to judge by this young woman sitting on the parapet, unwittingly living the dream of Chateaubriand. The French writer hoped to end his days in the nearby monastery of Sant'Onofrio, where Tasso was buried and whose little garden has a similar view.

surrounding gardens are formal in design and have been restored to their original splendor by recent renovation. They form a superb platform for the villa itself—a fine edifice built in the mid seventeenth century for Prince Pamphili by Alessandro Algardi, a great baroque artist who remains sadly neglected.

THE GARDEN OF ETERNAL REST

Finally, although it may appear paradoxical to mention a cemetery in a book devoted to lifestyle, it is impossible not to save a special place for one of Rome's most bewitching spots—the so-called "non-Catholic" or Protestant Cemetery designed not only for foreigners (mostly Protestant or Orthodox Christians who refused to recognize the supremacy of the pope), but also for atheists such as the political thinker Antonio Gramsci. The paradox is not so surprising when you recall that Rome usually presents death as a simple trip to a better world; unlike Naples and Palermo, where macabre images in churches are part of the everyday universe, in Rome religious faith dons a friendly air. Nothing is more revealing of this attitude than certain tomb sculptures

by Bernini where the deceased are shown in the prime of life, chatting to each other animatedly. The Protestant Cemetery nevertheless stands out from all others in the peacefulness and privacy of its triangular garden, dotted with tombstones, especially the movingly simple marker for the heart of an anonymous young English poet who turns out to be none other than Keats. It is just like being in an English country graveyard, except that the Pyramid of Caius Cestius rising above it and the age-old umbrella pines shading it remind us that we are still in Rome.

The gardens of Rome (unlike the English landscape garden) enhance nature rather than imitate it. They are striking for their constant—and sometimes obsessive—staging of the grandeur of ancient civilization. The Villa Borghese is thus populated with replicas of masterpieces of Greco-Roman statuary.

An angel of sorrow leans over a tomb in the Protestant Cemetery where Keats and Shelley lie (England's greatest romantic poets, along with Byron). Perhaps Shelley had a premonition of his fate when he wrote, "It might make one in love with death to think that one should be buried in so sweet a place."

Roman
Interiors

A PASSION FOR ART HAS GRACED ROMAN HOMES FOR CENTURIES. THIS LOVE OF BEAUTY CAN STILL BE SEEN IN ALL ITS FORMS, FROM THE UNMATCHED LAVISHNESS OF GRAND PALACES TO THE PURE SIMPLICITY OF MODERN APARTMENTS.

Since the center of Rome has few parks, residents have ingeniously created pockets of greenery. Even historic dwellings—such as the sixteenth-century Palazzo Caetani shown here—boast terrace gardens that produce lush vegetation offering flowers in spring and coolness in summer.

Preceding pages:
Palazzo Doria Pamphili.

Perhaps no other capital city in the world boasts as many beautiful houses as Rome. Magnificent or simple, anchored in the past or the present, they all display a love of art in every form. This key feature sometimes even takes precedence over the comfort or convenience so important in northern countries. Of course, Rome has had the luck to remain relatively untouched by wars and revolutions, helping it preserve the past's great decorative projects. But credit should go above all to the almost innate sense of beauty—not to say splendor—that has become the city's hallmark. Grand Roman interiors are striking, in fact, for their lavishness, generous proportions, and abundant artworks. Although they reflect a lifestyle limited to a social elite, they nevertheless represent the highest form of a profoundly historical taste

for everything that conveys majesty, grandeur and the expression of authority.

It is significant that the same word in Italian, *palazzo*, means both "apartment building" and "palace," an overlap perhaps best understood in Rome itself. Roman palaces seem integrated into the fabric of the city rather than detached from it. Although some of the more substantial mansions stand apart from their neighbors, the rupture is never complete. The two narrow streets running alongside Palazzo Farnese, for instance, seem more like hallways than true dividers. Meanwhile, a palace such as Palazzo Borghese—perhaps the most outsized of all—seems like a city within the city. Its austere architecture barely makes a break with its surroundings, even though its irregular shape has earned it the familiar nickname of *cembalo*, "the grand piano." A store or craftsman's workshop will often occupy the ground floor of these dwellings, something unthinkable in a comparable Parisian mansion. Many of Rome's palaces have been allocated to official occupants— Palazzo del Quirinale for the president of Italy, Palazzo Chigi for the prime minister— while others house embassies. Yet most remain inhabited, often by descendants of Rome's old aristocratic families, notably the "black nobility" that gave birth to popes and frequently came from other regions of Italy.

These palaces are not comprised solely of sumptuous salons, however; they formerly housed a multitude of relatives, friends and, of course, servants. The upper stories thus contain simpler rooms, which are actually

more suited to a modern lifestyle. Residents of the formerly less favored floors have been granted revenge by elevators and the modern desire for light and wonderful views, not to mention rooftop terraces that afford the possibility of having a patch of green in the heart of the city.

Less visibly noble neighborhoods and buildings on the fringes of the old center have long attracted artists, intellectuals and foreigners. This tradition applies not only to Piazza di Spagna but also, since the end of World War II, to Trastevere and, still more recently, to more or less dilapidated areas such as Testaccio, Termini train station and Piazza Vittorio Emanuele. All these developments reflect more than changing fashion, for they demonstrate that the city still holds, as it did in the past, an ever-

renewed power of attraction.

The interiors discussed in this chapter reflect this diversity, yet each one bears—in its own fashion—the hallmark of Rome. Our tour will start with stately apartments in the grand historic mansions, then lead to the upper floors of palaces where elegance becomes more intimate, before heading to neighborhoods less charged with history, where art stills remains ever-present although—and this is typical of Rome—in a form markedly more personal and eclectic as well as modern. Finally, our itinerary will reveal the Romans' love of the countryside, which occasionally prompted them to build "villas" on magnificent estates within the ancient walls of the city (in addition to the often magnificent ones they owned in areas outside Rome, such as Frascati).

A Roman *palazzo* should always offer a fine view, which might feature the charming little observatory overlooking the Villa Celimontana (left) or the famous inner courtyard of Palazzo Farnese (below). The courtyard arcade, designed by Michelangelo, was originally open. Although subsequent walling altered its overall rhythm, the arcade remains amazingly vigorous.

Left: Palazzo Pallavicini-Rospigliosi has one of the finest hidden gardens in Rome. Set on a terrace next to Casino dell'Aurora, it is reached by this double flight of elegant stairs. The austere color of the stone derives cheer from the busts that have acquired a fine sheen with time, and from the fountain flowing in its midst.

FAMILY PALACES

Unlike Paris, to take just one example, historic dwellings in Rome often still belong to descendants of the families who built or remodeled them down through the centuries.

The Massimo Family

Such is the case, for example, with the Massimos, one of the oldest households in Rome. Legend has it that they descend from the notorious consul Quintus Fabius Maximus, nicknamed Cunctator (meaning "delayer"), who played a decisive role in the defeat of Hannibal. When Napoleon expressed skepticism about the connection, one Massimo wittily replied, "I'm not claiming anything, Sire, but the legend has been handed down in the family for the past two thousand years."

The land on which Palazzo Massimo alle Colonne and Palazzo di Pirro are built has belonged to the same family since the tenth century. The street that corresponded to today's Corso Vittorio Emanuele long bore the Massimo name, as does the charming little square behind the edifice, Piazza de' Massimi, even today. From this square, which is adorned with a fine antique column, the two palaces join into a single facade decorated by sixteenth-century frescoes. A third dwelling completed the complex until it was demolished to make way for Corso Vittorio Emanuele. Palazzo di Pirro owes its name to the statue of an ancient warrior whose armor was decorated with elephants,

which Renaissance scholars immediately associated with Pyrrhus, the famous king of Epirus who was the first to use elephants against the Romans. The statue, however—found in the vestiges of Domitian's Theater which once stood on the site—is, in fact, Mars the Avenger. Bought from the Massimo family by Pope Clement XII, it is now in the collection of the Museo Capitolino. The palace, like the neighboring one, had to be rebuilt following the sack of Rome in 1527. Baron Coppa-Solari and the baroness (née Teresa Massimo-Lancellotti) have devoted remarkable energy in making the residence live again. It, too, was long thought to be the work of Baldassare Peruzzi, but the discovery of a drawing in the print department of the

Right: A strange mirroring effect has been created in Palazzo Massimo di Pirro—the reception room in the background can be seen in the gouache in the foreground (by French artist Philippe Casanova). Lined with green brocade, the salon offers a glimpse of the beautiful stucco and painting that decorate the frieze. Restored with great diligence by the owners, this delicate example of the work of a disciple of Raphael depicts the story of Aeneas, to whom the Romans attributed the ancient founding of their city.

Right: The grand salon in Palazzo Massimo di Pirro is an excellent example of a stately reception room designed to be imposing rather than comfortable or friendly. The classic decoration includes red silk brocade on the walls, tapestries, paintings and a frieze executed by a follower of Giulio Romano, another of Raphael's disciples. Light plays on the many colors of the floor, a fine modern reconstruction of traditional Roman flooring. Terracotta tiles, slabs of marble and squares of travertine are enhanced by the precious materials used in the middle for the heraldic emblems of the Coppa-Solari and Massimo-Lancellotti families.

At the time when this mosaic was found on property belonging to the Massimos, it was still possible to re-use ancient relics for private purposes. This geometrical masterpiece was therefore reconstituted in the first half of the nineteenth century in one of the salons of Palazzo di Pirro. The varying sizes of the small black and white cubes gave Roman mosaics a "shuddery" feel that tempered the rigidity of the pattern, an effect impossible to reproduce in modern copies. It is hardly surprising that a Bavarian monarch wanted to dance on this one, given the waltzing impression of its whirl.

Uffizi in Florence has established that it was in fact based on a design by Giovanni Mangone, an architect who collaborated on the church of San Luigi dei Francese but was known above all for his military fortifications. That may explain the extreme austerity of the exterior. The rooms on the piano nobile, or main floor, underwent major renovation in the first half of the nineteenth century, on the occasion of Donna Teresa's great grandfather's first marriage to a princess of the house of Savoy. At that time, the state apartments in both adjoining palaces were remodeled to enable them to communicate with one another. For many years now, the Coppa-Solaris have worked to undo these alterations, to rediscover and reconstruct the former setting, to return these magnificent spaces to their original luster. In the entrance hall, they managed to uncover a few fragments of the original frescoes, and have

placed over one doorway a marble inscription which records the date of these major restoration efforts, carried out *Deo adjuvante* ("with the help of God"). From the windows in this hall, you can see the small bell tower on top of the neighboring palace, the scene of one of Rome's most touching miracles. Saint Philip Neri, a highly venerated and popular figure in sixteenth-century Rome, had been called to the bedside of a young Massimo prince at death's door. Having arrived too late, the saint nevertheless brought the young man back to life, only to ask him if he would rather join his sister, who had died a short time earlier. Having glimpsed the light of heaven, the prince decided to return there immediately. The room where the miracle occurred was subsequently turned into a chapel, and every year on March 16 the Palazzo Massimo alle Colonne is opened to crowds of faithful who flock to hear the masses celebrated all day long.

The entrance hall of the piano nobile of Palazzo di Pirro affords a view of the chapel bell tower. It leads into a little salon that is more secular, intimate, and well lit. The salon is decorated with stucco and frescoes by the sixteenth-century artist Pierino del Vaga. A few years ago, the decoration was in a terrible state—the coffered wood ceiling had lost its color, the stucco was begrimed by thick coats of paint, and the frescoes, invaded by saltpeter or flaking off the walls, were threatened with total destruction. By calling on the skills of a great restorer, Maurizio Rossi, who had worked at the

The ornate back of a stately chair, still covered in its original upholstery, echoes the elaborate frame of a fine seventeenth-century painting inspired by Guido Reni. Roman furniture often tends to be designed for effect rather than comfort, with proportions adapted to the size of the huge rooms.

Vatican for many years, the Coppa-Solaris were able to save this remarkable cycle, which depicts the legend of Dido and Aeneas as recounted by Virgil in the first four books of the *Aeneid*. The salon opens onto a much larger room, which is used for major receptions and formal dinners. This large salon, notable for its frescoes, a collection of eighteenth-century porcelain from Saxony and a fine group of Flemish paintings, is also noteworthy for the beauty of its tiled floor, which as been restored by Donna Teresa with great care. Tiled in a combination of terracotta, travertine, porphyry and other precious marbles, the center of the floor is decorated with the coats of arms of the Coppa and Massimo-Lancellotti families, topped by a marquess's coronet (prior to receiving princely status, the Massimos were "marquesses of the baldachin," a title shared with a very restricted number of families—

the Costagutis, Patrizis, Sacchettis and Theodolis—who had the right to receive the pope in their homes).

The large salon leads to a succession of smaller but no less attractive rooms. First comes a small salon containing the dais of what was the throne room in the last century, but whose main attraction is the remarkable Roman mosaic on the floor. The thousands of small cubes comprising the mosaic were discovered on a family estate in 1818, and accurately reassembled here. The next little room was recently the site of a stirring discovery—a false nineteenth-century ceiling hid a painted decor of great beauty, including a frieze showing the main gods of the ancient pantheon in dress probably considered too scanty by a period that was far more prudish than the sixteenth century. The room is currently undergoing restoration.

Above: The Hercules salon, four stories high, is the most imposing room in the entire Farnese palazzo, giving a good idea of the building's proportions. Light enters through numerous windows, creating superb variations on the walls and the fine terracotta flooring. The colossal statue decorating the salon is a cast of the famous Farnese Hercules, now in Naples.

The Farnese Family

Not far from Palazzo di Pirro is the finest product of the open-mindedness displayed by great sixteenth-century ecclesiastics such as Alessandro Farnese, elected pope in 1534 under the name of Paul III. His palace boasts the famous gallery where Annibale and Agostino Carracci depicted *The Loves of the Gods* with refreshing irony. Thanks to its architecture, Palazzo Farnese is also generally considered the most beautiful in Rome. France is certainly lucky to be able to use the residence as its embassy in Italy. The embassy, along with the French School in Rome, has occupied the building since 1874, thereby perpetuating a tradition that dates back to the Ancien Régime, since the Farnese family had already rented the building to the French in the early decades of the seventeenth century. The restoration work which will soon return the entire edifice to its original splendor is being closely followed by the current ambassador, Jacques Blot, with his characteristic enthusiasm. His office—perhaps

Right: Niches were set into the walls around the Hercules salon to relieve the monotony. Each niche contains the bust of an emperor—a reminder that the Farnese dynasty claimed descent from Aeneas (thanks to some fancy genealogical work). Raked sunlight in daytime (or torchlight at night) throws these sculptures into sharp contrast helping to create a theatrical effect in the salon, now decorated with large tapestries.

Left: The light effects are equally warm in the private apartments fitted out for Cardinal Farnese, yet here they contribute to a more intimate atmosphere.

Above: This salon with its monumental marble fireplace is given a French touch thanks to classic Empire furniture, tapestries from the Gobelins Manufactory (set off perfectly by the scarlet silk fabric on the walls), and a vast carpet from the Savonnerie Manufactory.

Left: The red salon in Palazzo Farnese—a perfect setting for diplomatic receptions—is reflected in the fine old mirror set above a lavish baroque console table. The inner shutters and large curtains are no obstacle to the sun, which adds luster to the admirable patina of the tile floor.

Right: On seeing this detail from the famous Carracci gallery in Palazzo Farnese, it is easy to see why Stendhal, normally a religious skeptic, thought Catholicism was the faith most propitious to happiness, at least when compared to austere Protestantism. Cardinal Farnese displayed a striking sense of liberty when he commissioned *The Loves of the Gods* from the Carracci brothers about 1600. Rarely has the myth of virility been handled with so much irony—this panel makes Jupiter look foolish in the face of Juno's admittedly irresistible advances. The caryatids hide their faces or lower their glances (as does the eagle), all visibly shocked by the father of the gods.

the most beautiful in the world—is located in the Farnese archive room, where the painter Francesco Salviati depicted the epic story of the Farnese dynasty (supposedly descended—yet again—from Aeneas, although in fact of humble origins). Perfect settings for diplomatic receptions, meanwhile, are provided by the galleries flanking the courtyard designed by Michelangelo, by immense salons (such as the one that formerly featured the famous Farnese Hercules, now the pride of the Museo e Gallerie Nazionali in Naples) and by more human-sized rooms (decorated with magnificent Gobelins tapestries), not to mention the Carracci gallery itself. A masked ball given in the residence every year provides the touch of exuberance that these glamorous premises require.

Although perfect for celebrations and ceremonies, is the *palazzo* really suited to everyday life? Right from the start, the Farneses envisaged it as a place of almost regal presence rather than as a place to live. Ultimately, then, they did not reside there much, any more than did the Bourbons of Naples, who inherited the *palazzo* and retained it until 1911 (having rented it to France from 1874 onward). However, life at Palazzo Farnese is not limited, fortunately, to the stately apartments. There are more private rooms, including a small dining room located in Cardinal Odoardo Farnese's former *camerino*, where the ambassador and his wife like to receive guests. Furthermore, a garden and, above all, the terrace that formerly linked the main residence to its outbuildings make it possible to escape all that grandeur. The terrace offers a superb view of the rear facade of the palace with its majestic loggia, as well as the occasionally dilapidated roofs of neighboring buildings.

Intended above all for grandiose receptions, Palazzo Farnese nevertheless has a few rooms suited to a more private lifestyle. The *camerino* (little bedroom) used by Cardinal Farnese now serves as a dining room when the current resident—the French ambassador—has a small number of guests. The ceiling, also decorated by the Carraccis, predates *The Loves of the Gods*; it is also more moralizing, at least to judge by the Greek inscription which says that rest is the reward for work well done—a maxim that Hercules could never really appreciate.

Top right: Palazzo Caetani, whose main apartment has remained in the state it was left in by the last representative of that very old family, illustrates the way in which such spaces can be inhabited in modern times. The dining room is far from overwhelming, and the collector's items added by the current occupants, the Brazilian ambassador and his wife, personalize the setting.

Lower right: The severity of this tapestried salon is softened by the sweet expression on the face a fine eighteenth-century Brazilian virgin, placed on an amazing sixteenth-century table, a masterpiece of Roman marble work (mother-of-pearl was also used for such pieces).

Palazzo Caetani

Also allocated to an ambassador—although as a residence only—the piano nobile of Palazzo Caetani on Via delle Botteghe Oscure projects an image different from that of the Farnese palazzo. It is more or less contemporary with the latter, having been built in the second half of the sixteenth century for the Mattei family, who housed Caravaggio there. At Palazzo Caetani, however, the mark of Counter-Reformation austerity is more visible. Acquired by the Caetanis in the eighteenth century, the *palazzo* remained in their hands until the family died out just a few years ago. The building's heritage is zealously maintained by a foundation (which also administers the magnificent Ninfa estate on the road to Naples). Thus the apartment occupied by Brazil's ambassador to the Holy See remains in the state that the last members of the illustrious family left it, as though awaiting the return of its former owner. Yet the current ambassador, Marco Cesar Meira Naslausky, and his wife Sandra are themselves great collectors, and use this timeless setting to display objects acquired on their worldwide travels, thereby adding a touch of life and warmth to everything. The glittering colors of romantic opaline objects seem no more out of place on gilded console tables than do the South American madonnas of painted wood, or porcelain from China and Meissen, or a rare set of Indo-Portuguese ivories. The quarters comprise two parts, each different in spirit. First comes a succession of majestic sixteenth-century rooms, decorated with

Right: The heavy decoration of the grand salon in Palazzo Caetani is reflected in this mirror with elaborate frame. It is set on a console table topped by a Roman mosaic which reportedly came from the Tivoli villa of Emperor Hadrian. As is proper for an ambassador to the Vatican, a photograph of the pope figures prominently. This part of the *palazzo* has retained major decorative features executed about 1600 for Cardinal Girolamo Mattei, notably the fine landscape friezes painted by Paul Bril, a Flemish artist living in Rome.

Above: When the Caetani family acquired the palace, several rooms were refurbished in a pleasant, eighteenth-century spirit. This salon, for example, is drenched in light thanks to the presence of a huge mirror. Its silk wall covering has been preserved almost intact.

Right: The most successful renovation concerns the dining room. The ambassador and his wife have placed some personal objects on the table and sideboards, notably colorful parrots in Meissen porcelain.

coffered ceilings, tapestries and frescoes (including fine landscapes by the Rome-based Flemish painter Paul Bril); these rooms are entered by the gallery traditionally found in Roman palaces, paved with antique mosaics. This imposing atmosphere contrasts with the rooms the Caetanis built two centuries later, where proportions are more intimate. The decoration in these rooms was done by Cavalucci in a neoclassical spirit and the salons are hung with delicately patterned wallpaper, embodying a lifestyle as comfortable as it was graceful, typified by the elegant dining room whose refinement extends to the tiniest details.

Above: In contrast to the salons, the passage leading to the former palace chapel, flanked by a double curtain hanging from a gilded wood canopy, has a severe, solemn feel.

Left: A fine example of how to lend a personal touch to the historic setting of Palazzo Caetani. Photographs of the ambassador's mother and wife fit naturally on the fine late-eighteenth-century mantelpiece, along with personal knickknacks.

Palazzo Doria Pamphili

An entirely different sense of proportion is projected by Palazzo Doria Pamphili which, along with Palazzo Borghese, is one of the biggest in Rome. It was built over a period of four centuries, and has an imposing facade on Via del Corso that was completed in 1734. Other sections, however—notably the facade leading to the painting gallery—date from the same period as Palazzo Caetani and therefore project a more austere image. Once past this first impression, the palace presents visitors with dazzling interiors. Owned by the Doria Pamphilis—who still live there—it is well known for its remarkable collection of paintings. Yet the palace also has private apartments which the current prince, Jonathan Doria Pamphili, now allows to be visited. For everyday life, his family primarily used less solemn rooms, such as the little dining room decorated in a delicate harmony of greens. The Doria Pamphilis merely passed through the largest rooms,

which occasionally came to life as huge playrooms for the children.

That the palace is still an inhabited dwelling is indicated by a mass of portraits, souvenirs and family objects, such as the bust of Jonathan's grandfather playing the violin—an almost frivolous image that should not disguise the fact that he was a major opponent of fascism and the first mayor of Rome after World World II. A strange sled adorning the entrance is more of a toy than a useful object, snow being rare in Rome even though it falls heavily on the summits above the Tiber plain, whose snowy tips remain visible from the city until Easter. A smoking room, decorated in woodwork and furnished with dark leather armchairs, suggests the influence of England, to which the Doria Pamphili family has been closely linked for several generations now; one of the current prince's forebears attempted— unsuccessfully as it happens—to import the English tradition of having men and women separate after dinner. Such a custom would hardly have been compatible with the Roman lifestyle.

As in all great Roman collections, reminders of antiquity occupy a prime place. Their sheer abundance means that some pieces do not always receive the attention they merit. It is hard not to be moved, for example, by the evocative power of this figure of Silenus, to whom Socrates compared his own ugliness.

Left: Despite a basically Roman setting, the apartments in Palazzo Doria Pamphili sometimes recall the lifestyle of an English manor. Typically Roman, for example, is this magnificent gilded wood pedestal (bottom) with a graceful female figure supporting a haughtier, crowned eagle. In the study (top), a family bust seems ready to spring to life in a dark wood-paneled setting that recalls Victorian England, a country which the Doria Pamphilis have close ties with.

Right: A wonderful play of light in the private apartments of Palazzo Doria Pamphili. Through the panes of a small gilded rococo screen can be seen a frieze along the wall. The cherub—graceful without being cute—and the small genre painting create a much more intimate feeling than their counterparts in the stately reception rooms. Yet the decoration remains princely even when more adapted to private family life.

This bookstand, a veritable masterpiece of wood carving, serves as an easel for a small painting in the Pallavicini collection. The main apartments of the palazzo are still inhabited and boast a remarkable art collection begun in the seventeenth century. Rome's real "museums" are perhaps the places primarily designed to be homes.

Palazzo Pallavicini-Rospigliosi

Other nearby palaces remain in the hands of the families that built them, such as the Odescalchis (Piazza dei Santi Apostoli) and the Colonnas (whose residence on the slopes of the Quirinal Hill boasts one of the finest galleries in Rome). Yet one *palazzo* deserves special mention, although it may hardly be noticed when heading from Piazza Venezia to the Quirinal. Just before you reach Piazza del Quirinale there rises an imposing wall on Via XXIV Maggio, and through the gate can be glimpsed a vast, austere edifice in the background: Palazzo Pallavicini-Rospigliosi.

The exterior of the palace, built in the early seventeenth century for Cardinal Scipione Borghese before being purchased by Cardinal Mazarin, hardly hints at the riches it holds, notably the famous Casino dell'Aurora decorated by Guido Reni. Yet it is not a museum. The main apartments of the palace are still inhabited by Princess Pallavicini, one of the last great witnesses of a world and lifestyle that will soon be no more than a memory. Raised in Turin and Genoa, she came to Rome for her wedding just before World War II, and therefore never abandoned the rigorous, definite mentality that northern Italians find so lacking in Romans. "We're not going to let something so small come between us," a Roman upholsterer once told her on the day he was due to deliver some work, as he admitted that he had not even *begun* it: "Eternity is on our side." Such anecdotes pale beside the tribulations of the war—not only the loss of her husband, but also the risks taken in sheltering resistance

fighters sought by the Germans. Threatened with imminent arrest herself, one day the princess had to flee the palace along a gutter. She was given refuge in the Vatican, which led to unflagging loyalty to the memory of Pope Pius XII.

If Princess Pallavicini has a sense of eternity, it seems to apply mainly to the realms of religion and art. Like all patrician dwellings in Rome, the palace apartments include a chapel, whose spirit inevitably evokes the Tridentine liturgy even though the altar is usually hidden behind a drape. Yet the rooms serve above all as a setting for one of the finest collections of paintings anywhere, which the princess is determined to maintain. Whereas many other glamorous collections were slowly dispersed in the anonymity of auctions, at an early date she asked the great art historian Federico Zeri to establish a scholarly catalogue of her own collection—an unusual initiative at the time, which was only imitated later. Knowing that the future of the collection is assured in the very place where it started and grew makes for an even more moving experience when contemplating a mysterious painting long attributed to Botticelli—*La Derelitta*—placed on an easel in the corner of the library. Zeri attributed the work to Filippino Lippi, who had been a student of Botticelli's, and identified the weeping woman as a man, namely Mordecai. Appreciating that a masterpiece is part of real life will always be easier in Rome than elsewhere, and Princess Pallavicini's magnificent contribution to that tradition is certainly one of her finest titles.

Above: Marble flooring and green walls show off the red lacquer furniture typical of eighteenth-century Chinese-style decoration, also seen in the fine French tapestries on the walls. Perhaps the most astonishing object in the room is the carved cradle in the foreground.

Right: The music room in Palazzo Pallavicini probably represents one of the best illustrations of the art of fine living in a Roman *palazzo*. The harpsichord is an outstanding object, with its painted decoration and carved legs. Large paintings stand out wonderfully against the yellow silk, and do not appear overwhelming in this context. Rich Louis XV furniture from France provides comfort without diminishing the overall magnificence.

A marble fragment stands out against Roman roofs the color of burned toast. The apartment of Alvar Gonzalez Palacios, on the top floor of Palazzo Caetani, offers an admirable view of Rome's colors as they change with time of day and season. No city in the world is more beautiful in the eyes of this art historian from Cuba, also a connoisseur of French furniture.

PALACE HEIGHTS

Without a doubt, one of Rome's special privileges is its ability to offer a fairly large number of residents the possibility of living in a *palazzo*. Leaving the world of stately apartments with their impressive succession of salons, the upper floors of such palaces provide a more accessible way to appreciate the charm of Rome as it unfolds below.

The Top Floor of Palazzo Caetani

Such is the case for Alvar Gonzalez Palacios, one of the acquaintances who has most marked my time in Rome and to whom I owe my first visit to Princess Pallavicini. Readers will already be familiar with his address, since Alvar lives on the top floor of Palazzo Caetani. On my first visit, it was the Burmese cats that drew my gaze. He had bought these wonderful animals from an Englishwoman from Madras. They initially stare at the visitor, then slink away delicately among the highly fragile objets d'art, immediately projecting an image of sober elegance and unpretentious refinement. "I'd like to be just like them," said my host, who clearly has almost succeeded. Alvar Gonzalez Palacios is a singular character. Born in Cuba into a highly cultivated milieu, he was attracted to literature at an early age and moved to Italy in 1957. A decisive event in Florence was his encounter with the great art historian Roberto Longhi, which prompted him to renounce his initial calling of poet. The second phase of his life in Europe was marked by frequent stays in Paris, including a

1965 encounter with Pierre Verlet, the Louvre's head curator of objets d'art. Since that time, Alvar has developed into one of the finest connoisseurs of what are unfairly called the minor arts.

He has conducted a highly detailed study of the vast wealth of French furnishings preserved in the Palazzo del Quirinale, and has helped to promote the art of the great Roman goldsmith Luigi Valadier, father of the famous architect who designed the Piazza del Popolo; the elder Valadier's masterpieces were the pride of the Borghese family until Napoleon seized them. Rome has been Alvar's adopted home for some thirty years, but he had already fallen in love with the city well before moving there. It occurred on August 15, 1955, at the age of eighteen. He was dazzled by that first encounter. Perhaps the recollection explains why, even today, he likes best of all to be in Rome during the month of August, as well as other times when the city seems empty—the early hours of Sunday morning or the depths of night when the absence of cars makes it possible to hear the sound of footsteps ringing on *sanpietrini*. Rome is the place where, more than anywhere else, a sense of eternity makes itself felt. And yet maybe Alvar likes the city more than he likes Romans; sarcasm and a sense of irony, which he appreciates and occasionally displays, perhaps lead some Romans to reduce everything to the same level, to confuse wisdom with cynicism. Rome might be the city of faith, or maybe just a city of pilgrims. Awareness of the continuity of history—that

Right: Seen from Palazzo Caetani, the architectural purity of the dome of Sant'Andrea della Valle is striking. Christian Rome spawned an architecture symbolizing the union of heaven and earth even more than ancient Rome, which never managed to produce tall domes (as illustrated by the otherwise admirable Pantheon).

Above: The shape of this opening suggests a seventeenth-century landscape painting. In what may be irony (as suggested by the fragments of sculpture), it frames one of Rome's most controversial buildings, the notorious Vittoriano. Built to celebrate the unification of Italy, the Vittoriano's architecture is often compared to a typewriter, yet it has become an indelible part of Rome's image, not unlike the Sacré-Coeur basilica in Paris.

Right: Taken from the top floor of Palazzo Caetani, this high-angle view shows the scope of the buildings constructed in the sixteenth century by the powerful Mattei family. The vast ensemble is now divided into the Palazzo Mattei di Giove (background) and Palazzo Caetani (foreground). Whenever the architecture makes it possible, fine terraces planted with laurel or orange trees add the delight of an inner garden to the often austere beauty of the historic living quarters.

Alvar Gonzalez Palacios's extensive library of books on the decorative arts overlooks a vast, sun-drenched terrace. The fine spring sun shines on a marble bust beneath a trellis not far from arches of vegetation, constituting a fine urban version of the traditional Italian garden, designed to provide cooling shade as soon as the heat arrives.

powerful and sometimes exalting feeling of being a link in a long chain—can often degenerate into detachment and flippancy. *Morto un papa, se ne fa un altro* ("One pope has died, but another will succeed him").

Florence, which Alvar remembers fondly, is a tougher, more disciplined city where a true civic sense still prevails, no trace of which can he detect in the capital. Rome is more pliant, as is often the case with cities full of sojourners; the genius of Rome, which has ultimately spawned few artists, has been its ability to welcome talent from afar. For anyone who likes the visual arts, Rome offers everything, including a very strong sense of architecture that managed to sustain and rejuvenate itself, at least until the 1930s. The city boasts artworks of every provenance— Tuscan as well as Neapolitan, French as well as Flemish. One of the hallmarks of Rome is a sense of magnificence, which Cardinal Mazarin took with him to France in the seventeenth century. The great Bernini, when summoned to Paris by Louis XIV, noted that the Sun King thought in terms of crystal and embroidery where the pope would think only of marble and bronze.

Alvar's triple background—Hispanic, Italian and French—gives him an occasionally cruel insight into the

similarities and misunderstandings between the great Latin cultures. After long experience of them, he can only conclude: "I can know what an Italian is feeling, not what he's thinking."

From the top floor of Palazzo Caetani, Alvar's apartment offers several vistas on the city, notably a fine view of the Capitoline Hill and Palazzo Mattei di Giove (which readers will remember from the stroll by the Fontana delle Tartarughe). His entrance hall, meanwhile, affords a glimpse of a small collection of valuable marbles, next to a large mahogany bookcase full of precious bindings; but Alvar just shrugs his shoulders, as though it were an insignificant detail.

The heart of his home is his office. That is where he keeps most of his books devoted to the decorative arts. The mahogany bookshelves, designed by Alvar himself, provide a backdrop to this study where Italian paintings, objets d'art, Persian carpets, English furniture and eighteenth-century French chairs all distill a subtle charm. The room gives onto a fine terrace where the cats can sleep in the sun as soon as weather permits. Two other sitting rooms, furnished and decorated in the same spirit, will always remain associated in my mind with conversations in which the cultivation, wit and irony of the master of the house would have delighted Stendhal. As a European born in Christopher Columbus's America, Alvar is at home everywhere: in Paris, in London, but most of all in Rome, that most catholic—that is to say, universal—of cities.

Right: This double view illustrates the refinement with which Alvar Gonzalez Palacios wanted to decorate his apartment. A handsome canvas of David holding the head of Goliath sits above the books overflowing from the library. The red salon, with its many artworks, is a private, warm room in which a few eighteenth-century French chairs evoke the occupant's enthusiasm for the refined manners, conversation and wit of the Ancien Régime.

A painting by French artist Volaire, unusual in size and quality, shows a major eruption of Vesuvius in the eighteenth century, establishing a link between fiery Naples and stony Rome in Federico Forquet's living room. A porphyry bowl sits on the low table inlaid with a fine ancient mosaic, while

a pedestal table displays precious objets d'art evoking antiquity. The stenciled wall decoration is a modern interpretation of the coloring that Forquet, when a child, saw on painted vases produced in greater Greece.

An Interior Decorator's Apartment

Another seeker of heights is Federico Forquet, the most Neapolitan of Romans or, if you will, the most Roman of Neapolitans. He occupies the top floor of a fine building at the end of Corso Vittorio Emanuele, near the Tiber. Descended from a dynasty of bankers originally from France, Forquet is steeped in Neapolitan culture and proud of its past, yet also remarkably open to outside influences. Nothing relating to fashion or to design is alien to him; he cuts a figure of elegance and refinement down to the tiniest detail. After having worked with Balenciaga and then founded his own fashion house in Rome in 1962, he pursued a fertile career as a grand interior decorator. His faultless sense of color and taste has marked not only many interiors, but also several opera sets and exhibition designs.

Federico initially came to Rome for professional reasons rather than love. His heart will never forsake Naples, which he knew prior to the postwar upheavals, when the city with its surrounding landscape still resembled its romantic image. Fascinated by the grand Neapolitan taste that spread across Europe on the heels of the major archaeological discoveries of Herculaneum and Pompeii, Federico had no trouble pursuing this passion for antiquity when he moved to Rome. He is now profoundly attached to the city, although nostalgic for the period of the 1960s when so many great Italians and foreigners could be seen in Rome. "Fate has its cycles," he says, convinced that some day or other Rome will once again become the intellectual and artistic hotbed he remembers: "I see the city with the eye of someone doing the Grand Tour." Although the city has changed in the past thirty years, the neighborhood around Campo Marzio and Campo de' Fiori remains as it always was. Especially in the morning when not many tourists are around, Rome projects the charm of a small town. This comparison, pejorative in another context, is intended as a compliment here. For Federico, Rome is never so attractive as when it refuses to take on the airs of a capital city.

Federico's apartment reflects the perfectionist side of his personality. The views it offers on each of three levels are absolutely beautiful, taking in the city's major monuments, beginning with Saint Peter's. Sometimes they can be seen through large windows, sometimes through hidden

Right: In a corner of the living room restricted by a passage to the dining room, Forquet has arranged a fireside reading nook. The handsome painting of the outskirts of Naples is a discreet pendant to Volaire's monumental piece. A warming-lamp is set on an elegant late-eighteenth-century pedestal table, whose top is a masterpiece of marble inlay.

No space escapes Federico
Forquet's refined attention,
as seen in this reading corner
in the living room (above).
But attention to detail is
accompanied by a strong sense
of architecture, as demonstrated
by the handsome mahogany
bookshelves that greet visitors
in the entrance gallery (right).
The tone is set by an antique
god in terracotta—it is hardly
surprising that a Neapolitan
who has decided to live in Rome
should display a fascination
for Greco-Latin heritage and
its subsequent interpretations.

Left: On the upper floor, Federico Forquet has arranged an office in a corner of the salon. Above the armchair is a mysterious view of Solfatare, a sulfur mine near Naples, by Michael Wutky (an almost identical version hangs in the Belvedere in Vienna). The inkwell on the mahogany desk is a masterpiece by Luigi Valadier, a great Roman goldsmith in the late eighteenth century whose architect son, Giuseppe, designed Piazza del Popolo in its current form.

The little dining room, conceived as a kind of indoor garden, offers an intimate, private setting for Federico Forquet's parties. The limited size of the room prohibits much furniture or art, but everything is of high quality, notably the fine neoclassical porcelain service made at the Capodimonte Manufactory founded by the Neapolitan Bourbons. Federico's collection features other pieces of similar origin, notably a stunning centerpiece from the "Alexander service" commissioned by King Ferdinand IV.

gaps that recall the theatrical staging which, as a good Neapolitan, Federico adores. His own talent is expressed through architectural forms he paints onto walls the color of warm brick, through patterns he stencils onto parquet floors, through an ingenious piece of furniture that he designed to protect a superb collection of watercolors of ancient Egypt from the light even as they are being studied. Federico's preferences emerge from his vast number of artworks: evidence of antiquity that is not only Latin but also Greek (the heritage of Naples and Greater Greece), neoclassical furnishings and objects, and early-nineteenth-century Egyptomania. There are also, of course, a considerable number of images of Naples and the surrounding area, including Vesuvius and the islands. Nothing is left to chance,

neither the bathroom full of allusions to Pompeii, nor the hallways decorated in fine landscapes in oil, nor the bedroom which is a veritable little museum yet remains full of warmth. Federico knows how to play wonderfully on contrasts—the strict lines of an Empire console table on the one hand, a torrent of lava in a superb painting by Volaire on the other: reason versus passion.

On the top floor, with its collection of precious marbles, is a little desk lit by two tall windows, like embrasures in a fortress. It is hard to imagine any finer source of inspiration than the views of the city which appear like so many paintings. I cannot prevent myself, as I climb the stairway leading to this office, from thinking of the secluded observatories so beloved by the hero of Stendhal's *Charterhouse of Parma*.

Crazy About Rome

In a different spirit, Milton and Monica Gendel live in Palazzo Costaguti on Piazza Mattei, already mentioned during our stroll through the Campo de' Fiori neighborhood. They occupy spacious quarters just above the piano nobile, or principal floor, of the palace. Arranged in circular fashion, the apartment contains a succession of rooms of various sizes, from a salon with its original coffered ceiling and frieze showing the arms of Cardinal Costaguti to a small mezzanine studio used by Monica, who writes and illustrates books (notably a witty one on cats). Along the way there is a bedroom and studies for working or reading. Milton's die was cast when a Fulbright scholarship enabled the young American to come to Europe. That was in 1950. Ever since, the grand traveler could never bring himself to leave Rome. Initially a correspondent for *Art News*, he later took up photography and publishing, notably producing valuable histories on Italy and the papacy. Milton merely had a studio in Palazzo Costaguti prior to moving there. For some thirty years he lived in an apartment on Tiber Island in a former Franciscan monastery now owned by the city of Rome. The promotion of that history-laden place has become a crusade for Milton, and for years his fondest wish has been to open a museum there. The association which he founded in Rome to launch the Tiber Island museum has two counterparts abroad, one in Great Britain (chaired by Princess Margaret) and the other in the United States (headed by Mrs. Arthur Schlesinger).

The first stage of the project entailed converting the monastery's former pottery into a historical and pictorial database, to which Milton has contributed his own collection of images of picturesque characters of the past, such as a certain Padre Martini who was an amateur sculptor.

The apartment Milton shared with his deceased first wife on Tiber Island was a gathering place for artists and celebrities such as Peggy Guggenheim, Paul Getty, Alexander Calder and Willem de Kooning, in the days when everyone congregated in Rome, including a good number of Americans. Their photographs have been collected in Milton's book, *Incontri Romani* (Roman Encounters).

The Gendels' apartment on an upper floor of Palazzo Costaguti is imbued with the majestic spirit of the piano nobile. Several rooms are aligned in a row, including the salon and dining room. The soberly decorated ceiling dates from the sixteenth century. The flooring is more recent, but also has character. Inner shutters on the windows make it possible to modulate the light inside these large spaces.

The original atmosphere in the apartment is due to the personalities of Milton Gendel and his wife Monica. An American who has lived in Rome for fifty years, Milton loves history and photography; Monica comes from an old Roman family and is an illustrator. A mannequin with hat (below) sums up the wonderfully bohemian chic atmosphere infusing their home.

A well-stocked library (left) reflects a shared love of books, while a collection of medals commemorates important moments in Italian history. The little stairway in the distance leads to a mezzanine that serves as Monica's studio.

The Gendels can make a bold move seem natural. Cushions aligned on the sofa add a touch of strong, even tart, color to a setting dominated by softer tones. The low table is made from a fine Latin inscription carved in 1750 on Tiber Island, where Milton spent many years and whose past he hopes to preserve by founding a museum. The large mannerist canvas by a Bolognese artist, part of a series depicting biblical heroines, has no trouble standing up to contemporary works.

The apartment in Palazzo Costaguti contains numerous vestiges of Milton's previous home, notably some Queen Anne chairs in memory of his first wife. The bold contrasts and original decoration of the Costaguti apartment are striking. A portrait of Garibaldi keeps company with Pius IX in Lalique crystal, while large sixteenth-century canvases confront a work by de Kooning. Other paintings and antiques are reminders that Monica is related to the Chigi family, a famous dynasty of bankers and humanists from Siena that produced a pope in the person of Alexander VII, who commissioned Bernini to execute both the colonnade in Saint Peter's piazza and the magnificent glory in the apse of the basilica. The disparate objects gathered here lend a unique personality to this home, where highly contemporary items successfully assert themselves without disrupting the overall charm of the setting.

Living with Religious Paintings

A similar apartment, on the top floor of a *palazzo* in the old center of Rome, is home to Philippe and Isabelle. The palace is one of those imposing dwellings complete with antique statues in the courtyard, so it is almost startling to discover apartments of human proportions. Yet that is what makes it a very Roman setting, to which its occupants have contributed a southern touch, seen in the pale green color of doors, skirting boards and painted wood furniture. Whereas Isabelle is of old Neapolitan stock, Philippe is descended from a French family with a strange history—his grandfather, after having helped to build the Suez Canal alongside Ferdinand de Lesseps, died on the boat taking him home. His young widow, pregnant with a son, stopped at Palermo where her sister worked as a milliner in the famous Florio fashion house. That is how the family became Sicilian even as it remained attached to its French roots. It displayed the same sense of initiative in Palermo as it had in Egypt, spawning flourishing industries. This heritage perhaps explains Philip's love of travel, which Isabelle shares.

Over the years, both have built an extraordinarily refined collection of paintings, with a taste and sensitivity reflected in the apartment's overall atmosphere. Most of the works date from the seventeenth century, and include paintings by Pietro da Cortona, Guido Reni and Artemisia Gentileschi. In accordance with Isabelle's taste, many feature religious or biblical subjects—but displayed in a

Even the many austere religious paintings in the collection of Philippe and Isabelle acquire a familiar presence in this setting. In that respect they perpetuate the tradition of private devotional art, when great patrons would commission work from the best artists of the day.

A dramatic painting by
Artemisia Gentileschi of
Joseph and Potiphar's Wife
is reflected in the mirror of
Philippe and Isabelle's living
room, creating an unusual and
successful alliance between old,
museum-worthy works and a
resolutely modern interior.
Whereas plinths and doors are

surprisingly straightforward way. Where else
but Rome would anyone dare to place a cruet
set at the foot of a painting by Artemisia
Gentileschi or a fruit bowl under a rare
painting by the French artist Mellan, showing
an amazing Saint Bruno at prayer? "The
works have to be played down," says Isabelle,
but I notice that the familiar utensils

in wool or linen, heavy fabrics that tend to
make the body resemble a column. Bernini's
angels, on the contrary, are dressed in silk,"
namely the Chinese silk found in Rome in
Bernini's day, with a glittering, weightless
quality that wonderfully suited celestial
creatures. In Isabelle's home, fabrics from all
periods converse easily and naturally with
seventeenth-century paintings. It represents
a perfect example of the way tradition can be
reinterpreted in Rome—perhaps the city's
most attractive feature, and one found so
often among "outsiders" who have come to
love the place.

Philippe and Isabelle's
hobbies—reading, traveling
and growing roses (their country
garden has hundreds of
varieties)—are reflected in this
shot of their living room.
Splashes of bright color, such as
the red leather armchair on the
right, coexist happily with their
collection of baroque paintings.

painted a fairly pale green,
the orange-red sofa is striking
without being overwhelming. In
the hall leading to the entrance
glitters an amazing baroque
frame around a disturbing image
of the martyred Saint Agatha.

themselves have been arranged by an artistic
hand and eye, like some real-life still life.

Isabelle, who has an artist's studio
elsewhere, is also a connoisseur of fabrics
and textiles. Her enthusiasm runs from
precious, thousand-year-old Chinese silks to
humble rags. She is more interested in
texture than pattern or design—materials
which, like perfume, envelope the body,
either clinging to it or standing aloof from it
according to a complex grammar. "Antique
statues," she pointed out to me, "are dressed

Home as Museum

It may seem surprising at this point to
discuss the apartment of Fabrizio and
Fiammetta Lemme, who do not live in the
center of Rome. Pierre Rosenberg, director of
the Louvre, had told me they were
enthusiastic collectors and I knew that they
had managed to assemble a remarkable set
of paintings in nearly thirty years of
collecting. So the last thing I expected, the
first time I was invited to their home, was to
find myself ringing the downstairs entry-
phone of a 1960s apartment block in a new,
outlying neighborhood. On entering the
apartment itself, I was dumbfounded. There
were so many artworks that no patch of wall
was blank; and their luster, enhanced by the
beauty of the old frames, seemed unreal in
an apartment so different in spirit and
proportions from a *palazzo*. The rules for
hanging were the same as those applied in
princely galleries, but the stacking effect was

limited here to a height of 2 meters, rather than 6 or 8. The Lemmes' choice of apartment, in 1964, was dictated solely by professional requirements—strangely, the existence of the collection never made them rethink that decision. Of course, their first purchases followed no strict logic and the guiding principle behind their collection did not emerge immediately. An encounter with art historian Italo Faldi was the turning point, because it was he who advised the Lemmes to focus on Roman art of the seventeenth and eighteenth centuries—a sphere in which Italians, at that time, were less interested than the English, thus remaining affordable for private collectors.

Hence their veritable adventure began, abetted also by Federico Zeri. Little by little the initial core grew, and as the collection expanded, offers increased in number. Given the dimensions of the walls, there are not many large paintings. The biggest, by Luti, depicts the miracle of Blessed Ludovica Albertoni. I remember the spot it occupied, which made it seem immense, before it was placed on loan with the Galleria Nazionale in Palazzo Barberini. There are also a great number of sketches of modest size, whose very free handling is sometimes more to modern taste than the finished works. Fabrizio and Fiammetta, even as they constantly add to their collection, are in no way slaves to the idea of personal possession, much less to that of keeping their treasures to themselves. They are not afraid to show them to people who, for one reason or another, ask to see them. The

comparisons and connections it provokes make this collection a veritable research tool in the grand tradition of the private "cabinets" of connoisseurs in the past. The finest proof of their highly rare detachment is the Lemmes' two generous bequests, to the Galleria Nazionale in Palazzo Barberini and to the Louvre in Paris. Through his mother,

Fabrizio and Fiammetta Lemmes' collection turns their apartment into a living museum. It is typically Roman in the choice of artists and style of hanging, which is inspired by the grand palaces. Only by making major bequests, notably to the Louvre, can they add to their collection without being forced to move.

Fabrizio has deep affection for France, and has felt so at home there that he wished to make a donation to the great Paris museum.

Despite the number of works donated, the walls of their apartment are once again packed. Might not this presence become oppressive in the long run? Fiammetta admits to just one regret: her beloved books have been steadily obliged to give ground, emigrating either to her children's homes or to Fabrizio's office. Paintings cease to be inanimate objects, however, once you live

To get to Joseph Kosuth's studio, you cross the outbuildings of Palazzo Santacroce, a fine sixteenth-century residence now partly occupied by the Latin-American Institute. In the back, against a wall, is a magnificent fountain in gray stone (top). A fine sense of perspective is created by its semicircular arch and three stacked basins of different sizes. As is customary in Rome, figures that are more or less monstrous stand guard over the beneficial waters (bottom).

among them. Unnoticed details crop up years after a work was acquired, and certain figures can even spark an emotional relationship. The young Princess Altieri shown in Luti's painting, for instance, spurred Fiammetta into lengthy research until she ultimately located the princess's tomb in a church in Rome. Fabrizio went along with his typical enthusiasm. His verbal skills, which led to a brilliant career as a lawyer, allow him to pass easily for an expert in art history. And, sure enough, years of seeking and looking have considerably enhanced his knowledge and sharpened his eye. Like Fiammetta, however, he wants above all to remain a collector, thereby maintaining a grand Roman tradition.

Whereas the works collected by Philippe and Isabelle, as we have seen, mix with everyday objects in a disarmingly conspicuous way, those acquired by Fabrizio and Fiammetta assume an almost metaphysical dimension in their quest for the absolute. Both collections, so quintessentially Roman, thus present the city's two faces: one turned toward the appeal of the familiar, the other toward an almost abstract rigor. Yet both obey uncompromising artistic standards.

An American Artist's Studio

The Lemmes' apartment represents a paradox, so strong was my expectation of finding it in a majestic dwelling in the center of town. In a reverse paradox, Joseph Kosuth, one of the great names in American conceptual art, moved into a noble

sixteenth-century building in 1998 with his wife Cornelia and their two daughters. Palazzo Santacroce, on the edge of the Campo de' Fiori neighborhood, faces the fine church of San Carlo ai Catinari. Kosuth divides his time between New York and Europe, notably a Tuscan village where Cornelia organizes exhibitions in the summer. The artist's Roman studio is located in an annex to the *palazzo*, separated from the main building by a narrow street. After crossing a courtyard adorned with a large rocaille fountain, a rather steep stairway leads up to a space that has nothing of the standard studio about it. A true conceptual artist, Kosuth relies above all on his extensive library and a computer. The walls

Left: Steep, narrow steps lead from Joseph Kosuth's studio to this terrace, which, although small, creates the feeling of being in a special place where time no longer matters. Morning coffee is served in prototypes of a cup designed by the artist. This small patch of total serenity would be unthinkable in New York, Kosuth's other city of predilection.

A conceptual artist's workplace in no way resembles a traditional studio. There are no canvases, brushes or easels here, only books, documentation and computers. It is significant that an artist so committed to this radical approach should choose to work in Rome for much of the year. Perhaps some secret correspondence will be discovered between Rome's two-thousand-year-old tradition of inscriptions and Kosuth's own utterances, framed here like paintings or written in neon. One of the works that Kosuth used as a greeting card reads, "What you are regarding as a gift is a problem for you to solve."

nevertheless display evidence of his past work, every bit as packed as his future projects, which will take him in a matter of months from Frankfurt to Sarajevo and on to Istanbul and Japan.

Kosuth, an American who has not forgotten his family's European roots (he is the great-grandnephew of a famous Hungarian hero of 1848), likes Rome for its contradictions—simultaneously a hectic metropolis and a small town, an open-air museum and a dynamic city. He wittily describes it as an ideal place for "a postmodern existence against the backdrop of history. It's a wonderful place for an American." I came to appreciate the relevance of his approach during a solo show by Kosuth at the Villa Medici—after having done careful research on the sculptures that originally decorated the villa's now empty niches, he placed the names of the vanished works, in neon lighting, in those niches. The slight tremor of the lighting, the almost velvety softness of the ivory-colored light—which matched the color of the wall—and the power of the writing all combined to create an evocative and poetic effect.

Massimiliano Fuksas likes to compare his apartment to a large ship. The salon, seen from the dining room, features large rectangular windows (top). Furniture and decoration are resolutely twentieth century, with works by Guttuso and Matta in particular. The kitchen gives onto a terrace (bottom).

ARTISTS' NEIGHBORHOODS

Kosuth's studio in a *palazzo* right in the historic center of Rome is in many ways an exception. If we move out to the fringes of that center, we discover a lifestyle that is more in keeping with the usual idea of an artist's neighborhood.

An Architect's Level

Take, for example, architect Massimiliano Fuksas and his wife Doriana, who occupy the top floor of a 1950s building next to the church of San Giovanni dei Fiorentini, near the top of Via Giulia. Their brick building is unrelated to the neighborhood and seems to lie outside the old town. It is close, yet different—just like Massimiliano, an indefatigable traveler with a Lithuanian father and a Roman mother who nevertheless proclaims his "Romanness." His career as architect is the fruit of an unfulfilled calling as a painter. Fleeing convention and labels, never muting his convictions and commitments, Massimiliano has steeped himself in the great lesson offered by Rome: a city must constantly regenerate itself, building anew on the layers that preceding generations have piled on one another. For Massimiliano, radical modernity does not mean beginning with a clean slate. Every day, he travels on foot from his home to his office near Campo de' Fiori. "When I walk down Via Giulia," he told me, "I realize something obvious: in all the projects I've ever produced in my life, I've always had Rome in mind. Never a clean wall, always a

transition that slides into something else." The city seems to him like "one big sculpture" with its chiseling sunlight that can dazzle the eye at the end of the darkest alleyways.

The terraces of his apartment present a variety of vistas on the city, featuring some of the most glamorous sights: Castel Sant'Angelo and the dome of Saint Peter's, Via Giulia and the church of San Giovanni dei Fiorentini, the foliage on the Janiculum Hill. Massimiliano compares his apartment to an aircraft carrier, with its inhabited levels and layered terraces, its halls which seem like so many passageways. The summit of the upper terrace even seems to be on the same level as the nearby bell towers and the distant hills. Whereas the great views of the city from the top of the Janiculum or Pincio Hills show everything "in miniature," the Fuksas enjoy the privilege of seeing everything full-scale, so to speak, from the very center. Inside the apartment, paintings by Matta, works of primitive art, furniture that is resolutely twentieth century, and clean-cut interior decoration are all enhanced by large rectangular windows that divide the urban panorama into so many moving paintings. The Tiber passes almost at the foot of the building (the Fuksas's Paris apartment also overlooks the Seine) between its riverbanks overgrown with vegetation; at this point the river takes a bend that underscores the strange impression of being simultaneously on the edge and in the heart of the city. Great travelers always enjoy gazing upon rivers.

Above: A staircase from the Fuksas's kitchen leads to a vast terrace, serving as the ship's "deck," which leads in turn to a top level—or small watch tower—which offers an exceptional 360° view.

Right: The Fuksas's terrace offers majestic vistas on three sides, featuring sights like Saint Peter's and Castel Sant'Angelo. From certain spots the view is a dizzying drop, while from others dense greenery gives the delightful illusion of being on the same level as the horizon.

The Appeal of Trastevere

The neighborhood "across the Tiber" begins on the other side of the bridge overlooked by the Fuksas's apartment building. Trastevere, once Rome's most working-class district, is now prized by artists and intellectuals who appreciate the unconventional alliance of an ancient past with a totally non-aristocratic milieu.

Letizia, whom I knew through French friends prior to meeting her in Rome, lives in the heart of Trastevere. Now that Piazza di Santa Maria in Trastevere has been closed to car traffic, Letizia's house can be reached only on foot. Her profession of book restorer has something in common with that of my wife, Béatrice, who restores old wallpaper, and Letizia's spontaneous generosity immediately gave us the impression that we had always been part of the family. What immediately caught the eye the first time she opened her door was the abundance of books, an

A few pieces from Letizia's collection of crystalware are set on fine old fabric, where sunshine makes the bottles sparkle and the cloth shimmer (top).

Letizia's home is strikingly warm. The living room feels like a library, perfect for reading or for intimate conversation. Many family souvenirs recall Letizia's mixed Tuscan and Sicilian background. Two wooden chairs add a touch of modernity.

Books occupy all the shelves but leave room for small objects revealing Letizia's fondness for classical culture (bottom).

unmistakable sign of curiosity and an open mind. Unlike so many interiors where only "handsome books" are featured, here there were books that had been chosen to be read, to be thoroughly used—there was no affectation. "I hide the exhibition catalogues," she said with a smile. It was only in the dining room, where Letizia sometimes does restoration work on the table, that I believe I did not see any books. This love of books is hardly surprising when you learn that she is the daughter of a writer. The last book by her mother, Livia de Stefani, *La Mafia dietro le Spalle*, expressed the sorrow of seeing ancestral lands fall into the hands of the dreaded crime syndicate. Although her maternal roots are Sicilian, Letizia is Tuscan through her father, who made a name for himself as a sculptor by carving little portraits in gold. Perhaps that diversity explains the fact that, although born in Rome and completely at home there, Letizia has always had an urge to travel.

The apartment she occupies is all she now owns of the house that her father once owned entirely. She moved into the apartment in 1963 and has lived there since. At the time, Piazza di Santa Maria in Trastevere had just one restaurant (Galeassi, still there), not far from a wine seller who still served drinks on a marble counter (like the ones seen in the ancient ruins of Ostia) and the Peretti pharmacy, which is several centuries old. The neighborhood, which Americans from the film world were beginning to make fashionable in the 1950s, still had its working-class soul, the fruit of several centuries of sometimes stormy existence. Letizia appreciates its village spirit,

which creates a real bond between residents and even extends as far as Campo de' Fiori, easily reached by Ponte Sisto.

Her apartment, with its beautiful view of the church at all hours of the day and night, is a small-scale incarnation of the finest Roman spirit. Like the city itself, it harbors layers of familial and personal history—Sicilian furniture, thirteenth-century Persian ceramics, a Chinese statuette in lacquered wood (brought back by her great-uncle, an ambassador), drawings ancient and modern (including two washes by Guttuso dedicated to her mother) and the crystal objects that she herself has always collected. More or less everywhere, like an underlying theme, are vestiges of antiquity—the sign of a classical mind in the best sense of the term, curious about everything yet enamored of rigor. "All I lack is a little greenery," said Letizia as she took me outside. On that fine spring morning, the piazza had an almost provincial air. The effervescence of the 1950s was due to the arrival of Americans and a sense of new-found freedom. These days, the liveliness of the neighborhood is generated by tourists and for Letizia is more superficial. Rome is apparently lapsing into a peculiar attitude where a certain feeling of superiority—perhaps more defensive than anything else—leads to a turning inward, an indifference to strangers despite outward politeness; it is becoming less open than Florence, for example. Letizia delivers these impressions as we enjoy morning coffee opposite the church. But I cannot help thinking, as I listen, that the situation is not as drastic as all that.

Filtered by curtains and a half-open blind, the sun enters Letizia's apartment and illuminates two white roses in a crystal vase. A fine study of a hand and a small romantic portrait complete the delicately feminine setting. The baroque portico and statues of Santa Maria in Trastevere can be seen through the window, basking in the morning light.

A Figure from the Film World
in Piazza di Spagna

Marco Dolcetta lives at the other end of the old city, on Via Sistina, in the heart of the Piazza di Spagna neighborhood. Before it became a fashion district, the area leading toward Piazza del Popolo was already an artist's quarter. Ingres, before he was named director of the French Academy in Rome, lived on Via Gregoriana, a quiet little street overlooked by several of the rooms in Marco's apartment. In the eighteenth century, the building itself belonged to Rome's Academy of Fine Arts, which allocated space mainly to sculptors— Piranesi lived there, as did Canova. The Danish sculptor Bertel Thorwaldsen, in his day thought to rival the greats, lived on the floor where Marco now resides.

As a philosopher and film-maker, Marco has worked with famous names— intellectuals such as Raymond Aron, directors such as Federico Fellini, actors such as Catherine Deneuve and Carmelo Bene, art historians such as Federico Zeri. I first wanted to hear him talk about Fellini, whose assistant he had been. Their initial encounter occurred at Cinecittà during the shooting of *Orchestra Rehearsal*. French television had commissioned Marco to interview the master, who decided, for the occasion, to invent a whole host of anecdotes likely to please French audiences. This experience triggered a reciprocal friendship, and Marco became Fellini's assistant, a job that was not always easy. Every morning, his highly superstitious boss

would call a Jungian psychoanalyst, to whom he would recount the night's dreams. Subsequent to that conversation, which unvaryingly took place at 5 A.M., Fellini would completely alter the day's plans. The film's producers, in desperation, pleaded with Marco to find a way to put a halt to these daily upheavals. Marco therefore took it upon himself to call the master every morning just before the fateful hour, while another assistant would telephone the psychoanalyst, thereby blocking any interpretation of dreams. A rough job, but it was the only way that the shooting of *Orchestra Rehearsal* could proceed normally.

Fellini lived not far away, on Via Margutta, fairly close to the subway station linking Piazza di Spagna to Cinecittà like an umbilical cord. Both men shared the love that "provincials" can have for an adopted city. In *The White Sheik*, his first film on Rome, Fellini depicted the amazement of a young man fascinated by the myth of the Eternal City. Marco, who arrived in Rome from Milan at the age of ten, was shocked by the dilapidated streets and offhand manners which contrasted with the punctiliousness of northerners, yet immediately responded to the pleasant lifestyle. Fellini's perception was also a mixture of love and disappointment, like the image of Anouk Aimée in *La Dolce Vita*, beautifully alone in the early morning on Piazza del Popolo yet allowing herself, in another scene, to be kissed by a suitor even as she whispers words of love to Marcello Mastroianni through the mouth of a statue. This disenchanted gaze,

An eclectic spirit if ever there was one, Marco Dolcetta likes to collect vestiges of every civilization. Those from the Mediterranean obviously hold pride of place in his apartment on Via Sistina, such as strange funerary plaques of lead fished from the water near Byblos and a fine feminine bust whose Greek visage casts a shadow on the wall.

As Fellini's former assistant and a producer of cultural programs for television, it is only natural that Marco Dolcetta should line the wall of his kitchen with movie posters. This American-style decoration evokes the years when Rome and Cinecittà were the hubs of international cinema. The memory of occasionally riotous shoots with Fellini has not marred Marco's affectionate admiration for the *maestro*, who also lived not far from Piazza di Spagna.

simultaneously clear-sighted and affectionate, later took an extreme form in *Fellini's Roma*. That emblematic film grew from a commission by Italian television for a movie halfway between documentary and fiction, becoming a poetic vision of the clash between past and modernity: the wondrous discovery of ancient frescoes by workers tunneling a new subway (and their pained stupor on seeing the colors suddenly fade), the smile of a slumbering old princess who dreams of an ecclesiastical fashion show in her *palazzo* (capped by the appearance of a papal monarch whose majesty recalls that of Pius XII). The Catholic Church, in Rome, assumes a maternal image—an eternally young mother—as Fellini doubtless recalled in *La Dolce Vita* when Anita Ekberg is shown dressed as a priest climbing Saint Peter's bell tower.

Rome is a city where everything is pardonable. Although it can also be cruel, its sense of compassion perhaps seems greater than anywhere else. Relationships are based more on the heart than on intellect or money. Arrogance is considered inappropriate, but since all can be forgiven, there is also a tendency to relativize everything, to be surprised at nothing. A short story by Ennio Flaiano, for instance, recounts how a Martian rolled up to the Caffè Rosati, completely green and sporting antennas. A taxi driver in the café, depressed over a recent loss by Lazio—one of the city's two major soccer teams—notices the extraterrestrial. But does he show any amazement? On the contrary, in Roman dialect he asks the visitor to *facce ride* ("make me laugh"). Major capital, minor town.

The interior of Marco's apartment reflects this eclectic curiosity. The objects in it are all different, but form several coherent series. They express Marco's attraction to all forms of spirituality and the idea of rebirth. Christian symbols—such as Saint George slaying the dragon—can be seen alongside Buddhist objects, quotations from the Koran and the Kabbala, and even inexpensive Chinese statues given to him by a Taoist priest from Singapore. An unmistakably Roman touch is added to the collection by a magnificent antique head and some archaeological souvenirs brought back from Lebanon or found on family property in Latium. A copy of Arnold Böcklin's *Island of the Dead*, executed by the artist's nephew, overlooks his work table. And more or less everywhere, posters, photos and objects portray the heroes of the modern world, namely superstars of movie and comic-book fame.

This accumulation of things, in which items of great beauty are mixed with kitsch objects, is reminiscent of the great art historian Federico Zeri; the house he built in Mentana, outside Rome, also contained hackneyed paintings and a table displaying objects in provocatively bad taste alongside major works from antiquity and the Renaissance. As a symbol of his almost filial affection for Zeri, Marco keeps in his bedroom a sketch of the famous painting by Thomas Couture, now in the Musée d'Orsay in Paris, titled *Romans of the Decadence*. Zeri, who never stopped criticizing the mindlessness of his contemporaries, could hardly have presented Marco with a gift more in keeping with the historian's sarcastic wit and passion for art.

A Writer's Home in Piazza del Popolo

Heading toward Piazza del Popolo, I passed the building where Alexandra Lapierre has been writing books for the past five years. She lives in a little apartment on Via del Vantaggio which offers typical Roman views on every side: facades of buildings renovated for the year 2000 in the front, and a tangle of crumbling walls and baroque palaces in the back.

Having come to the city with the intention of writing a historical novel set in Rome, Alexandra latched onto the amazing and often dramatic life of Artemisia Gentileschi, trained as a painter by her own father, Orazio, one of the most highly reputed artists in the late sixteenth century. The extent of the research required would have discouraged many others. The first year was one of solitude, but Roman kindness and hospitality soon helped Alexandra to integrate. The theater, which she decided to attend regularly, came to her aid. "People greet you the first time, chat the second, and offer an invitation the third." In no other capital city would a stranger receive such a welcome. Romans nevertheless displayed discreet skepticism concerning her project.

Over the modest fireplace in Alexandra Lapierre's living room is a seventeenth-century oil, contemporary with her heroine Artemisia Gentileschi. Research Lapierre did for her novel revealed that the artisanal workshops on Via del Vantaggio were already there two or three hundred years ago. This tradition is probably coming to an end, but long colored life in Rome.

A few familiar objects that Alexandra Lapierre brought from Paris are assembled between two windows, through which can be glimpsed the facades of Via del Vantaggio, renovated for the year 2000. Many who plan a temporary stay in the city end up succumbing to its powerful attraction: although Lapierre feels the need to leave Rome often, she seems gradually to be cutting her ties to Paris.

Picasso's Former Studio
on Via Margutta

A similar fate befell Bertrand Marret, who decided to move to Rome with his wife Piera Benedetti over a quarter of a century ago. Born into an artistic milieu—he is the nephew of the great photographer Henri Cartier-Bresson and the great-nephew of writer Louis-René des Forêts—he is himself an art historian and lives in a former studio on Via Margutta. He recounts how, before he had a place of his own in Rome, his friend Giulio Turcato demonstrated an unforgettable sense of hospitality. Turcato, an artist, had embarked on a series of paintings titled *Superficie Lunari*, on which he employed a substance similar in consistency to rubber—so instead of recommending the name of a hotel as requested by Bertrand, Turcato simply spread three paintings on the floor, forming a mattress.

Thanks to a combination of events, Bertrand and Piera were able to buy the studio that Picasso used in 1917, when the famous artist had come to Rome with Jean Cocteau to meet Diaghilev and Massine in order to discuss the sets and costumes for their ballet, *Parade*. The two friends were staying at the Hotel de Russie, but Picasso spent his days working in one of the "Patrizi" studios. Then as now, the large north-facing window offered a fine view of the Pincio Hill and the Villa Medici, which Picasso sketched several times, representing a brief

confrontation between the greatest genius of modernism and an academy that, at the time, seemed like the bastion of artistic conservatism.

Piera, a well-known linguist who has worked with Umberto Eco, is also famous for her remarkable culinary skills, which she probably owes to her half-Venetian, half-Bolognese roots. Hence a small kitchen has been installed which, thanks to an ingenious mechanism, can be hidden from the living area by a sliding panel. The neighborhood has changed a great deal since Bertrand and Piera bought the studio. The arrival of the subway, in particular, meant that fashion boutiques pushed out most of the small workshops and cafés that had attempted to maintain the same tradition as the Caffè Greco. Via Margutta itself, meanwhile, because it is off the main track, has remained immutable, free from the clutches of time.

The Marrets' studio has gigantic north-facing windows. A whole series of such windows, typical of Via Margutta, can be seen from the heights of the Pincio. They offer not only ideal light for painting, but also an extraordinary view of the Villa Medici, which Picasso drew several times during his 1917 stay in Rome. Above the sofa, on the movable panel hiding Piera's kitchen is a canvas by Giulio Turcato.

Above: Simple volumes and pale colors: Bertrand Marret and Piera Benedetti respected the spirit of the original studios when they moved into Via Margutta. In this unique space, a staircase with pure lines leads to a mezzanine. The entire street is dotted with similar studios built in the early nineteenth century for the numerous foreign artists—many from northern countries—who wished to live in Rome. Picasso himself spent a year in the one now occupied by Bertrand and Piera. Right: A remarkable cook, Piera Benedetti has created an ultramodern kitchen for herself in the main studio space. An ingenious movable panel makes it possible to open or hide the kitchen.

Via del Babuino:
The Heart of the Artists' Quarter

Carla Accardi, one of the great names in postwar Italian painting, lives right near Via del Babuino. Her apartment, which also serves as her studio, occupies the top two floors of the building. The terrace crowning it offers magnificent views of the Villa Medici and the twin bell towers of Trinità dei Monti. Although she comes from Sicily, Accardi moved to Rome very early on, in 1947, to finish her art education. In the somewhat inward-looking atmosphere of the time, she founded an avant-garde group called Forma 1 along with other artists of her generation, such as Toccato, Consagra and Dorazio. They wanted to be part of the major European trends of the century, drawing inspiration from Kandinsky and Mondrian, among others. Accardi, whose oeuvre has evolved through several important stages, has always remained faithful to that spirit.

Although a great traveler—Paris and Turin have been very important in her life—Accardi always returns to Rome. This neighborhood and this home, a gift from her father, represent a fixed point around which she gravitates. She would often run into Fellini, who lived a stone's throw away, and de Chirico, who lived on Piazza di Spagna. Artists would meet at the Caffè Rosati on Piazza di Spagna (writers usually preferred Via Veneto), with the result that a certain number of them, such as Tano Festa and Mario Schifano, were often referred to as "the Piazza di Spagna school." Accardi perfectly remembers Picasso, having met him at the home of Visconti who, during his Roman sojourn, lived a few minutes away on nearby Via Margutta. So it is with regret that she has watched younger artists shun the neighborhood, which is probably too expensive now, in order to move closer to the center of town.

Although Accardi, like most contemporary artists, works in less conventional art forms, she still remains attached to painting. In terms of her own work, she avoids speaking of "abstraction" in favor of "an art of signs." As I went from one floor of her apartment to another, I got a better feel of the way in which everyday life and the demands of her art are inextricably linked. The studio where she paints her canvases receives no direct sunlight. In keeping with tradition, it faces north. But the facades opposite, with their fine yellow and ocher colors and the glass in their windows, reflect light into her studio all day long.

As to the terrace, it is not just a pleasant place to relax, but is also—and perhaps mostly—a place where the artist can drink in, so to speak, the light. "A light specific to Rome," she told me, "with an exceptional quality of color." That is where Accardi watches birds wheel above the city, an amazing show in autumn when thousands of starlings sketch constantly changing figures in the sky. Many of Accardi's works, produced on a transparent surface, evoke the countless wings fluttering over our heads. I knew that I would find some works by her in the homes of several friends who are ardent defenders of contemporary art in Rome.

Right: Several of Carla Accardi's own works are displayed at the entrance to her apartment. They feature bright colors on clear plastic and she often compares them to the flocks of birds that wheel above Rome before heading south. A large, long room in the back serves as her studio, which has a view of the Villa Medici and the bell towers of Trinità dei Monti.

Far left: Carla Accardi does not have a standard artist's studio, although the northern aspect is traditional. Large windows overlook Via del Babuino and provide generous light for part of the living space (top). A spiral staircase leads to the upper level, which includes the bedroom (below) and a large terrace where the artist likes to steep herself in Rome's ever-changing light.

Defending Contemporary Art
on the Esquiline Hill

Such is the case with Mario Pieroni and Dora Stiefelmeier who, after having managed one of the city's most important art galleries, now devote themselves to promoting cultural projects in Rome, Latium and Tuscany. Their Roman pied-à-terre is located on Piazza Vittorio Emanuele II (usually shortened to Piazza Vittorio), near where Ludovico Pratesi and Delphine Borione live. Ludovico, of Roman stock, is an influential art critic, while Delphine is from France and works for the United Nations. After having lived near Piazza Navona, they too moved halfway between the train station and Piazza Vittorio; the move represented a bold decision to leave the "gilded cage" of the historic center

Rome is not a city where contemporary art finds a natural place. Mario Pieroni and Dora Stiefelmeier have supported major artists as varied as Carla Accardi, Iannis Kounellis and Vettor Pisani. The curtains filtering the light in the small office of their apartment on Piazza Vittorio feature patterns suggesting birds in flight (left). The table in the dining room is wittily adorned with a ring of rabbits (above).

to live in a neighborhood that has deteriorated and become impoverished in the past fifty years. This whole part of town was designed in the late nineteenth century for a bourgeoisie infatuated with monumentality. But proximity to the station and the influx of a poor, immigrant population slowly modified the social makeup and now it is a mosaic of peoples. Artists and writers in recent years have been drawn to this melting pot—rather rare in Rome—to discover or create an atmosphere recalling Soho or Greenwich Village.

The apartment of Ludovico and Delphine, overlooks the former Aquarium—a fine nineteenth-century building which has gone through many incarnations (ballroom, theater, exhibition hall) and symbolizes the transformation of this formerly bourgeois environment into a laboratory of the future. Delphine wanted to create an "open house" feel, so she and her husband had the idea of inviting a critic, once a month, to present the work of a young artist who had not yet exhibited in Rome. The appeal of new discoveries is matched by the great diversity in the status of invited guests. But there is no question of transforming the apartment into a gallery; it truly remains a lived-in home, which gives these encounters a warm, spontaneous atmosphere and reminds us that art is a question not only of contemplation but also of commitment.

VILLAS, OR COUNTRY LIVING IN ROME

It is impossible to grasp the special quality of life in Rome without acknowledging a rural presence within the city. This presence has already been noted in the gardens of certain palaces and on flowery, trellised terraces where the eyes see only rooftops, domes and sky. Most of the grand aristocratic villas which flourished from the Renaissance onward have ceased being residences, but at least that allows us to visit ones open to the public, such as the Villa Borghese and the Villa Doria Pamphili. Some are still occupied, however, even as their use has changed.

The French Academy

Some villas have become the domain of artists, as is the case with the Villa Medici, which even today demonstrates the refinement of the grand Renaissance ecclesiastics. Cardinal Ferdinando de' Medici, fifth son of the Tuscan grand duke, already had a *palazzo* in town when he acquired this estate that another cardinal, Ricci de Montepulciano, had begun to establish on the Pincio Hill. He asked architect Bartolomeo Ammanati to recast his predecessor's project on an entirely different scale, in order to house his extraordinary collection of antique and modern artworks. But when Ferdinando succeeded to the duchy of Tuscany on the death of his elder brothers, most of the collection was progressively taken to Florence. Purchased in 1803 by France, the villa has since been home

Far left: Ludovico Pratesi, a critic and fervent defender of contemporary art, claims that Rome is not an easy-going town, despite appearances. "It's not a straightforward city like Paris, but one full of plotting." He worries that the city may become "a heap of stones usurped by tourists" instead of a modern capital, and that is why he and his wife Delphine Borione are passionate promoters of young artists. One of them drove a symbolic knife into the kitchen door of the apartment (top) while another produced a rather unconventional pedestal table (bottom).

Left: The terrace crowning the
Villa Medici offers a complete
view of Rome including,
on clear days, villas among
the pines in distant Frascati.

Above: Seen from the terrace,
the grounds of the Villa Medici
are a sea of greenery, although
the umbrella pines planted in
1832 are slowly dying of old age.

Balthus, director of the Villa Medici for seventeen years, overhauled the villa's interior decoration. He had a great number of tapestries hung and paid particular attention to the color of the walls. Using a technique that was complex and hard to imitate, he was able to give a remarkable patina and shimmer to the finished surface. The blue-green salon shown here sets off a fine seventeenth-century Italian chair.

Below: Though mutilated, this handsome head (said by some to be the work of Scopas, a Greek sculptor of the fourth century B.C.E.) has lost none of its appeal. Grafted onto another body, it long graced the Villa Medici gardens.

Right: This corner of the director's dining room shows the spirit in which Balthus renovated the villa. In place of standard decoration, he wanted to restore the aristocratic yet rural feel of a Renaissance villa. Garden vegetables on a rustic table contrast with elegant eighteenth-century chairs of Genoese origin and an antique cast transformed into a flower pot.

to the French Academy in Rome, an institution founded by Louis XIV in 1666 to enable the best French artists and architects to develop their skills within view of ancient and Renaissance masterpieces. The Academy recently regained some of its lost luster when the painter Balthus, who was director from 1960 to 1977, assembled around him some of the major figures on Rome's artistic and intellectual scene. He also undertook to restore the interior of the villa using a special technique—often imitated since—which helps to create a very special atmosphere of subtle colors conducive to meditation. He thus brought new life to the cardinal's apartments, decorated with friezes and ceilings painted by Jacopo Zucchi, as well as the famous Turkish bedroom, decorated in a Moorish style by artist Horace Vernet about 1830 when Vernet himself was head of the Academy. But it was not until the external facades were restored in preparation for the year 2000 that the villa recovered the brilliant whiteness of its original appearance.

The Villa Medici gardens have retained their sixteenth-century layout, but the vegetation has changed. Several dozen umbrella pines planted in 1832 still watch over the grounds, like friendly giants whose silhouettes are part of the Roman landscape. In May, lanes populated by antique statues are lit up by thousands of fireflies that flit between hedges of boxwood and laurel.

A small pavilion located above the ancient wall was converted into a *studiolo* by Cardinal Ferdinando. It comprises two rooms. In the first, a resident of the French Academy who was using it as a studio rediscovered a remarkable fresco. It shows a trompe-l'oeil aviary almost as dense as an encyclopedia, teeming with

Above: Several directors of the Villa Medici have left a visible trace of their presence. About 1830, well before Balthus, the painter Horace Vernet turned the top of one of the towers into a Moorish room. Now called the Turkish bedroom, this unusual place reflects not only Vernet's interest in the Orient but also offers an admirable view of Rome.

Right: Sunset warms a collection of objects, including casts of antique seals that will leave the villa when their owner's stay is up.

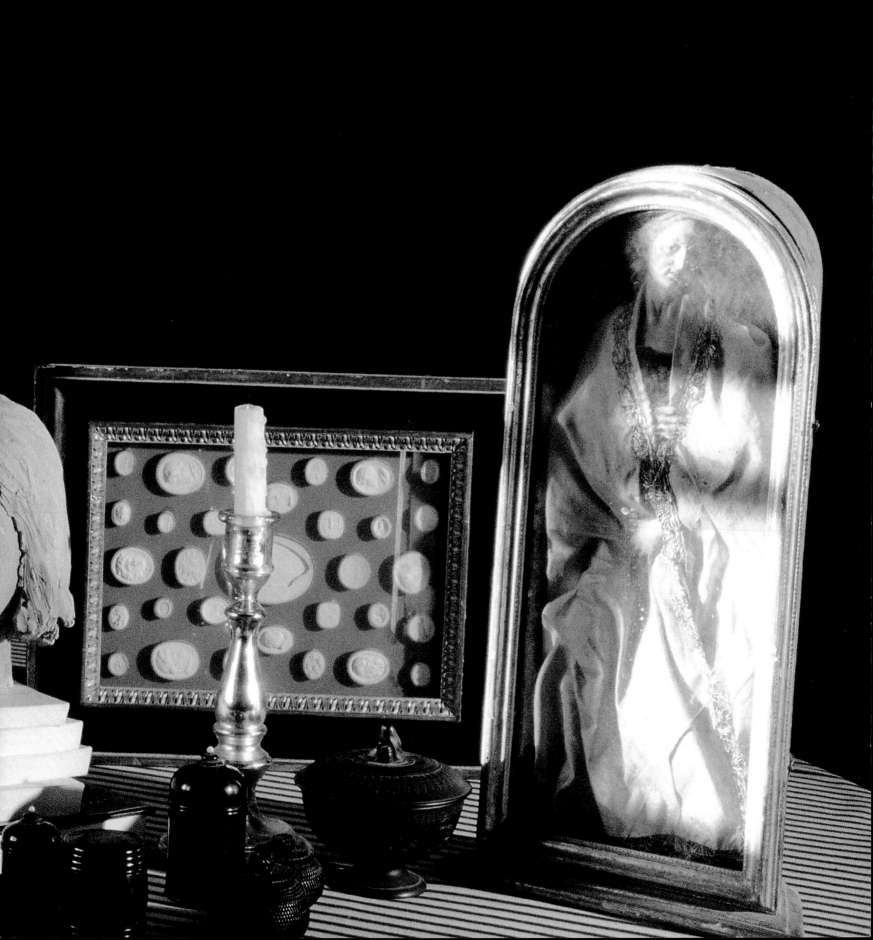

delightful details such as a viper caught by a heron, a weasel nursing her young, and one cat preening while another stalks a bird. The work reflects the cardinal's curiosity concerning the natural sciences, a curiosity that led him to set up a menagerie and lions in another part of the grounds. The second, very small room has a more refined decoration. Between the mythological figures and scenes from fables—the visible ancestors of La Fontaine—Zucchi inserted a view of the gardens as they looked at the time. Few spots provide such an evocative image of the lifestyle of an epicurean priest and art patron in the late sixteenth century.

The grounds themselves, extending over 17 acres, usually project a feeling of intimacy but display a certain solemnity just in front of the villa itself. Sixteen large squares framed by boxwood and laurel hedges contain as many surprises: an antique fountain, a little artist's house, a thicket of bamboo, a reconstitution of the Niobid group (the largest group of antique sculptures ever rediscovered during the Renaissance, the pride of Cardinal Ferdinando's collection). Sometimes luminous, sometimes shady, the grounds provide a multitude of varying perspectives on themselves and on the city. Velàzquez rendered all their poetic charm in two small oils which are now in the Prado in Madrid. Even today, resident members of the Academy (formerly winners of the Prix de Rome in France, now recruited from all over Europe) come to live and work there for one year or two, in the various houses and studios scattered through the grounds.

Below: A cast of an ancient statue in the Villa Medici. A marble copy of the same work stands in the grounds of the Villa Borghese nearby.

Left: These plaster casts at the Villa Medici were used in the past by artists to improve their drawing skills. Academicism has died, yet Rome still draws artists who have apparently abandoned that tradition.

Above: Studios in the Villa Medici have a northern aspect. Through the window can be seen the head of Dea Roma, one of the few items in the Medici collection that remained in place.

Left: Fountains dot the outer wall of the Villa Medici where artists' studios are located.

The American Academy in Rome, founded in the late nineteenth century, occupies a vast complex on the Janiculum Hill. The oldest edifice is the Villa Aureliana, built by a Borghese cardinal in the seventeenth century. The dwelling's elegant portico leads to the garden (above), where a fountain in the midst of boxwood hedges is conducive to meditation (right). The great architect Ferdinando Fuga, who rented a little house on the edge of the grounds, received a message from the cardinal one day asking him to vacate the premises without delay: "You will not have failed to notice," said the cardinal, "that the garden is not big enough for both of us."

Above: The Villa Aureliana has preserved some fine old decoration in the salons used for cultural events organized by the American Academy.

Lower right: A wing perpendicular to the main building houses residential artists for stays of several months, thanks to a system of privately funded prizes and scholarships. Two winners of the Nobel Prize for Literature have sojourned here.

The American Academy

The French model was imitated by others. The American Academy, for example, occupies the Villa Aureliana on the Janiculum Hill. Built in 1655 by Cardinal Girolamo Farnese, the edifice became Garibaldi's headquarters in his heroic and hopeless battle against the French army, which had come to restore Pope Pius IX to the throne in 1849. An American art patron bought the villa in 1885 and, after completely refurbishing it, bequeathed it to the American Academy in Rome in 1909. The Academy took possession in 1911, extending to other buildings nearby. Unlike the government-financed French Academy, the American Academy is a private institution. Since its founding in 1894 it has hosted famous architects, composers, historians, writers (including two Nobel literature prizewinners, Nadine Gordimer and Joseph Brodsky) and artists (the likes of Bruce Nauman, Frank Stella and Roy Lichtenstein). Its grounds basically reflect a late-nineteenth-century restoration undertaken in a Victorian spirit, and features a mixture of Mediterranean and tropical trees. Here, too, a splendid view of Rome is to be had.

Villa Bonaparte

Other villas are used as embassies nowadays. That is what has become of the Villa Bonaparte, another of those dwellings so dear to cardinals at the papal court who wanted all the advantages of the country within the city. Built in 1750 by Cardinal Silvio Valenti Gonzaga, secretary of state to Benedict XIV, the villa is surprisingly sober for the heyday of rococo art. Famous in its time for the Chinese paper lining its walls and for an amazing mechanical table that rose, fully set, from the kitchen to the dining room, the villa was also known for the exotic trees on the grounds. The estate's true fortune was made when Pauline Bonaparte Borghese decided to make it her Roman residence following her brother's downfall. She transformed the interior into a model of Empire taste, and made the residence a rendezvous for cultivated society. It is said that Pauline wanted to name it the Villa Bonaparte but that her mother, Madame Mère, who had taken refuge in Rome thanks to the generosity of Pius VII, did not find the house worthy of the family name. Since that time, it has often been called the Villa Paolina.

After Pauline died, the estate went to her nephews, sons of Lucien Bonaparte, whose branch of the family also settled in Rome and even produced a cardinal for the Church. Pauline's great-nephew, Prince Charles-Napoleon, was nevertheless a fervent supporter of Italian unity, to the extent of being forced to flee the pontifical state of Rome and seek refuge with his cousin, Napoleon III of France. The irony of the story is that Charles-Napoleon was being held

Right: The gallery of the Villa Bonaparte, designed as a loggia opening onto the main balcony, is decorated with a trompe-l'oeil pergola on the ceiling. The room's fine Empire furniture illustrates the intimate yet refined lifestyle of Pauline Bonaparte Borghese, Napoleon's favorite sister. After the disaster of Waterloo, she turned the villa into a place where Rome's finest minds would gather. Today the villa is the residence of French ambassadors to the Holy See.

The grounds of the Villa Bonaparte retain a special charm. They extend to the Aurelian Wall, where unifying Piedmontese forces entered Rome in 1870. The brick facade prefigured a return to classical forms.

prisoner by the Prussians in 1870 after the French disaster at Sedan, at the very moment that the unifying forces led by Victor Emmanuel were entering Rome through his own back yard—his grounds were ringed by the Aurelian Wall which was breached at that spot by Piedmontese artillery. On the other side of the rampart, a column topped by an allegory of victory now marks this deed. Even in their amputated state, the grounds of the Villa Bonaparte remain a place of great serenity. Faithful to the spirit that Pauline wanted to impart to the house, it has become once again the scene of an intense social life ever since France has made it the residence of its ambassadors to the Holy See. At the instigation of René Brouillet, highly respected by Pope Paul VI, it was clearly one of the places where ideas were most actively exchanged on the fringes of the second Vatican Council. The charm of its salons overlooking the garden and the beauty of the hundred-year-old pines on the grounds make it a very special place where the current ambassador, Jean Guéguinou, mobilizes his skill and courtesy (already tried and tested in London) in aid of a mission as contemporary as the Church is itself.

A More Recent Villa

There exists a modern version of the villa tradition, which has survived in Rome by becoming simpler and moving toward the outskirts of town, where many villas were built in the 1950s and 1960s to escape the noisy and sometimes annoying conditions of the historic center. A good example is the residence of Luigi de Conciliis, which has a purist 1960s architecture that fits comfortably into the landscape. Tall trees shade the pool and the flower-bedecked lawn next to a large meadow which once belonged to the Villa Incisa and is now used to pasture horses—in spring, when the grass is deep green, the area almost looks like the English countryside.

Luigi de Conciliis, descended from a Neapolitan family, lived in Milan before coming to Rome. With his wife, Pupa Raimondi (who died a few years ago), he built up a major collection of drawings and paintings that provide a good idea of the artistic effervescence of Rome in the 1960s. Like Carla Accardi, he waxes nostalgic about the days when Piazza del Popolo was one of the centers of artistic and intellectual life in Europe, where you could meet painters such as Cy Twombly and Renato Guttuso—a great friend of Balthus—and writers such as Alberto Moravia and Elsa Morante, not to mention celebrities from the world of movies and theater. De Conciliis's house offers a faithful reflection of those years, notably the staircase wall seen in the entrance, lined with relics from that period. Inside, an entire wall of the large salon is occupied by an immense triptych by Mario Schifano in tones of ocher, white and gray—it will one day join the Galleria Nazionale d'Arte Moderna in Rome, to which De Conciliis has recently bequeathed it along with other major works by Tano Festa, Franco Angeli and Mario Ceroli.

Part of the house's charm stems from the eclecticism of the works gathered there. Two superb landscapes by Paul Bril, originally from the villa that the Mattei family owned on the

Right: The office opens onto the garden and gives an idea of the owner's passion for a wide range of art objects, the most imposing being a majestic seventeenth-century portrait of the youthful Gian Gastone, last of the Medicis.

Below: Modern villas on the outskirts of Rome are filled with vestiges of the past. At the home of Luigi de Conciliis, a carved stone seat invites strollers to halt by the superb flowerbeds.

Caelian Hill, add a seventeenth-century touch to the dining room, which largely overlooks the garden. Here there are precious depictions of ruins by the likes of Clérisseau and Demachy, there a superb youthful portrait of the last of the Medicis, Gian Gastone, whose turbulent life inspired Dominique Fernandez. And over there are Byzantine plates, ceramics from Iznik, antique vases, views of Naples (a tribute to the collector's ancestors), and still more contemporary pieces, European as well as Italian: Hans Bellmer, Graham Sutherland, Otto Dix, and
so on. The collector's eclecticism embraces the most diverse items.

De Conciliis has a law office in the heart of old Rome, on Piazza dei Santi Apostoli, and although it took him time to adjust, Rome has now become indispensable to him. Following the footsteps of Renaissance predecessors, he owns country property within the municipality of Rome, a pleasant retreat which helps him forget the hassles of the city. Despite a soft spot for Paris, De Conciliis could not imagine living anywhere else. Rome constantly reveals new secrets to him, little by little, so how could he do without it? It is a never-ending story, one experienced by everyone who has succumbed to the enchantment of Rome.

Roman
Rendezvous

THE ROME THAT ROMANS LOVE: MUSEUMS NEGLECTED BY TOUR OPERATORS, VANISHING CRAFT TRADITIONS, ANTIQUE DEALERS, HOTELS WITH PANORAMIC VIEWS, CAFÉS AND RESTAURANTS WITH CHARM—EVERYTHING THAT MAKES LIVING IN ROME SO SPECIAL.

Although Romans enjoy receiving friends at home, they also benefit from countless opportunities for meeting elsewhere—if there is one city where "going out" is an ever-renewed pleasure, it must be Rome. Like long-time residents, you too can delight in discovering museums less crowded and less famous than those at the Vatican, and therefore more conducive to serene contemplation. You can find out about the crafts and workshops where centuries-old skills and traditions are perpetuated and, if necessary, updated. And you can simultaneously take advantage of the many cafés, hotels and restaurants where people meet over a cup of coffee—perhaps the best there is—or savor the authentic taste of local cuisine. The following pages cannot, of course, describe the city's charms in full: sampling them all would require more than a single lifetime. One of Rome's great attractions is the kind way a friend will reveal, almost under an oath of secrecy, the name of a particularly appealing *trattoria*, even indicating the name of the *cameriere* to ask for if you want to be waited on with special attention. In Rome, as seasons roll by and friendships form so simply, the pleasure of discovery is never ending.

Left: Palazzo Altemps has just emerged with new splendor from a long period of restoration. This is notably the case with the upstairs loggia, decorated like a pergola. The last time the residence sparkled was in 1883 when poet Gabriele D'Annunzio married Marie Hardouin de Gallese (whose father, Jules Hardouin, a lieutenant in the French army that protected the pope until 1870, married the sole Altemps heiress and was made duke of Gallese.) The marriage was a notoriously unhappy one.

Preceding pages:
The Zanon marble workshop.

MUSEUMS WITH CHARM

Museums in Rome are not as irreplaceable as they are in London, Paris and New York, given that the city itself displays timeless masterpieces in their original settings. Some Roman museums present countless stacks of archaeological finds uncovered since the Renaissance, while others display a profusion of paintings in an ostentatious way that discourages the modern visitor. Above all, the colossal mass of Rome's artistic heritage has led to temporary closures which may last—in the case of the admirable Villa Borghese—for a good twenty years. A considerable campaign is now under way to modernize Roman museums by improving displays,

Below: The Palazzo Altemps now houses the most remarkable pieces from the Ludovisi collection, including a famous Aphrodite. Several of the masterpieces were restored by Bernini and Algardi in the seventeenth century—tribute by great baroque sculptors to the beauty of ancient marble.

Left: Light plays inside Palazzo Altemps, whose walls and windows have recently undergone meticulous restoration. The interior retains interesting fragments of painted decoration, notably frescoes by Giovanni Romanelli, who also worked in the Louvre for the French queen, Anne of Austria.

The Museo Barracco is housed
in an elegant Renaissance
residence, seen here from the
loggia of Palazzo Massimo
alle Colonne. The charm of this
dwelling, which Romans call
the "Piccola Farnesina" ("Little
Farnese," due to a confusion
over heraldic emblems), is
not the least of the
museum's attractions.

highlighting key items, and providing the
facilities the public has come to expect. A
major part of the archaeological collections
of the Museo Nazionale Romano is thus
once again on view in premises
renovated for that purpose, namely
Palazzo Altemps and Palazzo Massimo
alle Terme. The long-term campaign has
included institutions as prestigious as
the Capitoline museums, the Galleria
Nazionale d'Arte Antica at Palazzo
Barberini and the Galleria Nazionale
d'Arte Moderna. This policy has often
entailed moving to little-known
buildings whose refurbishment is part of
the appeal of the new displays.
Any selection from such a vast range will
necessarily be arbitrary, but the few
examples that follow will provide, I hope,
an idea of what gives Roman museums
their special charm.

Museo Barracco

It seems natural to begin with museums
entirely devoted to antiquity. The Museo
Barracco is one of the smallest, but visitors
are rarely bothered by crowds. Named after
the collector who bequeathed it to Rome, it
is located right in the heart of the city, in a
charming Renaissance building on the corner of Corso Vittorio Emanuele and Via dei
Ballauri, opposite Palazzo Massimo di Pirro.
The edifice was designed by Antonio da
Sangallo the Younger in 1523 for a French
clergyman, Thomas Le Roy, who was
authorized by King Francis I to include the
French fleur-de-lis on his coat of arms.
Because of confusion with the fleur-de-lis of
the Farnese family (whose *palazzo* is nearby),
Romans took to calling it "Farnesina ai
allauri." A courtyard leads to the museum,
whose rooms are arranged on two floors. A
significant yet limited number of works offers

a more or less complete overview of Mediterranean civilizations, from Egypt to the Roman Empire and up to the early Middle Ages. They include a portrait of the young Ramses II, fine Roman replicas of Greek statues, and a refined bust of a child of the imperial family long thought to be Nero. Be sure to take the time to enjoy this rich if brief trip through the centuries.

Palazzo Altemps

Palazzo Altemps is on a completely different scale. Located not far from Piazza Navona, the palace has been restored to house part of the collection of the Museo Nazionale Romano formerly in the Baths of Diocletian. Built in the final years of the fifteenth century, its exterior has a certain elegance while still recalling the age of fortresses. It was renovated a century later for the powerful Cardinal Altemps, and its largely open, arcaded courtyard indicates the change in lifestyle. The *palazzo* was taken over by the Italian government in 1982, and has been meticulously and successfully restored, retaining its seventeenth-century frescoes and the mysterious beauty of its chapel. This magnificent building now serves as a setting for some two hundred antique sculptures from the Museo Nazionale Romano, notably masterpieces from the Ludovisi collection. One never tires of seeing the famous Ludovisi throne (in which a sense of holiness is matched by the delicate sensuality of the female figures). Equally wonderful are the statue of Aphrodite and the statue of Mars, which was magnificently restored by Bernini.

Palazzo Altemps still has some ancient statues belonging to the family that gave the palace its name. Four of them are placed under the arcade along one side of the main courtyard. This arrangement is typical of grand Roman dwellings, as also seen at Palazzo Odescalchi and Palazzo Borghese.

Dazzling Galleries

Other highly appealing museums directly reflect the lifestyle of the grand Roman families. The largest is the Doria Pamphili gallery near Piazza Venezia, recently modernized without undermining its original character. As the most dazzling of noble galleries, it boasts major works by the

grandest old masters, including Caravaggio's *Penitent Magdalene* and *Rest on the Flight into Egypt*, and Velàzquez's *Portrait of Pope Innocent X*, a figure whose cruel beauty so haunted the twentieth-century oeuvre of the British painter Francis Bacon.

Another gallery for which I have a particular weakness is the one in Palazzo Spada, which has also retained its authentic atmosphere. It houses a collection begun in the seventeenth century by Cardinal Bernardino Spada, patron to Guido Reni and

The loggia on the piano nobile ends with a gracefully decorated fountain. Worth noting on the pediment are two ibexes or wild goats, which were the heraldic emblem of the Altemps. Two rows of Roman busts representing the twelve Caesars line the loggia.

The wing of Palazzo Spada reserved for Italy's Consiglio di Stato includes a gallery of relatively modest size that is a masterpiece of mannerist decoration, a style that blossomed in Rome in the second half of the sixteenth century. Subjects inherited from the Renaissance—mythological figures and allegories of the virtues—began to take on movement (as seen in the youthful figures flanking the paintings), a movement that would become overpowering in the baroque age.

Right: The largest of the four rooms in the Galleria Spada gives a perfect idea of their charm. Less lavish than the others, less rich in major masterpieces, it provides a valuable example of the refined lifestyle of a high-ranking ecclesiastic. The paintings, mostly from the seventeenth century, are juxtaposed with classical sculptures and precious furnishings, including Dutch globes. The old tiling on the floor has a remarkable sheen.

Guercino. The gallery's four rooms—featuring old furniture and a tiled floor wonderfully polished by centuries of wear—present some important baroque works, including Guercino's magnificent *Death of Dido*. Also on display are a precious work by Jan Brueghel and an austere but moving still life by the French artist Lubin Baugin. The somewhat old-fashioned presentation is part of the charm here, as delightful as the scent of wax. From the gallery's windows the eye can appreciate the simple gardens and architecture of this part of the *palazzo*, which contrasts with the proliferating decoration in the courtyard and on the main facade. Special permission is needed to visit the rooms of the palace occupied by the Consiglio di Stato (supreme administrative court); there a gallery decorated in sixteenth-century painting and stuccois

certainly the high point, but the most intriguing detail is found on the barrel-vaulted ceiling of another room, where, at Cardinal Spada's request, a seventeenth-century French mathematician produced a kind of moon-dial—in Rome, even the passing of time becomes a work of art.

The Glory of English Romantics

I have saved for last the smallest of the charming museums. It is so small that it modestly bears the name "Keats-Shelley Memorial." Its door gives onto Piazza di Spagna, to the right of the Spanish Steps, yet goes unnoticed by most tourists. Thousands of them pass right by, although many may note the elegance of the pink house on the corner. Some tourists may even dream of having a room or apartment there, from where they could watch the

The apartment where English artist Joseph Severn lived in 1820 has been turned into a museum commemorating Keats and Shelley, both of whom were buried in Rome. A large north-facing window opens onto the Spanish Steps and the church of Trinità dei Monti. It is amazing—although not necessarily regrettable—that this spot in the center of town is known only to the few.

constant animation in the square. And yet nothing could be easier than to open the door and climb to the floor where Keats, suffering from tuberculosis, spent the last months of his life from November 1820 to February 23, 1821, in the house of his friend, artist Joseph Severn. The house includes a museum and a library that retain an air of old England. The bookshelves contain the complete works, in original bindings, of the major names of English romanticism, all of whom spent time around the Spanish Steps and Caffè Greco at one point or another in their lives. Not only Keats, Shelley and his wife Mary, and Byron, of course (whose bust was sculpted by Thorwaldsen in 1817), but also the next generation, epitomized by Robert and Elizabeth Browning.

In this meditative setting, souvenirs can create a unique emotional impact. The sight of objects belonging to Keats on the wall or in display cases in this tiny room—cut off from the hubbub of Piazza di Spagna— brings to mind the poet's lines: "Ye soft pipes, play on . . . play to the spirit ditties of no tone." And then there is the wax mask that Byron wore to the carnival in Ravenna in February 1820, and a strange silver reliquary containing locks of hair of John Milton and Elizabeth Browning. By a strange twist of fate, this object once belonged to Pius V, the very pope who excommunicated Elizabeth I of England.

The apartment includes various relics of the poets, some of which are very moving. The room where Keats died has remained more or less as it was in 1821, while a fine library (seen here in the background) contains an extensive collection of books devoted to nineteenth-century English poetry.

CRAFTS AND ARTISANS

Rome has not escaped the changes that have tended to squeeze out manual crafts and high-quality artisanal work everywhere. Some committed artisans and designers nevertheless refuse to be fatalistic: in their own way, whether in a spirit of tradition or renewal, they struggle to perpetuate the skills and the quest for beauty which have characterized Rome for centuries. Below are a few whose campaigns merit mention.

A Creator of Objets d'Art

After crossing the majestic Ponte Flaminio, a no doubt faithful reconstruction of the ancient bridge, you reach a northern neighborhood of Rome that bears the mark of Mussolini-style urban development. That is where Emanuele Pantanella has his workshop. Outside, stumps of olive trees flank the entrance, waiting to be transformed into objects and revealing that wood is the favorite working material of the master of the premises.

Despite the abundance of books piled in his workshop, Emanuele thinks primarily in images. The forms he adopts almost always have a geometric appearance, but there is nothing abstract or disembodied about his personal link to the objects. That is why he has great difficulty letting them go, and why his workshop resembles a limitless pile. There are stacks of books on art, catalogues of auctions and exhibitions, and documents of every kind; a small antique torso in precious marble sits next to modern scarabs

in basalt (tourist trinkets bought for a song in Egypt which will assume unexpected beauty once given a cabochon setting on a rosewood box). The two pieces in this amazing collection that touched me most were two superb blocks of serpentine, a marble-like stone highly appreciated by the emperors; they are called "martyr stones" because the blocks were originally used for

torturing Christians. Victims were hung from a kind of fork, while the weight of the stones attached to their legs slowly wrenched their limbs from their sockets. Two clearly visible holes are allegedly the sign of the hooks by which the stones were attached.

This sweeping ability to preserve and transform everything is wholeheartedly Roman. Today, as in the past, Rome provides an inexhaustible reservoir of ideas and forms. For some people, this abundance can lead to sterile skepticism—*Nihil novi sub sole* ("Nothing new under the sun"). That risk has constantly threatened the city for

French writer Julien Gracq has compared Rome to a "magnificent jumble of denuded urban materials awaiting reassembly or reuse." This pile of fragments in Emanuele Pantanella's workshop fuels his inspiration—these diverse forms and materials are reworked into contemporary objects with very pure lines.

centuries, which is why one of the clearest signs of its genius has been its ongoing ability to attract talent from outside.

Emanuele, meanwhile, followed an unusual path. He comes from one of the few industrial families to have emerged in nineteenth-century Rome. The Pantanellas founded the largest flour mills in the city and environs. Those built in Civitavecchia in the 1930s, now abandoned, are among the most interesting examples of industrial architecture in the area. But the family's first installations were located in the center of town, in the still fallow zone flanking the church of Santa Maria in Cosmedin. By a strange coincidence, that is where imperial Rome had its grain storehouses. Postwar economic consolidation induced the Pantanellas to sell the family firm, so the industrialist became

an artist, perhaps obeying some mysterious Roman law.

Objects as sober as they are refined spring from Emanuele's contemplation of his constantly growing, heterogeneous collection dominated by antique and Islamic art. Although some types of wood—Indian rosewood and African ebony—are now almost impossible to find, what really worries Emanuele is the loss of traditional skills.

A certain coherence can, in fact, be read into the extraordinary chaos that seems to reign at Emanuele Pantanella's place. The oval blocks called "martyrs' stones" (top left) are ancient weights used not only to measure wheat but aslo allegedly to torture early Christians. Despite their loaded past, these relics can also be appreciated as pure shapes. Pantanella is curious about all cultures, especially Islamic art with its calligraphy and colorful tiles (bottom left). His studio (right) is a place of research rather than manufacture, because the objects designed by Pantanella (whose favorite medium is wood) are made elsewhere. Here, art is above all *cosa mentale* ("a mental thing").

Everyone remembers the dazzling costumes in Visconti's great films. Fewer people, however, know the name of the Tirelli firm, which produced them with the help of great costume designers. The firm's collections include legendary items such as the black gown that Maria Callas wore in *La Traviata*. Thanks to these dummies (above), the dresses worn by Romy Schneider in *Ludwig II* and by Sophie Marceau in *Anna Karenina* reappear before our eyes (right).

A Costume Maker

The Tirelli firm, located in one of the residential neighborhoods built in the early twentieth century on the right bank of the Tiber near the Vatican, is known worldwide for the opera and movie costumes it makes. The unusual story of the company's founder, Umberto Tirelli, was recounted to me by Dino Trappetti, the current director.

Born near Parma in one of the wealthiest regions of northern Italy, the young Umberto felt no desire to take over his parents' vineyard. He got a job as a courier for a fabric store. By chance—or fate—he found himself at La Scala in Milan lending a hand to the costume maker. Visconti, who was directing a production of *La Traviata* starring Maria Callas, noticed the young man bursting with ideas and energy, and invited him to join one of the city's major costume makers, SAFAS. Thanks to his outstanding qualities, Tirelli became head of the company, located on Via Margutta, which worked with the leading directors of the 1950s. Then he decided to set up on his own, beginning with four employees. Two weeks later, he had to hire three times as many.

Success has been unwavering, thanks in particular to close collaboration with great costume designers such as Piero Tosi (ever at Visconti's side), Pier Luigi Pizzi and, more recently, Gabriella Pescucci and Maurizio Millenotti (who worked on Fellini's last films), not forgetting Ann Roth's costumes for *The English Patient*. Tirelli has also worked for Zeffirelli, Bolognini, Milos Forman and many others.

In addition to making costumes, Tirelli was an enthusiastic collector. Over the years he accumulated one of the finest private collections of historical clothing, whether found in family attics and wardrobes or at flea markets in Paris. He very generously donated some of them to the Metropolitan Museum in New York and the Musée des Arts Décoratifs in Paris, while hundreds of others have gone to Palazzo Pitti in Florence and a similar number are reserved for Rome's future costume museum. This veritable "costume archaeology" explains why Tirelli's specialty is historical reconstitution, which is not necessarily incompatible with a fanciful and creative approach, as witnessed by Fellini's *Casanova* in which the magnificent garments were modern inventions. The firm's business is certainly not threatened, given the considerable needs of the film industry and opera scene, not to mention more unusual orders such as all the costumes for Siena's Palio in the year 2000.

Right: An office lined with sketches of costumes tracing the history of the firm also features the dress worn by Catherine Deneuve in *Time Regained*, along with the one worn by Winona Ryder in *The Age of Innocence*.

Two Marble Works

Marble has been used so widely in Rome in the past two millennia that this symbol of luxury and magnificence seems almost ordinary. One of the leading connoisseurs of this inspiring stone is Raniero Gnoli, whose book *Marmorata Romana* remains a key reference work, covering the history and uses

of marble, and the problems connected with its care and restoration. He laments the inexorable disappearance of top-notch artisans and typically Roman techniques (such as the secret of imitation-marble stucco, *marmoridea*, and microscopic mosaics) and tries to keep the tradition alive by designing rare objects.

It is thanks to Gnoli that I was able to meet Priscilla Grazioli, heir to the Medici firm founded by her ancestors in 1838. In the sphere of marble, this company is the oldest

and most sought after in Rome. Its workshops are located near the Tiber, in nineteenth-century buildings set on a site with easy access for the heavy blocks. The Medici firm moved there in 1929, after having had various addresses, including the Vatican, where it still has an office; indeed, for five generations now, the family has worked for the Holy See and Rome's major basilicas.

In the delightful office where Grazioli received me, I noticed a clutch of certificates attesting to the gratitude of a succession of popes since the mid-nineteenth century. She showed me watercolors that her mother would execute prior to every project. The archives contain almost five thousand drawings and photographs illustrating the quality of the work done since the early days, including in particular the paving for Saint Peter's and for Saint Patrick's Cathedral in New York. Also, since the 1929 concordat which settled the dispute between the papal state and the Italian government, the firm has received public commissions, notably at the Quirinal. Private customers have become scarce due to the cost of traditional techniques.

In the adjoining garden is an impressive quantity of marble of all kinds, ancient and modern, giving an idea of the material's rich variety—coralline breccia, incarnadine red (used on Versailles and the Trianon), *portoro* (with its fine gold veins on black), Greek pink, Assouan granite, and so on. This rich variety is essential for high-quality work, making it possible to employ all shades of stone, for instance, to create the illusion of light and shadow.

The large, luminous workshops pieces being restored or executed. The firm has a

Nothing better demonstrates continuity down through the ages than a visit to the Medici firm, the largest marble works in Rome. Stocks of the precious material are required for new pieces and for restoration work, sometimes including varieties not quarried since antiquity. The garden flanking the workshop is thus an amazing open-air museum, displaying an incomparable range of marble in a more or less raw state, often cut into slabs or carved fragments.

staff of ten, and it is becoming increasingly difficult to find and train artisans who have both skills and taste. I could not help wondering, as I passed the offices on my way out, whether the examples covering walls and floor represented an art and a craft that are also on the way out, perhaps even doomed to extinction. It is so much more economical to have inscriptions engraved by machine, and yet, for as long as people such as Priscilla Grazioli are around, there is reason to hope that high standards can be maintained.

In order to reinforce that hope, I wanted to visit a more modest marble workshop, so I went to Dante Zanon on the recommendation of Alvar Gonzalez Palacios. Heading out from the center of town, I took the Via Appia to a small patch of countryside still within city limits. On my arrival, I was surprised by the horde of dogs—more noisy than aggressive—which announced the presence of a stranger. So what riches were hidden in this out-of-the-way place? The answer is marble, in a whole range of magnificent, rare varieties. Founded in 1975, the workshop took over from an older firm, created generations earlier by the Maiorani family. It restores objects in marble and other types of hard stone, as well as execu-

ting modern works to order. A path strewn with marble and travertine rubble led to the mechanical saw that has replaced an old hand tool which became obsolete some thirty years ago. Cutting the blocks into slabs of varying thickness no longer takes months—or even years—as it once did, but will still take weeks given marble's resistance to the combined forces of steel saw, water and sand.

In the yard behind the workshop, impressive blocks wait to be handled. Inside, workers—who require years of training— restore ancient sculptures or inlaid table-tops, working and polishing stones of all sizes. I wondered whether some were more precious than others. Dante anticipated my question, and led me to a heavy armored door. It enclosed a multitude of blocks of antique marble on which water had just been poured, bringing out the colors in all their splendor. In the adjoining room were smaller fragments, ready to be worked and therefore all the more sought-after: porphyry, African serpentine, antique yellow, coralline breccia, florid alabaster, lapis-lazuli and—even more difficult to work than porphyry—agate. The beauty of these jewels of nature is as fine as the poetry of their names.

Marble was once worked entirely by hand but machines have now largely taken over. Blocks, in particular, are no longer cut by mechanical saws which required months or, in the case of porphyry, years of toil. As in the old days, however, abundant use is still made of water and sand (for its abrasive qualities).

A Stucco Worker

Thanks to the infinite range of possibilities it offers decorators, stucco is closely identified with the baroque spirit, undoubtedly one of the finest expressions of Rome's genius. I wanted to discover whether the skills that produced all those flitting angels on church ceilings still existed, and therefore paid a visit to a workshop run by the Baiocco family on Via della Luce.

It is located in the heart of Trastevere, on one of those narrow streets that were formerly the realm of artisans. Right from the doorway, I was struck by the whiteness of the workshop, as though plaster dust covered every single object. Raising my eyes to the ceiling, I saw a wide variety of sample decorations, ornate cofferings and garlands,

all part of a real-life catalogue that included dozens of numbered moldings and cornices lining the walls. More or less everywhere were copies of famous sculptures, some reduced in scale, some life-sized, such as the Christ from Michelangelo's *Pietà* which greets visitors at the entrance.

The grandson of Fabrizio Baiocco, who founded the firm, was working among sacks of plaster on a huge travertine table. He discussed the old way of preparing stucco—using a certain quality of plaster, marble dust and lime—which he now only uses for restorations. The firm's most noteworthy projects include the framing of Raphael's frescoes at the Vatican, as well as work at the Palazzo Barberini and the Capitoline. Most business, however, employs another kind of plaster which makes it possible to economize on the other ingredients. Modern decorations and furnishing such as wall fixtures and table legs are made from the new material.

His mother, who has always lived in Trastevere, regrets that artisans are gradually vanishing from the neighborhood. Their successors—when there are any—have now moved out to the outskirts. "But our crafts are artistic, not industrial," she said. "We couldn't survive if we moved to the outskirts." There seems to be no lack of business for the firm, nor of love for the profession, which is handed down from generation to generation. But there is a fear of being driven from a neighborhood, once the most authentic in Rome, which is now inexorably changing.

Even the Baiocco family dog has taken on the color of plaster. Stucco is traditionally made from lime powder and marble dust, and makes it possible to cast or sculpt every decorative form imaginable, such as bas-reliefs, moldings and ceiling rosettes. The wall of the workshop is lined with models numbered according to the firm's catalogue.

Right: This reproduction of the Christ in Michelangelo's *Pietà* is the work of the founder of the Baiocco firm, and therefore a valuable souvenir of the family history. Still operating in the center of Trastevere, the third generation perseveres in trying to maintain fast-disappearing artisanal traditions.

A Family of Antique Dealers

Despite its considerable artistic heritage, Rome's art market is not as important as the ones in Paris and London. The main reason for this situation, I think, stems from the lack of a conquering bourgeoisie in the nineteenth and early twentieth centuries,

In Franco di Castro's antique shop, a large Venetian painting hangs above a fine Italian Renaissance table discovered in England. The precious objects and small paintings displayed on the table give an idea of the rich collections assembled by Roman antique dealers, often in business for several generations.

one that would have wanted to demonstrate its social rise by owning works of art. Legal and administrative complications, plus an occasionally extreme concern to remain discreet, did the rest.

Fortunately, the city still has a respectable number of antique dealers, centered around Via Giulia, Piazza Navona and Piazza di Spagna. The only antique shop located on Piazza di Spagna itself is Alberto di Castro, which has a long and intriguing history. An ancestor, Angelo di Castro, was

the first member of this old Jewish family to leave Rome's ghetto, in the mid-nineteenth century. An ardent advocate of Italian unity, he jumped into the Tiber to join Garibaldi's troops on the Janiculum Hill, battling the French and papal forces at Mentana. It was his two sons Leone and Alberto who founded an antique shop near the Vatican, later moving to Via del Babuino, the first of its kind on a street where such stores are now legion. The firm really took off under one of Leone's sons, also called Alberto. However, the racial laws of the fascist regime of the day forbade Jews from dealing in ancient objects, obliging Alberto to find a dodge. By acquiring an "Aryan" partner, he managed to continue doing business until the tragic moment when the Germans decided to deport the Jewish community from Rome. Alberto, like a certain number of fellow Jews, found refuge with the Catholic clergy, hiding in the Genoese church in the heart of Trastevere. By a twist of fate, while digging a secret passage he found the tomb of a certain Marchese del Grillo, known in the eighteenth century for his hatred of Jews. When peace returned, Alberto took up business again, going international. He began in Vienna, where he bought a fine portrait by Rembrandt, and then went to England where his young son Franco got his own start.

Franco speaks of those days as a kind of golden age, when the break up of the British empire resulted in an amazing circulation of artworks. He remembers, among others, an unusual character in the shape of a

A drawer filled with gold thread evokes the lavishness of the liturgical vestments made by the De Ritis firm, which was founded in the late thirteenth century. It is hardly surprising that Rome is the world capital of ecclesiastical dress and that it even counts Protestant ministers among its clientele.

clergyman from northern England who had assembled a remarkable collection of religious paintings. Among the works stored in the vicar's dimly lit cellar, all framed in dark wood, there glowed an El Greco. The Di Castros, meanwhile, have won the trust of Rome's grand families, gaining an entrée to that closed world with its treasures. It now looks as though the family tradition will be perpetuated by a new generation, trained in London and Rome, that seems determined to carry on the venture.

Church Tailors

The same family tradition recurs in another realm, that of tailoring for the clergy. The second Vatican Council granted priests and other clergy a freedom of dress that they had not known for centuries. The 1980s, however, saw a marked return to sartorial strictness among clerics. Rome itself had never been a city for laxism in this sphere, so specialized firms—some of which had existed for generations—were hardly threatened with extinction.

Most ecclesiastical tailors are found in the Pantheon neighborhood, especially on Via di Santa Chiara and Via dei Cestari. Two of the better known are perhaps Annibale Gammarelli, who boasts the title of the pope's official tailor, and the De Ritis firm, which is known among other things for its ready-to-wear line for nuns. Competition occasionally leads to a certain division of labor—thus De Ritis began to specialize in liturgical vestments and decorations made of fabric, work that was formerly the prerogative of nuns whose skilled hands made

lace and embroidered chasubles. It was only natural that, having adopted this work, De Ritis should also begin to focus on the way nuns dressed.

Conventional black cassocks are giving way to more comfortable vestments. The "clergyman look" is no longer restricted solely to Protestants (who, in these days of ecumenism, sometimes come to the papal city to buy clothing). An almost infinite range is offered, from bespoke to ready-to-wear, from buttons to silk socks. Gammarelli proposes over seventeen fabrics, four for summer, eight for winter and five for spring and fall; some are inexpensive and some are costly, silk being theoretically reserved for Vatican dignitaries. The most difficult period for Gammarelli comes during the conclave, just before the white smoke indicates the election of a new pope; the firm reportedly prepares several series of vestments and accoutrements likely to suit leading candidates whose measurements are as different as those of, say, a Pius XII and a John XXIII.

This shot of the De Ritis store, with its glittering silk and embroidered chasubles, should not give the impression that only priests shop here. Anyone can make purchases, whether seeking embroidery, lace, fine gloves or socks (the same is true across the street at Gammarelli's, tailor to the pope).

HOTELS WITH A VIEW

Rome not only hosts millions of tourists every year but must also cope with floods of pilgrims that accompany grand papal ceremonies, beatifications and canonizations. One of my most striking childhood memories concerns the 1958 funeral of Pius XII, the last truly "monarchical" pope. I will never forget the cortege from Castel Gandolfo, the pope's summer residence, arriving in Rome by the light of torches as an entire people watched his mortal remains inch forward. The jubilee in the year 2000 will probably draw bigger crowds than did the one in 1950, humorously described in a famous novel by Alexis Curvers, *Tempo di Roma*.

The city is therefore endowed with hotels of all kinds, not to mention the facilities offered by numerous convents and monasteries. Given such abundance, special mention will go to those that combine a sweeping vista with the privacy or coolness of a garden. The brief itinerary that follows, featuring either garden terraces or terrace-and-garden combinations, hardly claims to exhaust the city's endless possibilities, yet it offers a good glimpse.

Hotels on the Heights

The first terrace restaurant in Rome opened just after World War II atop the Hassler Villa Medici hotel. Even today it is perhaps unrivaled for the beauty of its vista. Landmarks on the horizon include the Villa Medici, the dome of Saint Peter's and the Palazzo del Quirinale. For people who dare to lean over the railing, the steep view of the

Left: The terrace of the Hassler Villa Medici hotel boasts an unforgettable view of Rome and its main buildings. The dome of San Carlo al Corso is seen in the middle ground, with Saint Peter's in the distance. The Hassler was the first hotel to open a restaurant with a panoramic view. Their example was imitated by others and now seems an inevitable part of the charm of grand hotels.

Left: The Hotel Eden, on the edge of the grounds of the Villa Medici, also has a terrace-garden where you can enjoy a drink in the shade before dining. The pergola creates an intimate yet tasteful atmosphere. The prospect is superb and alternates close-up perspectives with a panoramic view, as does the roof of the Hassler (above).

Spanish Steps is dizzying. On the ground floor, meanwhile, after crossing a lobby with decoration worthy of an ocean liner of yore, you can appreciate the charm of an enclosed garden and bar.

I find the Hotel de la Ville, along Via Sistina, pleasing above all for the quality of its 1930s interior decoration by Josef Vago, a

Europe-spanning Hungarian who left his mark in Paris and Geneva (Palais des Nations). Its finest feature is perhaps its elegant inner garden.

Located on the edge of the Ludovisi neighborhood near Via Vittorio Veneto, the Hotel Eden has not only one of the city's best-known restaurants but also a terrace with a far-ranging view which, unlike the Hassler, includes in the foreground the greenery of the Villa Medici and Trinità dei Monti. It thus evokes one of ancient Rome's

supreme luxuries, revived during the Renaissance: being able to contemplate the city from a rural vantage point.

Terraces in Town

Terraces situated on the plain, so to speak, offer a different impression, but the city should also be admired from the level of its rooftops with their fine tiles the color of burned toast. The ivy-covered facade of the Hotel Raphael is a stone's throw from Piazza Navona; it is worth having a drink on the terrace, where the eye can take in the entire Campo Marzio neighborhood with the churches of Sant'Agnese and Santa Maria della Pace, while the bulk of Saint Peter's rises in the background. Not far from there is the Portoghesi Hotel, with a small terrace that offers a view of the center of Rome which is simultaneously rare yet typical. Apart from the nearby Portuguese church—whose interior is one of the highlights of Roman baroque art—you can see a statue commemorating a miracle performed in the neighborhood by the madonna.

Finally, the Forum Hotel should be mentioned, for its terrace provides a view not only of the great archaeological ruins but also of the rooftops in this charming neighborhood, which was known as Suburra in antiquity, when it was a sleazy Pigalle-like district. The view takes in Via Tor dei Conti below, lined by the impressive wall of the temple of Mars the Avenger, while the horizon is marked by the Palatine and Capitoline Hills.

Like the Hassler, the Hotel de la Ville is located on Via Sistina. Although its view is less heady than that of its famous neighbor, it has an indoor garden that can be glimpsed through the remarkable interwar architecture (left). It has all the charm of little-known places, evident in this delicate composition of statue, sculpture and greenery (above).

Right: Perhaps there is no more sensual image of the delight of living in Rome than this breakfast on a balcony at the Hotel Eden, in the morning light before the summer sun begins to weigh on the city. The silhouette of Palazzo del Quirinale, flying the Italian tricolor flag, can be seen in the distance in its new-found whiteness.

GASTRONOMY: MARKETS AND RESTAURANTS

In comparison with other large cities in Italy, Roman gastronomy might seem somewhat feeble. It has neither the extraordinary wealth of recipes from regions such as Piedmont and Emilia-Romagna, nor the aristocratic cuisine which is still the pride of Naples. Not only did the area around Rome long remain unproductive, but the papal court, given its constant changeover, hardly favored the development of a tradition proper to a local elite—some Florentine, Venetian or Neapolitan cardinal would arrive with his entire household, which would then vanish along with him. Yet it would be risky to conclude that Rome has nothing to offer gourmets.

Two Authentic Markets

More or less everywhere in town there exist little street markets where a few carts overflow with brightly colored flowers, fruit and vegetables. These markets cannot rival the big ones, however. In addition to the one in Campo de' Fiori, right in the heart of the old city, two markets merit special attention for the variety of their merchandise and for the authentic, much less "touristy" picture of Rome they present.

The market on Piazza Vittorio Emanuele II (or Piazza Vittorio), in the middle of a neighborhood built by the Piedmont contingent after the unification of Italy, is without a doubt the most multi-ethnic in Rome. Organized around a large rectangular

garden, this vast market presents a wide range of products from all corners of the earth. As though in some exotic market, a fish will be pulled live from the tank before being stunned, scaled and gutted before your eyes. Garlands of tripe hang from carts alongside gleaming fruit from the southern

hemisphere. Not far from the bustling, colorful crowd are local elderly citizens and a few lovers who sit on the benches in the garden, which, as soon as the stalls are closed, is invaded by an incalculable number of cats. Fans of the mysteries should not miss the esoteric signs on Porta Magica, an antique doorway located at one end of the garden.

Another place worth knowing is Testaccio market, with its apparently more ordered appearance. Also located in a square shaded by fine plane trees, it is composed of

Taking advantage of a local *trattoria* is one of Rome's unending pleasures, especially when fine weather draws the tables outdoors. A few plants and umbrellas are the only decoration in the narrow streets and tiny squares of the old neighborhoods such as Piazza del Drago in Trastevere.

Two typically Roman, if contrasting, ambiances: the Caffè Rosati (left), pride of Piazza del Popolo, is elegant and refined, a meeting place for celebrities with its old furnishings and pastry cart; Piazza Sant'Apollonia in the heart of Trastevere (right), on the other hand, is nocturnal, relaxed and simple. Dining outside on a summer night, when the air is cooler, is one of Rome's great joys.

permanent stalls aligned like an ancient Roman camp. The atmosphere is more conventional but certainly no less lively than Piazza Vittorio.

Roman Specialties

As with all cuisines that derive from the common people rather than aristocrats, it is the excellence of the local ingredients that determines the quality of what you eat in Rome. While pasta and rice are key elements, like everywhere else in Italy, Roman cuisine is notable for the importance traditionally given to offal such as tripe and oxtails. Some specialties are typically Roman—*spaghetti alla carbonara*, seasoned with bacon, fresh cream and egg yolks, or *saltimbocca alla romana*, a

veal cutlet fried with raw ham and a sage leaf. Jewish cuisine in Rome has also produced original dishes, the most widespread being Jewish-style artichokes and the famous *filetti di baccalà* (cod fillets in batter). My own preference is for certain delicious hors d'oeuvres such as *suppli* (cheese-flavored rice cakes), *fave in guanciale* (local beans simmered in bacon and onions, a seasonal dish I discovered in a little restaurant in Frascati), and above all *fiori di zucca* (fried zucchini flowers, a delight to both the eye and the palate, crispy on the outside and soft within).

The wines of Castelli Romani and Colli Albani, a region of volcanic formation near Rome where popes and elite families liked

A good example of the way luxury and simplicity can coexist in Rome: on Largo Febo, a modest *trattoria* at the foot of the Hotel Raphael benefits from the shade of some venerable trees (which are rather rare in the old central neighborhoods). Here, the delightful setting counts for as much as the quest for gastronomic pleasures.

to go in summer, will please wine-lovers who are not overly demanding. Some vintages of Orvieto, another region not too distant from Rome, might leave a more lasting impression, but the ancientness of vineyards in Frascati and a few other Castelli villages adds an extra dimension to the pleasure of a glass of cold white wine accompanied by *bruschetta* (delicious morsels of toast seasoned with tomatoes and herbs).

Restaurants and *Trattorie*

Roman restaurants reflect a certain lifestyle—their charm is due as much to their warm and easy-going atmosphere as to any culinary prowess or innovation. The city does, of course, boast restaurants known for refined service, much closer than small local eateries to notions of international elegance. And some chefs try to be bold and inventive in their interpretations of traditional recipes. When, in addition, such restaurants benefit from a superb view (as on the terraces of the Eden and Hassler hotels), a dinner will give a fairly good idea of luxury. But the charm of Rome can be appreciated just as much, if not more, in some unpretentious *trattoria* where tables will be set on the sidewalk behind a hedge of greenery during fine weather, and where you can linger in the warm evening air.

In often attractive settings, many wine bars offer a vast range of Italian wines to accompany the dishes they serve. Some establishments still propose family cuisine—usually intended for a clientele of regulars—providing, perhaps, the best

This shot of the Sabatino restaurant on Piazza Sant'Ignazio shows the extent to which a rather elegant spot can be hard to distinguish, at first sight, from a local *trattoria*, especially when tables are placed outdoors (top). For anyone wanting a quick lunch without resorting to a snack bar, wine bars often accompany their wide selection of wines with antipasti, as shown here at Bottega del Vino (bottom).

opportunity to sample traditional Roman cooking. I am thinking in particular of Der Pallaro, a *trattoria* on Largo di Pallaro where you first have to be accepted by the female owner before you can enjoy a series of dishes, each one as delicious as the next, although you will not have any choice in the matter.

Whether in Trastevere or Campo de' Fiori, the possibilities are infinite. In winter, I like to duck into the Roman vaulting of the Pancrazio or the Costanza, located on the site of Pompey's Theater, where the owner greets you by cutting a thin slice of raw ham. And then there's Piperno, in the heart of the Ghetto, which has maintained the tradition of Jewish cuisine since the nineteenth century. Next to Giolitti, the famous ice-cream parlor near the parliament, Piccola Roma offers good Roman specialties (as does its sister restaurant near the Pantheon)—you are supposed to ring the bell near the door on leaving, if your meal was satisfactory.

In summer, countless terraces offer a more or less lively setting, depending on the neighborhood. The predominance of tourists, particularly noticeable in the old center, alters the atmosphere somewhat, but I like to wind up at Vecchia Roma on Piazza Campitelli, whose rooms have a great deal of charm. Anyone who remembers the scenes from *Fellini's Roma* with the

unforgettable dinner in the street would be advised to try his or her chance in sectors less endowed with artistic treasures, notably Testaccio (which has the advantage of its own market) where Roman traditions are perpetuated by several establishments such as Perilli and Cecchino (this latter more expensive, but with a wine cellar

worth sampling). There is also the San Lorenzo neighborhood, full of students, where Florence Patrizi introduced me to Da Franco, one of the most delightful fish restaurants around—its owner, when in the mood, will prove that bel canto is still an art of the people.

A terrace restaurant would be unthinkable without its umbrellas, especially at lunchtime when the summer sun can be scorching. Every square inch of the table should be shaded, as seen here in a well-known restaurant in Trastevere, La Cornucopia.

Right by the Villa Medici on the heights of the Pincio Hill, the tables and umbrellas of the Caffè Ciampini surround a pool with turtles (top), while the Caffè della Pace spills into the street of the same name below a screen of Virginia creeper in a scene typical of the Piazza Navona neighborhood (bottom).

CAFÉS AND ICE-CREAM PARLORS

It is not necessary to extol the well-known excellence of Roman coffee in all its forms—*espresso*, *macchiato* (with a drop of milk) or *corretto* (with a dash of alcohol), not to mention frothy *cappucino*. I have always preferred espresso, just a few drops in the tiny cup, downed in one swallow before the sugar cube has completely melted. Attempting to give the address of "the best café in Rome" would be both pointless and unfair. The same can be said of the ice cream, sherbets and crushes which, as soon as the June heat arrives, become a mandatory pleasure. In this sphere, the most modest bars sometimes rival the better-known establishments like Rosati on Piazza del Popolo or Giolitti (the ice-cream parlor whose original outlet, near the Pantheon, is one of the most popular places in town). Perhaps Rome's greatest pleasure is being able to stop almost anywhere without being disappointed.

A Few Addresses

For people who, despite everything, seek a recommendation, Tazza d'Oro near the Pantheon smells so strongly of freshly roasted coffee that the beverage seems to take on special flavor. But similar pleasure can be found nearby at Sant'Eustachio on Piazza Sant'Eustachio, remarkable for its collection of old coffee grinders, or at Antico Caffè della Pace, which is also among my favorites, probably because I feel the

neighborhood incarnates the soul of the city.

On Piazza Navona itself, perhaps due to an unconscious memory of Venice and Piazza San Marco, I almost always order chocolate: steaming hot chocolate with a dollop of whipped cream in winter, when the cold bites, but in summer a piece of Tre Scalini's famous *tartufo*, a dark ice-cream cake, crunchy and soft at the same time (which I also order at the Caffè Ciampini below the Villa Medici, run by the same family).

I have saved two extremes for the end: first, for its beautiful decoration and the memories it evokes, the famous Caffè Greco on Via Condotti. Founded by a Greek in 1760, it was frequented by all the great figures who have haunted Piazza di Spagna, becoming the favorite meeting spot of the artistic and intellectual elite in the nineteenth century. Romans and tourists still flock there, the former generally preferring to have an espresso at the bar while the latter like to sit at tables below the portraits of great travelers of the past. Anyone who likes contrasts can go from the Caffè Greco's evocations of the past to the resolutely modern setting of Gusto, whose large windows overlook the Mausoleum of Augustus. Frequented by a young and trendy clientele, in the evenings it features a pianist. Despite appearances, however, this is not New York—the sight of ruins overgrown with vegetation, surrounded by 1930s buildings of brick and travertine, symbolizes a city which, even when it wants to be part of the present, must always reinterpret its own past.

Right: Seen through the window of the Caffè della Pace, a waiter prepares a tray under the watchful eye of Emperor Augustus. In Rome, even cafés are charged with history.

Following page: A halt at the former confessors' residence (Palazzo dei Penitenzieri) with its superb sixteenth-century frescoes—now the Hotel Columbus on Via del Conciliazione—might be in order prior to a promenade or pilgrimage to Saint Peter's Square, seen here with the fountains playing beneath Bernini's statues.

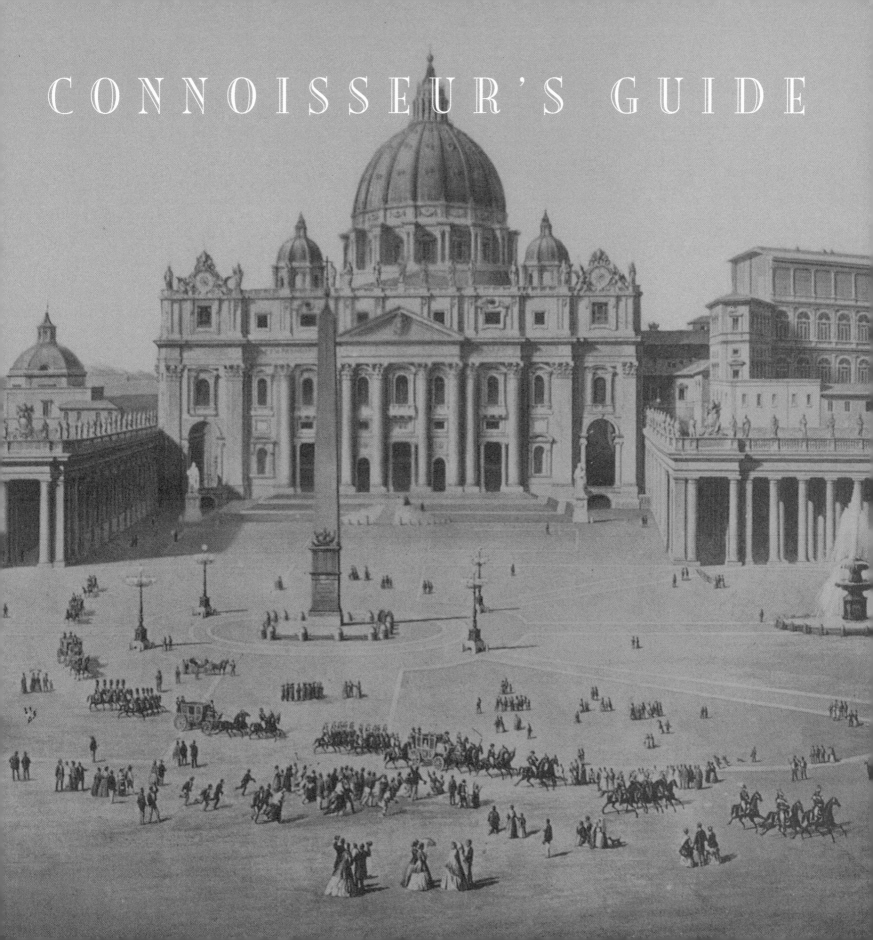

CONNOISSEUR'S GUIDE

This guide is both subjective and selective. It includes a number of "musts," together with a range of good addresses and personal favorites of the authors and their friends. Most of these are concentrated in the center of the city, but the guide also explores Latium, the region for which Rome is the administrative center. It provides the address and telephone number (and, for hotels, the fax number). Because they are subject to change, opening hours and prices are not included.

HOTELS

It is not easy to find cheap comfortable accommodation in Rome. The city is one of the most important tourist and religious destinations in the world, and in certain periods accommodation is full. Only January and February could be called quiet months.

The following list focuses on hotels which have a particular charm. About ten years ago many of the large hotels were renovated, a practice which subsequently spread to establishments in other categories as the new millennium approached. The hotels situated near the train station do not generally have a good reputation, but many have made remarkable efforts to improve their accommodation.

The area around Piazza di Spagna and Piazza del Popolo offers many possibilities, as do the Pantheon and Piazza Navona neighborhoods: their central location and their charm make them particularly worthy of recommendation. The Ludovisi neighborhood, around the Via Veneto, has a large range of hotels, some of which are luxurious, but the golden age of the 1960s is now just a memory.

There are a range of hotels and boarding houses in the areas around the Vatican and the station, and also on the edge of the city center. These districts are a little lacking in the charm which is particular to Rome, but this is not always the case and there are some pleasant surprises.

Piazza di Spagna

ALBERGO D'INGHILTERRA
Via Bocca di Leone, 14
Tel: 06–69981; fax: 06–69922243
This hotel, with its beautiful ocher facade, is situated near Piazza di Spagna, in a little street which intersects the Via dei Condotti, home to the big names in fashion. It is a historic hotel which was already well known in the middle of the nineteenth century. Recently restored, its past guests include Anatole France, Mendelssohn, Liszt and Hemingway. The most sought after tables are naturally those on the top floor, which have terraces with magnificent views.

GRAND HOTEL PLAZA
Via del Corso, 126–127
Tel: 06–69921111; fax: 06–69941575
"Albergo Splendido" says the inscription in bronze letters at the entrance. The entrance hall alone, with its woodwork and marble, is worthy of this epithet. There are magnificent views from the terrace.

GREGORIANA
Via Gregoriana, 18
Tel: 06–6794296; fax: 06–6784258
Situated in a relatively quiet street near the Trinità dei Monti, and not far from the sixteenth-century palace whose front door is set within an astonishing monster's mouth, this hotel, which has less than twenty rooms, has an intimate atmosphere and a reputation for providing a warm, hospitable welcome.

HASSLER VILLA MEDICI
Piazza Trinità dei Monti, 6
Tel: 06–699340; fax: 06–699340
Overlooking the whole city, the Hassler offers an incomparable panoramic view, particularly from its terrace, which serves as a restaurant. Popular with important personalities and passing celebrities, for decades it has epitomized the idea of luxury in Rome, even if the competition for top

spot is fiercer now. An inner courtyard, adorned with greenery and a fountain, provides a cool and peaceful spot for a drink.

HOMS
Via della Vite, 71
Tel: 06–6792976; fax: 06–6780482
A little hotel well situated near Piazza di Spagna. The rooms are small, but the good service, the reasonable prices and the beauty of the view from the terrace will ensure a worthwhile stay.

HOTEL DE LA VILLE-INTERCONTINENTAL
Via Sistina, 67–69
Tel: 06–67331; fax: 06–6784213
Very well located near the Trinità dei Monti, slightly less luxurious than the neighboring Hassler but still refined and elegant. The Hotel de la Ville is notable for its 1930s decor and architecture, the work of Josef Vago, the architect of the Palais des Nations in Geneva. Its garden is also charming. The Sunday morning brunch has become a classic.

MOZART
Via dei Greci, 23
Tel: 06–699400411; fax: 06–67842271
Situated halfway between Piazza di Spagna and Piazza del Popolo, in the heart of a lively neighborhood but in a very quiet street, this hotel has been decorated with great taste. It is next to the beautiful Renaissance church of Sant'Atanasio dei Greci, where the Sunday service is celebrated in accordance with the Byzantine rite.

SCALINATA DI SPAGNA
Piazza Trinità dei Monti, 17
Tel: 06–69940896; fax: 06–69940598
This little hotel, with its charming eighteenth-century facade, is tucked into a corner of the piazza, opposite the Hassler. It makes it possible to stay at the top of the famous Spanish Steps. The view from its terrace has a view which is almost as sublime as

that of its prestigious neighbors. Although not cheap, prices are markedly more affordable. The classical decor is of impeccable taste.

Ludovisi, Vittorio Veneto

EDEN
Via Ludovisi, 49
Tel: 06–478121; fax: 06–4821584
Built at the end of the nineteenth century, for many years the property of the family which owned the Hassler, the Eden was magnificently renovated a few years ago. Benefiting from a unique view of the gardens of the Villa Medici and the city from its upper stories, it is now without doubt one of the most beautiful hotels in Rome, and also one of the most luxurious. An apéritif on the terrace, especially at sunset in the summer when the city glows, is a delightful experience.

Fontana di Trevi

DEI BORGOGNONI
Via del Bufalo, 126
Tel: 06–69941505
Close to the Fontana di Trevi, but in a quiet street, this hotel has an elegant decor, exemplified by the paintings in the entrance hall. Centrally placed and easy to reach, this is a very pleasant place to stay, even though there is no view.

Piazza Navona, Pantheon

HOTEL DEI PORTOGHESI
Via dei Portoghesi, 1
Tel: 06–6864231; fax: 06–6876976
Situated next to the beautiful baroque church of San Antonio dei Portoghesi, this hotel has been furnished with great taste, both in the communal areas and in the bedrooms, most of which are fairly small. It has a very pleasant roof-height terrace and offers a peaceful place to stay in the Piazza Navona and San Luigi dei Francesi neighborhood.

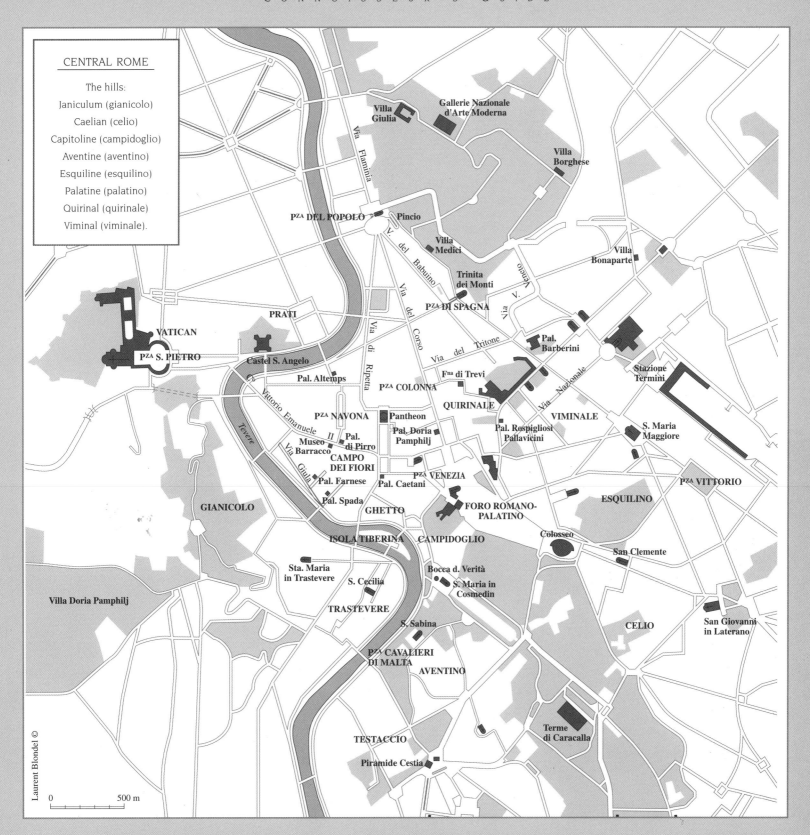

CENTRAL ROME

The hills:
Janiculum (gianicolo)
Caelian (celio)
Capitoline (campidoglio)
Aventine (aventino)
Esquiline (esquilino)
Palatine (palatino)
Quirinal (quirinale)
Viminal (viminale).

Villa Giulia

Gallerie Nazionale d'Arte Moderna

Villa Borghese

P^{ZA} DEL POPOLO   Pincio

V. del Babuino

Villa Medici

Villa Bonaparte

Trinita dei Monti

PRATI

P^{ZA} DI SPAGNA

VATICAN

P^{ZA} S. PIETRO

Via del Corso

Via del Tritone

Pal. Barberini

Castel S. Angelo

F^{na} di Trevi

Stazione Termini

Pal. Altemps

P^{ZA} COLONNA

Via di Ripetta

Via Nazionale

QUIRINALE

P^{ZA} NAVONA   Pantheon

Pal. Doria Pamphilj

VIMINALE

Pal. di Pirro

Pal. Rospigliosi Pallavicini

S. Maria Maggiore

Museo Barracco

Vittorio Emanuele II

CAMPO DEI FIORI

Tevere

Pal. Farnese

P^{ZA} VENEZIA

P^{ZA} VITTORIO

Via Giulia

Pal. Caetani

ESQUILINO

Pal. Spada

GHETTO

FORO ROMANO-PALATINO

GIANICOLO

ISOLA TIBERINA   CAMPIDOGLIO

Colosseo

San Clemente

Sta. Maria in Trastevere

Bocca d. Verità

S. Maria in Cosmedin

S. Cecilia

Villa Doria Pamphilj

TRASTEVERE

S. Sabina

CELIO

San Giovanni in Laterano

P^{ZA} CAVALIERI DI MALTA

AVENTINO

Terme di Caracalla

TESTACCIO

Piramide Cestia

Laurent Blondel ©

0   500 m

203

RAPHAEL
Largo Febo, 2
Tel: 06–682831; fax: 06–6878993
Frequented by politicians whose fates can be unpredictable (as in the recent case of Bettino Craxi), but also by writers such as Jean-Paul Sartre and Eugenio Montale, this is one of the best-situated hotels in the center of Rome: Piazza Navona and Via dei Coronari, a magnet for antique dealers, are close by. It occupies a beautiful building clad in vegetation, and this mixture of ocher and greenery is one of its greatest charms. Some of the rooms are quite small, but the panoramic terrace will leave an indelible memory.

SANTA CHIARA
Via Santa Chiara, 21
Tel: 06–6872979; fax: 06–6873144
Very close to the Pantheon, surrounded by stores selling ecclesiastical clothing or ornaments, this classy hotel offers reasonable prices in the heart of Rome. The rooms are spacious and well furnished. This was where, in 1919, the movement which led to the political mobilization of the Catholics began, leading in 1945 to the birth of Christian Democracy.

SOLE AL PANTHEON
Piazza della Rotonda, 63
Tel: 06–6780441; fax: 06–6878993
Another favorite of Jean-Paul Sartre, one of the historic figures after whom the rooms have been named, this is a very old establishment, dating back nearly five centuries. The sun symbol appears in the different elements of the decor, such as the floor and the door handles. It has been modernized in a refined style, but its main asset is that it looks onto the Pantheon.

Campo de' Fiori

CAMPO DE' FIORI
Via del Biscione, 6
Tel: 06–68806865; fax: 06–6876003
This simple little hotel, which has less

than thirty rooms, has been very successfully renovated. In addition, it has two charming terraces which offer a beautiful view of the Campo de' Fiori and its market. An excellent address offering reasonably priced accommodation in the heart of historic Rome.

SOLE
Via del Biscione, 76
Tel: 06–68806873; fax: 06–6893787
Not to be confused with the hotel of the same name near the Pantheon, this is a pleasantly simple establishment with something of a family atmosphere. It has a terrace on the top floor.

TEATRO DI POMPEO
Largo del Pallaro, 8
Tel: 06–6872812; fax: 06–68805531
Close to the Sole, on a site occupied by the first stone theater of ancient Rome, this hotel is distinguished by the elegant simplicity of the decor and furniture, as well as the welcoming atmosphere. It only has twelve rooms and is thus in high demand. The Costanza restaurant, with its ancient vaults, is next door.

Esquiline Hill, Termini

CANADA
Via Vicenza, 58
Tel: 06–445770; fax: 06–4450749
A good example of the relatively basic but well-run hotels found in the neighborhood around the station.

MASSIMO D'AZEGLIO
Via Cavour, 18
Tel: 06–4880646; fax: 06–4827386
In the heart of the district built immediately after unification, situated on one of the main roads which is emblematic of the moment when Rome became capital, this hotel will please all those who enjoy the *fin de siècle* atmosphere created by the meticulously maintained decor and furniture. It conserves the charm of

nineteenth-century Italy, a state proud of its history and yet very young. The Termini station is nearby.

MECENATE PALACE HOTEL
Via Carlo Alberto, 3
Tel: 06–44702024; fax: 06–4461354
Situated very near the basilica of Santa Maria Maggiore, one of the oldest in the city and famous for its admirable mosaics, this hotel has just been refurbished from top to bottom. The prices inevitably reflect this, but a lot of the rooms look onto the church and it is possible to have breakfast at the Terrazza dei Papi.

VENEZIA
Via Varese, 18
Tel: 06–4457101; fax: 06–4957687
Excellent address near the station, with very reasonable prices. Special mention should be made of the decor, which features beautiful old church furniture.

Forum, Colosseum

FORUM
Via Tor dei Conti, 25
Tel: 06–6792446; fax: 06–6786479
Situated in an old Renaissance convent, and constructed partly out of ancient building materials, this is the most charming of the hotels near the great archaeological remains. It is in a picturesque street with high fortified towers which has hardly changed since the Middle Ages. Its terrace is one of the most attractive in Rome.

Aventine Hill

SANT'ANSELMO
Piazza Sant'Anselmo, 2
Tel: 06–5750845; fax: 06–5783604
This little hotel belongs to the same group as the Villa San Pio and the Aventino. It is the pleasantest of the three, and if you have to choose between the other two, go for the San Pio. The Sant'Anselmo enables you to sample the charms of the Aventino,

one of the greenest and quietest hills in Rome. Simple but pleasant with old-style decor, it has its own private garden and, for some of the rooms, beautiful views.

Caelian Hill

CELIO
Via dei SS. Quattro, 35c
Tel: 06–704953333; fax: 06–7096377
Each of this hotel's few rooms is named after an artist. Intimate and elegant, it offers the opportunity of staying on one of the hills where the charm of old Rome has been best preserved. In particular, do not miss the fortified monastery of the Four Crowned Saints, which gave its name to the street: occupied by nuns, it has one of the most moving cloisters in the city. Its location, near the Colosseum and the astonishing ensemble formed by the super imposed levels of San Clemente, is relatively central. San Giovanni in Laterano lies at the opposite end of the street.

Vatican, Prati District

COLUMBUS
Via delle Conciliazione, 33
Tel: 06–6865435; fax: 06–6865435
Very near Saint Peter's Square, this is one of the most beautiful hotels in the city. Occupying what used to be the Palace of the Penitentiaries, it has a marvelous enclosed garden and the former refectory still has its sixteenth-century frescoes. They were painted by the Florentine artist Francesco Salviati, who also decorated the interior of the Palazzo Farnese. At dinner time one often meets important ecclesiastical figures.

GIULIO CESARE
Via degli Scipioni, 287
Tel: 06–3210751; fax: 06–3211736
This elegant hotel occupies a beautiful late-nineteenth-century building in the residential area of Prati, which was

built following the unification of Italy. The furniture and the decor respect the spirit of the place. In fine weather, it is possible to use the private garden.

Suburbs

VILLA DEL PARCO

Via Nomentana, 110
Tel: 06–44237773; fax: 06–44237572
If being quite far from the center is not a problem, this hotel is worth considering. It is located on a main road in the heart of a residential neighborhood which dates from the beginning of the twentieth century and contains some interesting relics from the past, including the Villa Torlonia. The house, with its beautiful ocher-pink rendering and the plane trees in the garden, is not without charm.

CONVENTS

There are numerous convents in the city and on the outskirts, many of which provide accommodation, chiefly for pilgrims. For the jubilee year 2000 they have carried out extensive building work to modernize their capacity and bring it up to standard. However, it would be inappropriate to consider them as hotels or boarding houses. Many close their doors long before midnight in the interests of peace and quiet. It is possible to get information from the pastoral reception center near San Luigi dei Francesi, Via Santa Giovanna d'arca, 12 (tel: 06–68803815, fax: 06–6832324). Of the convents located in the historical center, the Bridgetine sisters have their headquarters at the Piazza Farnese. The religious of the Sacred Heart are lucky enough to occupy the convent of the Trinità dei Monti, founded by the king of France Charles VIII, who established the Minims there. Driven out by the Revolution, the monks were replaced at the beginning of

STROLLING AROUND THE HILLS

Three of the seven original hills have retained a particular poetry, as if they had somehow escaped time, and are still covered in greenery. The Palatine, which has become an archaeological zone, is visited with the Forum. The Aventine and Caelian Hills, which are part of the modern city, are also well worth wandering around.

Aventine Hill

The Aventine, where the plebeians retired to in their struggle with the Roman aristocracy, lies a little outside the center. A place of contemplation, it has the beauty of a cloister, but a cloister with a view of the city. It should be visited on foot, taking Clivo di Rocca Savelli which starts at the Lungotevere Aventino. This street, which has no cars, is like a trip back into the nineteenth century. It leads to the Parco Savello, which is planted with orange trees. From here, the view of the city is perhaps even more beautiful than the view from the Pincio or the Janiculum. Next to the garden rises the basilica of Santa Sabina, a dazzling example of early Christian art, with its carved wooden doors—the oldest in Rome—and its cloister with its captivating atmosphere.

Continuing along the Via di Santa Sabina, you reach the church of Sant'Alessio, an old church which has been extensively renovated, and then, a bit further on, the mysterious Piazza dei Cavalieri di Malta, a masterpiece by Piranesi, one of the greatest engravers in history. Do like everybody else and look at the view of the cupola of St. Peter's through the keyhole of the gate of the Priorato di Malta. The dome appears strikingly white in the center of the perspective formed by one of the garden's trellises. This unreal vision concludes the walk on the Aventine.

Caelian Hill

A complete itinerary to explore the Caelian Hill begins at the Piazza San Giovanni in Laterano which, taking Via dei Quattro Santi Coronatti, leads to the beautiful fortified church of the same name. Ask the nuns for the key to the San Silvestro chapel and for permission to take a look at the very attractive thirteenth-century cloister. Below, in Via di San Giovanni in Laterano, the church of San Clemente is a major monument which consists of three superimposed levels: a shrine to Mithra, a fourteenth-century church, and another from the twelfth century, the apse of which is still decorated with the most beautiful mosaic in Rome.

Via Celimontana, a turning on the left, takes you straight to the fountain of the Navicella in the square of the same name. It is possible to begin the walk here for a shorter but more evocative circuit. Begin with the church of Santa Maria in Dominica, right in front of the fountain. The interior is heavy with the atmosphere of Carolingian basilicas. The mosaic, which dates from around 820, is one of the most beautiful creations of the epoch. Pope Paschal I is represented in it, not with the saints' halo, but with a square nimbus.

On the right, as you come out of the church, can be seen the Villa Celimontana. Take the time to wander around the magnificent park, which is little known to tourists. At most times it is possible to leave it at the Piazza dei Santi Giovanni e Paolo at the top of the hill. If this entrance is closed, return to the Piazza della Navicella and take the very evocative Clivo di Scauro, which will lead you to the same place.

This peaceful square has remains of the temple of Emperor Claudius and leads to a church where centuries overlap. The interior, refurbished in the eighteenth century, is built on a fourteenth-century house, transformed into a Christian place of worship by its owner and decorated with interesting paintings. Continue up the Clivo di Scauro until you reach the square of the church of San Gregorio Magno, but make sure you turn to admire the beautiful apse with small columns of the basilica of Santi Giovanni e Paolo.

The church of San Gregorio, renovated in the baroque period, is interesting chiefly for the three chapels in the adjoining garden. The one on the right has a famous fresco by Guido Reni, the *Concert of Angels*. The one on the left houses an ancient marble table which has an admirable sheen: it is said that an angel came and sat here while St. Gregor was giving some poor people a meal. This place is one of the most poetic places in Rome and offers a precious moment of serenity before heading back into the urban maelstrom.

the nineteenth century by the current congregation, whose mission is to teach. The buildings are more or less intact and contain important works of art. The church adjoins one of the prettiest cloisters in Rome, where all the kings of France from the Merovingians on can be seen, with the exception of Louis-Philippe, of course, who was regarded as a usurper.

RESTAURANTS

Rome's restaurants are often more affordable than the city's hotels, which are not among the cheapest in Europe. This is partly because only those with particularly large appetites will be able to cope with a complete meal, which normally includes one or two antipasti, a plate of pasta or a risotto, a meat or fish dish, and a dessert. The portions are nearly always large.

There exist a few luxurious restaurants, notably in large hotels, but the Romans do not attach a lot of importance to sophisticated settings. That is why there is less of a difference between the city's various establishments than there is in, say, France. You have as much chance of getting a good meal in a trattoria or a neighborhood restaurant as you have in a supposedly elegant establishment.

Innovation is unusual: a city of tradition, Rome remains faithful to its down-to-earth traditions, although fish and seafood from the nearby sea are also prominent. However, the large numbers of visitors poses a threat to authenticity. Generally, Rome is much less open than other European capitals to foreign cuisine, despite the appearance of a few Asian restaurants and a McDonald's in Piazza di Spagna. On the other hand, the regional traditions of the rest of Italy are more in evidence.

Ludovisi, Vittorio Veneto

LA TERRAZZA DELL'EDEN
Via Ludovisi, 49
Tel: 06–47812552
With its panoramic view, the restaurant

of the Hotel Eden is one of the swankiest in the city. It offers very refined cooking, Mediterranean in inspiration, which is original and creative. The chef has a predilection for fish and seafood. Also worth trying is the Sunday morning brunch.

LA VERANDA DELL'HOTEL MAJESTIC
Via Veneto, 50
Tel: 06–486841
This is the restaurant of a prestigious hotel founded at the same time as the Eden. It was renamed Maestoso ("majestic") under Mussolini, who was opposed to names which sounded foreign. The Veranda is notable for its dishes based on age-old traditional recipes, an approach which helped win it an award in 1996.

Villa Borghese

DELLE ARTI
Via Gramsci, 73
Tel: 06–32651236
The cafeteria of the Galeria Nazionale d'Arte Moderne, where it is possible to have lunch or dinner outside, is one of the pleasantest places to relax during a walk in the gardens of the Villa Borghese.

Piazza di Spagna

AL 34
Via Mario dei Fiori, 34
Tel: 06–6795091
This restaurant offers traditional cooking, including some good preparations of fish and seafood, such as tagliatelle al nero con gamberetti for those who do not have an aversion to cuttlefish ink. Via Mario dei Fiori is a peaceful little street, making it possible to dine outside in the summer.

DA MARIO
Via della Vite, 55
Tel: 06–6783818
Situated in a fairly quiet street, this family restaurant specializes

in Tuscan cuisine, particularly braised beef (brasato di manzo) and game, accompanied by a large choice of excellent wines from the same region.

OSTERIA I NUMERI
Via Belsiana, 30
Tel: 06–6794969
This restaurant/steak house specializes in red meat dishes, but remains true to the Italian tradition.

OTELLO ALLA CONCORDIA
Via della Croce, 81
Tel: 06–6781454
Founded in 1860, much frequented by people from nearby Via Condotti, this restaurant has a charming courtyard garden and offers local cuisine, particularly spaghetti alla Otello.

SETTIMIO ALL'ARANCIO
Via dell'Arancio, 50
Tel: 06–6876119
Situated in a quiet street where it is possible to dine outside, this restaurant offers the delicious and copious rib of beef alla fiorentina, brought to your table on its broiler made of lava stone and accompagned by various vegetables.

Piazza del Popolo

DAL BOLOGNESE
Piazza del Popolo, 1–2
Tel: 06–3611426
This elegant establishment frequented by politicians and business people offers the great culinary tradition of the rich province of Bologna.

Fontana di Trevi

AL MORO
Vicolo delle Bollette, 13
Tel: 06–69940736
True to the tradition of old trattorie, this restaurant is one of the best representatives of local cuisine. Try for example the macaroni alla pajata or the cod, baccalà al Moro.

COLLI EMILIANE
Via degli Avignonesi, 22
Tel: 06–4817538
In a simpler, more informal setting than the Al Moro, this restaurant also offers specialties from Emiliane, which you can sample before making a wish at the nearby Fontana di Trevi. In the autumn, the spaghetti with white truffles is memorable.

Piazza Venezia

ABRUZZI
Via del Vaccaro
Tel: 06–6793897
This trattoria is located very close to the noisy Piazza Venezia in a small street leading to the Piazza Santi Apostoli, which is dominated by the imposing Palazzo Odescalchi. It offers a welcome place to stop, where one can enjoy a plate of spaghetti alle vongole for lunch.

Piazza Navona, Pantheon

FORTUNATO
Via del Pantheon, 65
Tel: 06–6798147
A fashionable restaurant popular with people from business and politics.

HOSTARIA PICCOLA ROMA
Via Uffici del Vicario, 36
Tel: 06–6798606
This restaurant, next door to the ice-cream maker Giolitti, is a congenial place offering true Roman cuisine, particularly the excellent roast sucking lamb (abbacchio). A bell enables you to show your satisfaction as you go out.

IL CARTOCCIO D'ABRUZZO
Via di Tor Sanguigna, 4
Tel: 06–68802427
In the summer, this restaurant offers a delightfully shady terrace on the Largo Febo, opposite the Hotel Raphael.

IL CONVIVIO
Via dell'Orso, 44
Tel: 06–6869432
This pleasantly decorated restaurant

offers interesting variations on classic Roman dishes.

LA ROSETTA
Via della Rosetta, 8–9
Tel: 06–6861002
This elegant restaurant near the Pantheon dates back to 1760 and offers innovative cooking, such as spaghetti with zucchini blossoms, shrimps, and Pecorino Romano cheese.

L'EAU VIVE
Via Nonterone, 85a
Tel: 06–68801095 or 06–68802101
Located at the foot of the Palazzo Lante, this restaurant is on two floors corresponding to two price levels. Served by nuns and frequented mostly by French people and clerics, it serves cooking with a French slant in an atmosphere of prayer which would be inconceivable outside Rome. In this respect, it is a unique place.

LE CAVE DI SANT'IGNAZIO DA SABATINO
Piazza Sant'Ignazio, 169
Tel: 06–6791012
This restaurant has an ideal location, in front of the church of Sant'Ignazio, in one of the most intimate baroque squares in Rome.

PAPÀ GIOVANNI
Via dei Sediari, 5
Tel: 06–6865308 or 06–68804807
This address, in a quiet street near Piazza Navona, can be recommended for its inventive cooking, which is quite rare in Rome, where the gastronomic world tends to be conservative. In the style of nouvelle cuisine, it tries to lighten traditional recipes while retaining their flavor, notably specialties with truffles. It is renowned for its wine cellar.

QUINZI E GABRIELI
Via delle Coppelle, 6
Tel: 06–6879389
Well situated between Piazza Navona and the Pantheon, this restaurant is famous for the quality of its fish specialties and its setting. The display of freshly fished produce in the entrance hall is impressive.

SANT'EUSTACHIO
Piazza dei Caprettari, 63
Tel: 06–6861616
On summer evenings, the restaurant sets out its tables on this charming square adjoining Piazza Sant'Eustachio, opposite the large Palazzo Lante. It has all the charm of the Pantheon neighborhood without the crowds.

TAVERNA DI GIOVANNI
Via di Banco di S. Spirito, 58
Tel: 06–864116
Pleasantly located near the Ponte Sant'Angelo, this place offers good classic specialties, such as *bucatini all'amatriciana*.

Campo de' Fiori, Ghetto

COSTANZA
Piazza del Paradiso, 63–65
Tel: 06–6861717 or 06–68801002
Travel back through the centuries by having a meal under the vaults of the ancient theater of Pompey. The manager greets regulars at the entrance by cutting a fine slice of ham. The cooking is rich and tasty.

DA PANCRAZIO
Piazza del Biscione, 92–94
Tel: 06–6861246
Also located in the remains of Pompey's theater and offering the same kind of cooking, this restaurant opens onto a picturesque square which joins the famous Campo de' Fiori. A small, dark and neglected passage can be seen near the entrance to the restaurant: a lamp burns there continuously at the foot of an effigy of the Madonna.

DEL PALLARO
Largo del Pallaro, 15
Tel: 06–8801488
The archetypal Roman *trattoria* where the whole family comes—providing it has been admitted by the manageress. The different dishes which make up the complete meal appear one after the other on your table, from the cocktail snacks which come before the pasta and the risotto to the desserts, via the meat dish. It would be unseemly to turn anything down or to want to make one's own selection.

HOSTARIA DEL CAMPIDOGLIO
Via dei Fienili, 56
Tel: 06–6780250
Opposite the famous Tarpeian Rock where traitors were thrown to their death in antiquity, this restaurant is a good introduction to the cuisine of the southern province of Basilicata, where all the Mediterranean civilizations met. The lamb dishes are excellent.

IL DRAPPO
Vicolo del Malpasso, 9
Tel: 06–6877365
A pleasant place which provides an opportunity to discover the originality of Sardinian cuisine.

LA CARBONARA
Piazza Campo dei Fiori, 23
Tel: 06–6864783
The writer and film director Pier Paolo Pasolini liked to come to this place which, in summer, sets out its tables in the Campo de' Fiori. It offers the traditional rich and copious cuisine of Rome and Latium, in particular the *pajata di vitella alla cacciatora*, which must be sampled during a stay in Rome.

PIERLUIGI
Piazza dei Ricci, 144
Tel: 06–6868717
This restaurant in a small square near the Via Giulia offers, among other things, excellent fish in salt crust.

PIPERNO
Via Monte de' Cenci, 9
Tel: 06–68806629 or 06–6861113
This restaurant's deserved reputation is founded on a century of tradition. It specializes in traditional Roman cooking and its Jewish variants, the heritage of a community which has survived the vicissitudes of history for two hundred years. Its wine list is one of the most renowned in the city.

SORA LELLA
Via Ponte Quattro Capi, 16
Tel: 06–6861601
Another establishment known for its Judo-Roman specialties, it offers in addition a very beautiful view of Isola Tiberina.

VECCHIA ROMA
Piazza Campitelli, 18
Tel: 06–6864604
This place looks onto one of the prettiest squares in the historic center, at the foot of the Capitolino. Its open-air terrace and eighteenth-century decor make it a place worth visiting in any season to enjoy the varied classic Roman cuisine.

Testaccio

CECCHINO DAL 1887
Via Monte Testaccio, 30
Tel: 06–5743816
This restaurant in the heart of a neighborhood undergoing redevelopment continues to serve traditional Roman cuisine of the purest kind, beginning with tripe specialties, such as *pajata*, or oxtail (*coda alla vaccinara*). The manageress and her sons are characters. The wine cellar, dug out of the ground of this hill formed by the accumulation of pieces of pottery and broken amphorae, is quite astonishing.

MESSICO E NUVOLE
Via dei Magazzini Generali, 8
Tel: 06–5741413
This Mexican restaurant offers a short journey through the cuisines of the world. The atmosphere is quieter than is usual for this type of establishment.

For those who want to enjoy the Estate Romana (a summer festival several events of which take place in the neighborhood) it is possible to have a drink here after midnight.

PERILLI
Via Marmorata, 53
Tel: 06–5742415
Another upholder of authentic Roman cuisine, although in a more popular vein than Cecchino and with little concern for elegance. Do not be put off by the noise. The portions are generous.

Trastevere

ALBERTO CIARLA
Piazza san Cosimato, 40
Tel: 06–5818668 or 5816068
This elegant restaurant in Trastevere is known for its excellent fish dishes. If you are looking for a typical dish, taste the cod à la nage, *baccalà in guazzetto alla romana*.

CHECCO ER CARRETTIERE
Via Benedetta, 10
Tel: 06–5817018
Located next to the Piazza Trilussa, named after the poet from the first half of the twentieth century who wrote in the Roman dialect, this is a good representative of local cuisine, with a strong emphasis on fish and seafood.

DA MEO PATACCA
Piazza de' Mercanti, 30
Tel: 06–5816198 or 06–5882193
For those who want to sample an atmosphere worthy of Montmartre, this very touristy restaurant near the church of Santa Cecilia in the heart of Trastevere proposes musical entertainment which should be taken with a pinch of salt.

ER COMPARONE
Piazza in Piscinula, 47
Tel: 06–5816249
This excellent family restaurant,

founded in 1900 and located in one of the most delightful squares of Trastevere with its little Roman bell tower, offers tasty cooking in the form of specifically Roman dishes, such as *bucatini all'amatriciana*.

GALEASSI
Piazza Santa Maria in Trastevere, 3a
Tel: 06–5809898
This restaurant is the oldest one in the Piazza Santa Maria in Trastevere, the heart of this fashionable neighborhood.

LA CORNUCOPIA
Piazza in Piscinula, 18
Tel: 06–5800380
In the same square as Er Comparone, this rather elegant restaurant has a very pleasant terrace in the summer.

PARIS
Piazza San Callisto, 7
Tel: 06–5815378
This restaurant, founded in the nineteenth century, is a good representative of traditional cuisine in a part of Trastevere where the large number of tourists often leads to compromises. The *carciofi alla giudia* are remarkable, but it also offers all the specialties of local cuisine, such as tripe and *coda alla vaccinara*.

ROMA SPARITA
Piazza Santa Cecilia, 24
Tel: 06–5800757
Adorned with engravings of old Rome, this restaurant offers pizzas and traditional dishes in a charming square which, during the day, is rarely overrun with tourists.

Esquiline Hill

AGATA E ROMEO
Via Carlo Alberto, 45
Tel: 06–4465842
An elegant restaurant not far from Santa Maria Maggiore and the Opera. The cuisine is creative, with delicious specialties such as fish carpaccio

with tomato jelly, which is most welcome on hot summer days.

CROSTACERIA IPANEMA
Via dei Capocci, 26
Tel: 06–4824758
This pleasant restaurant is unusual in that it only serves dishes with shellfish or seafood, notably an excellent Catalan-style shellfish salad.

PULCINELLA
Via Urbana, 11
Tel: 06–4743310
A pleasant address to discover some of the infinite resources of Neapolitan gastronomy, from fish or seafood dishes to famous pastries.

San Lorenzo

DA FRANCO AR VICOLETTO
Via dei Falisci, 1b
Tel: 06–4957675
The San Lorenzo neighborhood, still working class and unaffected by tourism, is an area whose regeneration is attracting Romans, and in particular students because of the proximity of the university. It takes its name from the basilica of San Lorenzo Fuori le Mura, consisting of two churches joined together, one of which dates back to the time of Constantine. The restaurant specializes in fish and seafood. In summer, the tables are set out in the street, and sometimes the manager demonstrates his considerable vocal talents. An address worth visiting for its food and atmosphere.

POMMIDORO
Piazza dei Sanniti, 44
Tel: 06–4452692
This restaurant, where Pier Paolo Pasolini used to come, offers authentic Roman cuisine. It bears the surname of its owner, the winner a few years ago of the Premio Simpatia, the guarantee of a welcome that is always warm.

PIZZERIAS

Although it originally came from Naples, the pizza has adapted well to Latium. In addition to the pizza rossa (with a tomato base), try the pizza bianca, a kind of flat loaf which can be eaten on its own or supplemented as you wish.

The flood of tourists has considerably increased the demand for pizzas and production has risen, but sometimes to the detriment of quality, particularly in the numerous tavole calde, snack bars where you can dine quickly and cheaply. Here are a few addresses to which this criticism does not apply.

Piazza Navona

DA BAFFETTO
Via del Governo Vecchio, 11
Tel: 06–6861617
For some pizza enthusiasts, this is the best pizzeria in the city. It is located in a charming neighborhood, not far from the Piazza Navona, in one of the most evocative streets of Renaissance Rome.

Campo de' Fiori

ANTICO FORNO CORDELLA
Piazza Costaguti, 31
Tel: 06–68803012
In the heart of the Ghetto, this oven has belonged to the same family for more than half a century and does not compromise on quality.

IL FORNO DI CAMPO DE' FIORI DI BARTOCCI E ROSCIOLI
Piazza Campo de' Fiori, 22-22a
Tel: 06–6880662
This old oven, situated in a corner of the square, is very popular with Romans, who flock to it at all times of the day.

Piazza del Popolo

PIZZARÉ
Via di Ripetta, 14
Tel: 06–3211468

This pleasant new establishment, opened by Neapolitans, has quickly carved out a solid reputation for being true to the authentic flavors of their home town.

Trastevere

FRONTONI
Viale Trastevere, 52
Tel: 06–5812436
You will find here a seemingly infinite number of suggestions to accompany your *pizza bianca*, together with all the tasty hors d'œuvres that Roman cuisine can offer, such as zucchini blossoms and croquettes, accompanied by a wide selection of beers.

PIZZA TRILUSSA
Piazza Trilussa, 42
Tel: 06–5883096
Located in one of the squares near the river, this old establishment offers a vast selection of pizzas, including one with boletus mushrooms, as well as traditional dishes.

TABERNA PISCINULA
Piazza in Piscinula, 50
Tel: 06–5812525
Each one of the six rooms is named after a historical figure.

CAFÉS, TEAROOMS AND ICE-CREAM PARLORS

Inseparable from the Roman lifestyle, with its mixture of indolence and insouciance that is not found in the north of Italy, cafés and ice-cream parlors can offer both a restful moment of tranquility or an animated conversation.

It should be noted that the legendary cafés of the Via Vittorio Veneto, in particular the Doney at No. 145 where Fellini shot one of the scenes from La Dolce Vita, have changed in character. It is well worth indulging in the pleasure of discovery, which is part of the charm of Rome, as are the bonds which form between regulars and the waiters and waitresses.

From the morning cappuccino, with its foam and sprinkling of chocolate, to the ice cream enjoyed on a hot afternoon and the after-show drink, the stops are endless, yet never monotonous. The very strong espresso, which you can down in one go, has never prevented true coffee-lovers from sleeping.

Some establishments have several functions—café, tearoom, restaurant, bar—according to the time of day or night.

Piazza di Spagna

CAFFÈ GRECO
Via Condotti, 86
Tel: 06–6782554
This historic café, founded more than two centuries ago and frequented by numerous artists and writers from many different countries, steadfastly upholds the tradition, although the clientele has largely changed. The rooms, with their old decor, evoke this illustrious past and retain their charm. Having breakfast here in the tourist off-season is a wonderful experience.

CIAMPINI
Viale Trinità dei Monti
Tel: 06–6785678
This café was founded by the same family as the Tre Scalina in the Piazza Navona and serves the famous *tartufo*, ice cream and dark chocolate with or without cream. Situated in the open air on the banks of the Pincio, at the foot of the Villa Medici (and therefore shut in the winter), it also offers lunch and dinner. In season, try the risotto with boletus mushrooms, *funghi porcini*.

Piazza del Popolo

CANOVA
Piazza del Popolo, 16
Tel: 06–2612231
This was where Fellini invariably liked to have his breakfast, for the café is situated on the side of the Piazza del Popolo which is shady in the morning. There is also a piano bar.

GUSTO
Piazza Augusto Imperatore, 9 and Via della Frezza, 23
Tel: 06–3226273
This café opposite the Mausoleum of Augustus has an uncompromisingly modern decor. It is also a wine bar, tearoom, bookstore and "cigar club," and there is live music in the evening.

ROSATI
Piazza del Popolo, 4
Tel: 06–3225859
One of the most refined tearooms in Rome, where you often bump into celebrities who are not trying to remain incognito. Many artists used to meet here during the 1960s. There is a beautiful sunny terrace in the morning.

SOGO
Via di Ripetta, 242
Tel: 06–3612272
This café-restaurant, known for its Japanese specialties, also offers delicious croissants at breakfast time—something which is not that common in Rome.

Piazza Navona, Pantheon

ANTICO CAFFÈ DELLA PACE
Via della Pace, 3–5
Tel: 06–6861216
An unforgettable place opposite the beautiful church of Santa Maria della Pace, very near the Piazza Navona. Popular with artists and intellectuals, the café is filled in the evening with lively conversation. The rooms have a timeless charm, and in summer, when the tables spill out onto the little square, it is impossible to resist stopping here.

BAR DEL FICO
Piazza del Fico, 26–28
Tel: 06–6865205
This bar, which has a youthful atmosphere, is in a pretty little square near the Santa Maria della Pace. It stays open very late and, because Rome is not Madrid, thus attracts nighthawks. It also organizes exhibitions, notably of photos.

CAMILLONI A SANT'EUSTACHIO
Piazza Sant'Eustachio, 54
Tel: 06–6864995
This café, the nearest to the church of Sant'Eustachio, serves excellent pastries. If you sit outside, you have a pretty view of Borromini's quirky campanile for the church of Sant'Ivo.

DELLE PALME
Via della Maddalena, 20–23
Tel: 06–68806752
The decor may be of dubious quality, but no other ice-cream parlor offers such a rich selection. And children will be fascinated by the giant lollipops in the form of palms.

IL DOMIZIANO E CAFFÈ DI COLOMBIA
Piazza Navona, 88
Tel: 06–6879647
Located on the side of the square that catches the sun in the afternoon, this place offers a beautiful view of the church of Sant'Agnese and the Fontana dei Fiumi. In the past one might have bumped into Moravia, who lived nearby.

SANT'EUSTACHIO
Piazza Sant'Eustachio, 82
Tel: 06–6861309
The Sant'Eustachio is situated in one of the most charming squares near the Pantheon. Its espresso is one of the most highly regarded in the city and the interior is decorated with a collection of coffee grinders from different epochs.

TAZZA D'ORO
Via degli Orfani, 84
Tel: 06–6789792
Here you can buy the coffee of your choice freshly roasted and ground. The delicious aromas waft out into the little street which leads to the Pantheon. It is virtually impossible to pass by without stopping.

TRE SCALINI
Piazza Navona, 28
Tel: 06–6880199
Although its fame can result in a rather offhand manner with tourists, nothing beats sitting on the terrace here for a drink of chocolate, either hot or as a *tartufo*. The experience is particularly pleasant in the morning, when the Piazza Navona is at its best.

Piazza Colonna

GIOLITTI
Via Uffici del Vicario, 40
Tel: 06–6991243
Located near the Parliament, this is the best-known and most popular café and ice-cream parlor in Rome. It has a Louis XV decor and offers a wide range of ice creams in diverse flavors.

LA CAFFETTERIA
Piazza di Pietra, 65
Tel: 06–6798147
This place is housed in an ancient Roman temple in the Borsa neighborhood. It offers remarkable Neapolitan pastries which give some idea of the refinement of this culinary tradition. Particularly worth trying are the *sfogliatelle*, with their flaky pastry.

Esquiline Hill

PALAZZO DEL FREDO
Via Principe Eugenio, 67
Tel: 06–64464740
A delight for lovers of hand-made ice creams of various flavors.

WINE BARS

*M*any wine bars grew out of wine merchants who used to offer wine for tasting at the counter accompanied by snacks (mescita). A number of them now offer hot and warm buffets and are becoming more like local *trattorie, providing fast food in the best sense of the term.*
It was in Rome in the second half of the 1970s that the fashion for wine bars in

Italy started. Many have succeeded in retaining or re-creating the atmosphere of traditional wine merchants.

L'ANGOLO DIVINO
Via dei Balestrari, 12
Tel: 06–6864413
This is a very old family establishment near the Campo de' Fiori. Its name is a Roman play on words (the divine or wine corner).

BEVITORIA NAVONA
Piazza Navona, 72
Tel: 06–68801022
A genuine wine bar, which is ideally situated. Wine is served with canapés of toast or cold meats. If there are not too many customers, ask if you can have a quick look at the remains of the Stadium of Domitian preserved in the cellar.

CUL DE SAC
Piazza Pasquino, 73
Tel: 06–68801094
Situated near the Piazza Navona, close to the old statue known as Pasquino, which, under the popes, used to be covered at night with satirical comments, this long narrow establishment is lined with bottles. Its main attractions are its old interior and the choice of wines. It is possible to have hot or cold meals.

ENOTECA BUCCONE
Via di Ripetta, 19
Tel: 06–3612154
This historic store in an eighteenth-century building near the Piazza del Popolo was founded before 1900. The interesting decor is typical of a traditional wine merchant, and it offers a good selection of quality products, with the possibility of wine tasting.

IL GOCCETTO
Via dei Banchi Vecchi, 14
Tel: 06–6864268
This place near the Campo de' Fiori is a favorite with wine-lovers, who enjoy chatting with the knowledgeable owner.

LA BOTTEGA DEL VINO
Via Santa Maria del Pianto, 9a, 11, 12
Tel: 06–6865970
This place in the Campo de' Fiori neighborhood also offers a cold buffet, featuring a large range of antipasti with vegetables, cold meats and seafood. When you come out, remember to take a look at the butcher shop opposite, housed in the ground floor of a very old palace.

PASTRY SHOPS

*R*ome does not have the same reputation for producing pastries and similar delights as Naples, but there are some good addresses all the same, several of which offer foreign specialties. The dividing line between such places and some ice-cream parlors is sometimes narrow.

BELLA NAPOLI
Corso Vittorio Emmanuele II, 246
Tel: 06–6877048
The best-known Neapolitan pastry shop in the historic center. This is the place Federico Forquet prefers for *sfogliatelle.*

CECERE
Via Musolino, 53
Tel: 06–5895014
This is doubtless the best-known pastry shop in Trastevere, renowned for its delicious *torta alla ricotta.*

CINQUE LUNE
Corso Rinascimento, 89
Tel: 06–68801005
This pastry shop near the Piazza Navona is one of the best in the city.

DAGNINO
Via V.E. Orlando, 75
Tel: 06–4818660
Recommended for its Neapolitan specialties, particularly the *cassate.*

FORNO DEL GHETTO
Via del Portico d'Ottavia, 2
Tel: 06–6878637

This address in the heart of the Ghetto provides an opportunity to try some Roman Jewish pastry specialties, notably donuts.

IL CIGNO
Viale Parioli, 20
Tel: 06–8082348
This pastry shop serves the more exclusive neighborhoods. It sells, among other things, a fine and varied selection of tarts, as well as candy.

LA DOLCE ROMA
Via del Portico d'Ottavia, 20
Tel: 06–6892196
Despite the name, there is nothing Roman about the delicacies on offer here. This place is a must for its Austrian specialties, including the famous *Sachertorte* which Nanni Moretti is so fond of, and American pastries.

RUSCHENA
Lungotevere Mellini, 1
Tel: 06–3204652
This charming address is located on the banks of the Tiber, not far from the imposing Palazzo di Giustizia. You will hesitate for a long time between a delicious Montblanc and a particularly tasty patriotic cake with pistachio (green), meringue (white), and raspberry ice cream (red).

FOR FOOD LOVERS

*G*ood Roman grocery stores sell a range of products—including the famous, expensive, and delectable white truffle—and always have a pleasant, welcoming atmosphere. As with restaurants, the sophistication of the interior is not an indication of quality. Some stores, such as Achilli, could be classified as wine bars.

ACHILLI AL PARLAMENTO
Via dei Prefetti, 15
Tel: 06–6873446
Well known for the diversity and quality of its wines, this establishment offers wine tastings accompanied by a

slice of bread with *bruschetta*, or small sandwiches called *tramezzini*.

AI MONASTERI
Corso Rinascimento, 72
Tel: 06–688027837
This unusual address sells nothing but products made by hand in monasteries, such as honey, liqueurs and candy.

ANTICA NORCINERIA VIOLA B. E FRATELLO
Piazza Campo de' Fiori, 43
Tel: 06–68806114
The delicate cold meats here are delicious, and connoisseurs eat them with their *pizza bianca* bought at the pizzeria at No. 22 (see page 208).

CASTRONI
Via Cola di Rienzo, 196
Tel: 06–6874383
Belonging to a chain which has several stores in Rome, this is one of the grocery stores with the biggest selection of local and international specialties.

FRANCHI
Via Cola di Rienzi, 200
Tel: 06–6864576
This store, not far from Castroni (see above) and equally popular, is notable for its selection of cold meats and cheeses of every kind.

PALOMBI
Via Vittorio Veneto, 114
Tel: 06–4885817
With its old oven, this establishment offers a vast range of breads, pizzas and pastries (there are said to be three hundred kinds of bread in Rome). Needless to say, there are many kinds of fresh pasta, with their different flavors.

PASTA ALL'UOVO
Via della Croce, 8
Tel: 06–6793102
When it comes to pasta, the imagination has no limits with regard

to shape, taste and color. The ones sold here are fresh, or course, and should be eaten within a few days for maximum flavor.

VOLPETTI
Via della Scrofa, 31
Tel: 06–5742352
This store, which in the autumn is filled with the aroma of truffles, has a remarkable choice of cold meats of all kinds.

VOLPETTI FORMAGGIOMANIA
Via Marmorata, 47
Tel: 06–5746986
Situated in the Testaccio district, this grocery store for gourmets specializes in Italian cheeses (190 in all), but doesn't neglect the different types of bread or cold meat. The merits of this old establishment are vaunted in little poems written in the Roman dialect.

MARKETS

R ome has a large number of small street markets with a few stalls selling *fruit and vegetables, as well as fish, cheese and salt meat. But there are also some very large ones which attract big crowds and which reflect Rome in all its diversity.*

Campo de' Fiori: *one of the most picturesque in the old center; florists predominate, but not to the exclusion of food and clothing.*

Piazza Vittorio Emmanuele, *generally called the Piazza Vittorio: this market is one of the best provisioned and cheapest in Rome. It is becoming increasingly multi-ethnic and all the immigrant communities of the city meet here to buy such things as exotic spices, semolina and flavoring for couscous.*

Testaccio: *this lively and pleasant market situated in the heart of the neighborhood has everything, in particular excellent fruit and vegetables, and marked-down clothes and shoes.*

Mercato dell'Unità: *situated on the Via Cola di Rienzo, on the same side of the Tiber as the Vatican, this is doubtless the*

Gastronomy: What to Bring Back from Rome?

T he city is full of grocery stores of different sizes, but they all have a slightly family feel. Even in the best-known establishments, the welcome is as simple and warm as it is in more modest stores. Most of the products come from Italy, but you can also find such things as French wines and Spanish ham. What is immediately striking is the art with which the articles are arranged and the distinctive odor. Many of the preparations should be eaten immediately: the delicious croquettes of fried rice filled with mozzarella (*suppli*), fritters made with zucchini blossoms or artichokes (*fiori di zucca, carciofi fritti*), or a simple but delicious *pizza bianca* still hot and seasoned with rosemary.

The cheeses, such as *pecorino romano*, can travel if they have been correctly wrapped, which is not the case for delicious *mozzarella di bufala*. Volpetti Formaggiomania, in the Testaccio district, offers a bewildering selection from the many different kinds of Italian cheese.

The elegant bottles of pure or flavored olive oil, or of vinegar (notably *aceto balsamico di Modena*) are

classics. You can also find, in glass jars, all the different kinds of olive and a host of vegetables preserved in plain or flavored olive oil, from sweet onions to little artichokes (*carciofini*), from peppers to hot peppers and capers, the choice is endless. If it is not the season for fresh white truffles, such preserves will give you an idea of the splendor of this delicacy. Italy is renowned for its cold meats and, as throughout the peninsula, hams are often suspended from the ceiling. Obviously, there is a wide variety of pastas. From *penne* and *bucatini* (short or long tubes), to *farfalle* (butterflies), *fusili* and *tortiglioni* (twists), one is struck by the variety and color that the Italian imagination has found for them. It is important to remember that fresh pasta should be eaten within a few days of purchase.

As for the wines, with their elegant bottles and labels, it is best to visit a wine bar and, when there is a wine tasting (the *mescita*, accompanied by canapés), to choose according to personal preference and the suggestions of the owner.

most interesting market architecturally. The quality of the produce is above reproach.

MUSEUMS

R ome has a large number of museums, which belong to the state, to the municipality, or to private foundations (in addition, of course, to those of the Vatican). The sum of their riches is incalculable, and therein lies the problem, aggravated by the fact that churches, to which entry is generally free, contain a

similar number of treasures.

A considerable effort is currently being made to bring Rome's museums into line with what the public expects today and with what the works themselves deserve. The Galleria Nazionale d'Arte Antica in the Palazzo Barberini and the Galleria Nazionale d'Arte Moderna, for example, are in the middle of long-term refurbishments. Former barracks to the north of the Villa Borghese should soon become an exhibition site for contemporary art. The landscape is changing radically and this is cause for celebration.

The finished results will be a delight for eyes and mind.

However, as a result of this upheaval it is important for visitors to check if a particular museum or collection is open before visiting. Refurbishment entails long-term closures or the theoretically temporary transfer of works.

The list which follows, in keeping with the spirit of this book, lists above all charming or unusual museums. Monday is the usual closing day for state museums and those belonging to the Comune.

ACEA ART CENTER
LE MACCHINE E GLI DEI
Via Ostiense, 106
Tel: 06–5748030
During the renovation of the Musei Capitolini, some of the exhibits were transported to the former power station at Montecatini (located not far from the Piramide Cestia), which belongs to the ACEA power company. The juxtaposition of the large turbines with the marbles was so popular that this temporary scheme was made permanent, except that the works are changed periodically
(the vast collections of the Musei Capitolini make it possible to supply both locations simultaneously).

GALLERIA COLONNA
Via della Pilotta, 17
Tel: 06–6794362
Open Saturday mornings only, the Galleria Colonna, which is in the palace of the same name near Piazza Venezia, illustrates superbly the power and extravagance of one of the oldest families of Latium, descendants of the counts of Tusculum who wielded great influence in the Middle Ages. The Great Hall, decorated with mirrors and frescoes depicting incidents from the life of Marcantonio II Colonna, hero of the victory over the Turks at Lepanto, is one of the most beautiful and impressive in Rome. The collection of paintings is commensurate with this magnificent setting and contains works by Ghirlandaio, Tintoretto,

Veronese and Bronzino, among others.

GALLERIA DORIA PAMPHILI
Piazza del Collegio Romano, 2
Tel: 06–6797323
The jewel of a colossal palace that still belongs to the family that had it built between the sixteenth and nineteenth centuries, the Galleria Doria Pamphili contains a remarkable collection of sculptures and paintings, displayed in a dazzling setting. Of particular interest are two works by Caravaggio, *Rest on the Flight into Egypt* and *Penitent Magdalene*, and above all the *Portrait of Innocent X* by Velázquez, one of the artist's greatest masterpieces. The Gallery of Mirrors represents an accomplished example of Roman baroque at its peak, combining in an inimitable way elegance and prodigious wealth. The gallery has longer opening hours than the Galleria Colonna and is very centrally located near the Piazza Venezia—two further reasons why it should be visited by all lovers of Rome. It is also possible to visit the private apartments.

GALLERIA SPADA
Piazza Capo di Ferro, 3
Tel: 06–6861158
In the superb white palace which houses the supreme court, the Galleria Spada, which dates back to the time of a powerful eighteenth-century cardinal, protector of Guido Reni and Guercino, is one of the most charming in Rome. With its human scale and original decor, it is delightful as much for its atmosphere as for the works on display, which are typical of aristocratic taste of the period. Borromini's trompe l'oeil perspective—baroque illusionism at its most cerebral—can be visited at the same time.

KEATS-SHELLEY MEMORIAL
HOUSE
Piazza di Spagna, 26
Tel: 06–6784235
Although it overlooks the busiest

square in Rome, this tiny museum has few visitors. It occupies the apartment where the English poet Keats, suffering from consumption, spent his last weeks in 1821. Carefully maintained and enriched since 1906 by the Keats-Shelley Memorial Association, this is one of the most moving places in the city. It conserves a number of souvenirs of Shelley, who died tragically in 1822 when he drowned off the Tuscany coast. It is said that it was possible to identify his body because he was carrying a copy of the poems of Keats. The beautiful library, chiefly devoted to nineteenth-century English poetry, adds to the striking charm of the place.

MUSEI CAPITOLINI
Piazza del Campidoglio
Tel: 06–67102071
This museum, located opposite the Palazzo dei Conservatori on the piazza designed by Michelangelo, is currently being refurbished. The Museo Capitolino itself, in the Palazzo Nuovo, houses the oldest collection in the modern world, created in 1471 by Pope Sixtus IV.

MUSEO BARRACCO
Via dei Ballauri, 1
Tel: 06–68806848
Housed in a charming little Renaissance building built for a French prelate, this museum contains a collection assembled by Giovanni Barracco which consists of a fairly small number of sculptures. Some of these, such as the head of Ramses II as a young man, are of great value. The collection, which illustrates the principal Mediterranean civilizations, cannot claim to be exhaustive but it does reflect the eye of a discerning amateur. The different rooms offer a rich journey through time and space, from Egypt and Mesopotamia to the beginning of the Middle Ages.

MUSEO BORGHESE
Piazza Scipione Borghese, 5

Tel: 06–8548577
A key part of any visit to Rome, this museum has recently reopened after two decades of conservation work. The restored late-eighteenth-century decor provides the setting for a dazzling collection of masterpieces, featuring ancient and baroque sculptures, including major works by Bernini, neoclassical pieces, the statue of Pauline Borghese by Canova, and exceptional works by Raphael, Titian and Caravaggio. Everyone will have their own favorites, whether it be the *Diana* by Domenichino, which Cardinal Borghese only managed to acquire from the artist by threatening to imprison him, *Cupid and Psyche* by Zucchi, or the mysterious *Circe* or *Melissa* by the artist from Ferrara, Dosso Dossi. For reasons of security and conservation, numbers are restricted, and it is necessary to reserve a ticket by telephone. The park, currently being improved, is a delight.

MUSEO CANONICA
Viale Pietro Canonica, 2
Tel: 06–8842279
Located in "La Fortezzuola," a sixteenth-century annex of the Villa Borghese resembling a small medieval castle, this was formerly the studio of the sculptor Pietro Canonica, who produced many commemorative monuments. The interior is unchanged since the artist's death in 1959. Evocative of an artistic tradition which has largely disappeared today, this little-visited museum has a unique charm, to which the delightful garden contributes.

MUSEO DELLA CIVILTÀ ROMANA
Piazza G. Agnelli, 10
Tel: 06–5926135
This museum provides a good reason to visit the EUR district, which was built for the 1937 Universal Exposition and is a typical example of Mussolini town planning. The museum, which explains Roman civilization using

reproductions, is essentially didactic, but it houses the largest model in the world showing Rome at the end of the fourth century, when Constantine converted to Christianity.

MUSEO NAPOLEONICO
MUSEO MARIO PRAZ
Via Zanardelli, 1 and 2
Tel: 06–68806286 and 06–6861089
In a palace situated near the Palazzo Altemps, Count Primoli, descendant of Lucien Bonaparte, brother of the emperor, assembled a remarkable collection of imperial family souvenirs. In the same palace is the collection of Mario Praz, indicated by an inconspicuous sign. You will hardly ever hear a Roman mention the name of this famous art historian, for Rome is a more superstitious city than might appear and Praz had a reputation for putting curses on people.

MUSEO NAZIONALE ETRUSCO DI VILLA GIULIA
Piazzale Villa Giulia, 9
Tel: 06–3201951
Situated on the edge of the gardens of the Villa Borghese and housed in one of the most beautiful Renaissance villas, built for Pope Julius III, this museum displays masterpieces of the Etruscan civilization, which had a decisive influence on Rome. The terracotta sarcophagi where the dead are represented reclining as for a banquet are invariably moving. Those who like looking at major works in a serene atmosphere should visit this museum.

PALAZZO ALTEMPS
Via di Sant'Apollinare, 8
Tel: 06–6897091
The Palazzo Altemps, a beautiful construction dating from the fifteenth century, has recently been restored to accommodate the masterpieces of the former Ludovisi collection from the Museo Nazionale Romano, previously displayed in the Baths of Diocletian. The beauty of the

architecture and the elegant restraint of their presentation enhance the Greek and Roman sculptures. Inside the palazzo, some interesting old decors as well as the chapel have been conserved. This palazzo, situated very near the Piazza Navona, is well worth visiting.

PALAZZO MASSIMO ALLE TERME
Piazza del Cinquecento, 68
Tel: 06–48903500
This museum, which opened in 1998, also contains works which were previously in the collections of the Museo Nazionale Romano, whose historical seat, the Baths of Diocletian, is nearby. It contains, among other things, an astonishing collection of painted decors which give a particularly vivid idea of how people lived in antiquity. Because of their fragility, access is limited.

In addition to the permanent collections of the museums, it is well worth finding out about big exhibitions taking place in Rome. The principal public institutions are:

PALAZZO VENEZIA, on the square of the same name or Via del Plebiscito, 118 (tel: 06–6798865).

PALAZZO DELLE ESPOSIZIONI, via Nazionale, 194 (tel: 06–4742216 or 06–48854651), a vast neoclassical building dating from the end of the nineteenth century which offers an eclectic and interesting program.

GALLERIA NAZIONALE D'ARTE MODERNA, Viale Belle Arti, 131 (tel: 06–3224151).

Also worthy of mention is the contribution of foreign institutions, particularly the VILLA MEDICI (Viale Trinità dei Monti, 1; tel: 06–67611), the seat of the French Academy in Rome, which is fortunate enough to have beautiful exhibition rooms and whose magnificent gardens can also be visited at certain times .

ANTIQUES

*T*he art market in Rome is not as *extensive as one might think. Exceptional objects from the great aristocratic collections, when these are not untransferable, are not usually seen in the windows of antique dealers or in auctions, which are rare.*

The city, which has only really been growing for 130 years, did not experience the same mania for buying that the bourgeoisie in Paris and London went through in the nineteenth century.

The antique shops are principally concentrated in three areas: Campo de' Fiori, especially Via Giulia; near Piazza Navona, essentially Via dei Coronari; between Piazza di Spagna and Piazza del Popolo, particularly Via del Babuino and Via Margutta.

The following addresses are not cheap, but they certainly offer the stuff of dreams. In the back rooms not visible from the street, where the atmosphere is more confidential, you might meet the curator of a great Italian or foreign museum looking for something to buy.

ANTONACCI
Via del Babuino, 141a
Tel: 06–32651679
Here one finds above all depictions of the Rome and Latium of yesteryear. Many were produced by foreign artists who stayed in the city.

APOLLONI
Via del Babuino, 133–34
Tel: 06–36002216
The vast store window gives some idea of the items sold by this establishment, which has an international reputation.

DI CASTRO ALBERTO
Piazza di Spagna, 5
Tel: 06–6792269
An establishment that has been in the family for generations. I have seen here, among other things, a remarkable series of drawings by the French artist Vinchon, dating from the beginning of

the nineteenth century, devoted to Rome and the surrounding country. Curiously, it is not related to the antique dealers of the same name in Via del Babuino and Via Margutta.

GASPARRINI
Via Fontanella di Borghese, 46
Tel: 06–6786658
Its superb paintings can be glimpsed from the street which leads to Palazzo Borghese.

LAMPRONTI
Via del Babuino, 69
Tel: 06–6782947
This is a very old store which has been at the same address since 1914. Carlo Lampronti, grandson of the founder, had the happy idea of showing part of the family collection in a small adjacent museum.

Also of interest is the MERCATO DELL'ANTIQUARIATO DI FONTANELLA BORGHESE, on the square along one of the massive facades of the Palazzo Borghese. This market offers second-hand books, engravings and prints, the latter consisting for the most part of old views of Rome.

For old books, a historic address:

ANTICA LIBRERIA CASCIANELLI
Largo Febo, 15
Tel: 06–68802806
One of the oldest stores in the city, and well known in its field. The interesting decor, preserved intact, dates back to about 1850.

CRAFTS

*I*n Rome, as in all big cities, the crafts are *threatened with a slow death, even in neighborhoods where not so long ago they occupied an important place, as in Trastevere. Because of the importance of the city's heritage, trades relating to restoration tend to fare better than those involved in the production of new objects.*

Nevertheless, there are some neighborhoods where craft activities survive. Of the places worth exploring, do not miss Palazzo Taverna at Via di Monte Giordano, 1, near Via del Governo Vecchio. Built on a mound resulting from the conglomeration of previous buildings, which included the medieval fortress of the Orsini family, it houses, among others, cabinetmakers and artistic ironworkers. Their presence is due to the proximity of Via dei Coronari, one of the main centers for antique dealers in the city. Here are a few other addresses:

DANTE ZANON
Via Castel di Guido, 190–92
Tel: 06–66890517
This workshop, almost in the country, makes mosaics or marble marquetry to order. It has an impressive store of ancient blocks and hard or semi-precious stones, such as agate and lapis lazuli.

DITTA MEDICI
Via dei Papareschi, 32
Tel: 06–5561646
The most illustrious of the firms specializing in marble, in existence for five generations. Priscilla Grazioli, descended from the founder, strives to maintain traditional standards and practices. The workshop executes commissions from the Vatican for the floors of the great basilicas. The firm has an astonishing store of marbles, some of which cannot be found elsewhere, from quarries which had already been exhausted in antiquity.

EREDI BAIACCO
Via delle Luce, 3a
Tel: 06–58331068; tel and fax: 06–5818854
This workshop, which has been based in Trastevere for three generations, specializes in stucco and plaster. It can reproduce old plaster and its range of techniques includes moldings and decoration applied to walls, reproductions of sculptures, and wall lights.

FERRAMENTA BORRA
Via Torre Argentina, 78
Tel: 06–68308577
This metal workshop has occupied the ground floor of this seventeenth-century palace since 1911. From the street there is no indication of the size of the spaces inside or the incredible quantity of objects and models conserved on the hundreds of shelves and drawers, such as hasps, handles and knobs. Over the years, a large number of Roman craftsmen in bronze and brass have learnt their trade in this foundry.

VALENTINI ALBERTO
Via Angelo Brunetti, 30
Tel: 06–3610358
A good address for work in bronze, representative of a tradition that used to flourish in Rome but is now under threat.

VINCENZO PIOVANO
Via dell'Orso, 27
Tel: 06–6869920
There is an extraordinary abundance of gilt wood and stucco in Rome, mainly found in furniture or picture frames, and Piovano's is one of the best wood carvers and gilders in the city.

VITO CIPOLLA
Via Sambuco, 8
Tel: 06–4820597
This craftsman works marble according to traditional sculpture techniques and makes high-quality copies.

CLOTHING AND JEWELRY

When it comes to clothing and jewelry, Rome, a city where people take great care over what they wear, offers many temptations. Today, the Italian fashion industry is based in Milan, but Rome still counts. The Piazza di Spagna neighborhood, in particular Via Condotti, has become the fashion center of the city—something which

---

THE PORTA PORTESE MARKET

The Porta Portese flea market is the largest in Rome. Located on the outer edge of Trastevere, it is open on Sunday mornings. It has its enthusiasts, as well as its detractors: the myth of the miraculous find against that of pickpockets. It has to be said that the invasion of secondhand clothes has rather altered the overall look of the place, but as long as you are not searching for a masterpiece, the range of bargains is vast. The typically Roman atmosphere, with the sound of Roman dialect filling the air and the endless theater of facial expressions and banter between buyers and sellers, makes it one of the places that must be visited in Rome.

Entering by the Via di Porta Portese, the first thing you see are bicycle stores and places selling automobile parts. Starting from the Piazza Ippolito Nievo, you will come across a jumble of old objects, together with craft items from all over the world. The Via Parboni side has been the Russian sector for some years. The variety is considerable even here and will be of particular interest to those looking for old records, watches or cameras. Many of the goods date from the 1950s and 1960s and a number of these are already becoming collector's items.

---

has caused the disappearance of a number of traditional cafés, together with almost all the artisans who used to meet in them.

On Via Condotti, GUCCI is at No. 8 (tel: 06–6789340), MAX MARA at 46 (tel: 06–6783465), TRUSSARDI at 49–50 (tel: 06–6990457), ARMANI at 77 (tel: 06–6991460) and PRADA at 92–95 (tel: 06–6790897), without forgetting such distinguished places as BATTISTONI, on the street and at the end of a double courtyard, at 57 and 61a (tel: 06–6976111 and 06–6786241). FENDI is at Via Borgognona, 38–40 (tel: 06–69761128) and VALENTINO is at Via Bocca di Leone, 16 (tel: 06–6795862), while UNGARO is at 24 (tel: 06–6789931) and VERSACE at 26 in the same street (tel: 06–6780521).

The legendary boutique of the SORELLE FONTANAS is at Salita di San Sebastianello (tel: 06–6798652), the little street which leads to the Villa Medici from Piazza di Spagna. GENTE, with a more youthful outlook, is at Via Frattina, 69 (tel: 06–6789132)

and at Via del Babuino, 82.

The Via del Babuino is a long succession of fashion stores alternating with major antique dealers: at 102, ETRO (tel: 06–6788357) makes magnificent use of silk and velvet; at 91, RUFFO (tel: 06–3213457), at the corner of Via Alibert, has a more modern outlook; at 97 is MISSONI DONNA (tel: 06–679797), while the men's clothing store is on Piazza di Spagna. CARIERI RITZ-SADDLER, which also has a range for smart children, is at 185 (tel: 06–3611001) and displays a list of autographs left by personalities from art and literature.

A few mythical names from haute couture have remained at the top of the steps leading to Piazza di Spagna: VALENTINO, Via Gregoriana, 24; Balestra, Via Sistina, 67 (tel: 06–6795537); and CAPUCCI, Via Gregoriana, 56 (tel: 06–6795180). SARLI, the famous Neapolitan designer, is now based at Via Gregoriana, 40a (tel: 06–6795210).

BOMBA
Via dell'Oca, 39
Tel: 06–3612881
This place, it is said, is very popular
with the intelligentsia.

DEGLI EFFETTI
Piazza Capranica, 79/93
Tel: 06–6791650
A trendy if rather expensive store,
where young designers rub shoulders
with more established names. The
goods change constantly, and the
fashion is original and resolutely
unconventional.

DULCE VIDOZA
Via dell'Orso, 58
Tel: 06–6893007
The architecture is reason enough
to visit this boutique.

JOSEPHINE DE HUERTAS
Via di Parione, 19–20
Tel: 06–6879995
An independent designer who makes
full use of a diverse range of materials.

ZAMPIERI
Via Molise, 13–15
Tel: 06–4827267
An unusual address. This tailor
specializes in uniforms of every kind,
whether it be those of maître d's—
particularly elegant in Rome—or
the nurses who accompany the sick
to Lourdes.

Particular mention should be made of
firms which specialize in ecclesiastical
and liturgical clothing. In the
Pantheon neighborhood, the best
known are also the oldest. It is not
necessary to be a member of the
clergy to acquire prelate's gloves,
shoes or embroideries. You will be
given a delightful welcome, providing
you do not enter with the idea of
indulging in inappropriate humor.

DE RITIS
Via dei Cestari, 48
Tel: 06–6865843

Founded in 1800, this firm specializes
in liturgical ornaments, as well as
nun's habits. The explanation for this
dual vocation lies in the fact that it
was the nuns who in the past
embroidered chasubles and made
lace. The store has a certain charm,
with its wooden armchairs.

SARTORIA GAMMARELLI
Via di Santa Chiara, 34
Tel: 06–68801314
Situated opposite De Ritis and dating
from 1798, this establishment bears
the title of official tailor of Saint Peter's.

Shoes and leather goods are also
concentrated around Piazza di Spagna.

AVC ADRIANA CAMPANILE
Piazza di Spagna, 88
Tel: 06–6785670

FRAGIACOMO
Via dei Condotti, 35
Tel: 06–6798780

FURLA
Piazza di Spagna, 22
Tel: 06–69200363

HERZEL
Via del Babuino, 123
Tel: 06–6783384

SALVATORE FERRAGAMO
Via dei Condotti, 73–74
Tel: 06–6791565

For jewels, the legendary BULGARI is
based at No. 10, Via Condotti.
BUCCELLATI is at 31 in the same street
(tel: 06–6790329) and ELEUTERI, for old
jewelry, is at 69 (tel: 06–6781078).
There are also workshops where new
jewelry is made, drawing on the
inexhaustible supply of artistic ideas
which has accumulated in Rome over
three millennia.

ALCOZER
Via delle Carrozze, 48
Tel: 06–6791388

For those who want to impress
without bankrupting themselves, this
goldsmith can supply copies of ancient
pieces of jewelry so good they cannot
be distinguished from the originals.

**CLEMENTINA IMPERIALI
DI FRANCAVILLA**
Tel: 06–3234672
This artist produces remarkable
bronze jewelry, but can only be visited
by appointment.

MASSIMO MARIA MELIS
Via dell'Orso, 57
Tel: 06–6869188
A goldsmith who specializes in
mounting very old pieces on modern
settings with impeccable taste.

SERGIO E ROSANNA CORRADINI
Via Bocca di Leone, 53
Tel: 06–6793487
This little firm of goldsmiths makes
superb jewelry inspired by antiquity,
using in particular pieces of hard stone.

HISTORIC SHOPS

Although they have disappeared in their
tens if not hundreds in recent decades,
Rome is without doubt the European
capital with the largest number of stores
still more or less in their original state.
The municipality organized a survey and
the setting up of a particular appellation,
Urbs Mirabilis ("The Admirable City").

A number of the cafés, notably the
Caffè Greco and the Caffè della Pace,
together with ecclesiastical tailors and the
Borra ironworks have already been
mentioned in this guide. Here are a few
others which are worth visiting.

ABBIGLIAMENTO SCHOSTAL
Via del Corso, 158
Tel: 06–6791240
This clothing store, founded in 1870,
does not pretend to be fashionable.
Its charm lies in the warmth of the
welcome, its many drawers and the
quality of the merchandise. There is

an interesting anecdote attached to
this establishment. When the racial
laws came into force in 1939, the
fascist authorities wanted to remove
the Austrian name, which sounded
Jewish to them, but the owners, the
Bloch brothers, persuaded them not
to by convincing them that the name
was an acronym.

ANTICA ERBORISTERIA ROMANA
Via di Torre Argentina, 15
Tel: 06–6879493
Probably established at the end of the
eighteenth century, this store seems
to have come down through the ages
intact. It has several hundred drawers
which contain everything imaginable
in the way of herbs, plants and different kinds of extract. The decor and
the furniture retain some original
elements, although they date mostly
from the nineteenth century.

CAMICERIA BAZZOCHI
Via del Tritone, 141
Dating from before World War I, this
store was proud to count Burt
Lancaster as one of its loyal
customers. Although the items are
more ordinary today, the store is one
of the last—perhaps the last—in Rome
to have retained its Liberty decor.

CAPPELLERIA VIGANO
Via M. Minghetti, 7–8
Tel: 06–6795147
Founded in 1873, having borne
the title of supplier to the *sacri palazzi
apostolici*, this store is a rare survivor
of the hatters of old. Inside, there is
a photo taken in 1885 in the workshop
which used to be upstairs, together
with a number of souvenirs, including
a letter from Garibaldi and two fezzes
belonging to Mussolini.

D'AURIA
Via Due Macelli, 55
Tel: 06–6793364
Historic glove-maker, whose store
has conserved its beautiful, brightly
colored, baroque-style furniture dating

from early twentieth century. The atmosphere is that of a bourgeois salon propitious for conversation.

MACELLERIA MASTRODDI
Via di Ripetta, 237
Tel: 06–3612269
In the same street as the Buccone wine bar you will find this extraordinary butchers shop, which has conserved its late-nineteenth-century Art Nouveau decor. A winged dragon watches over the counter.

MEROLA
Via del Corso, 143

Tel: 06–6791961
Another traditional glove-maker, whose origins can be traced back to a Neapolitan who settled in Rome in 1855 after having learnt his craft in France. The walls are lined with diplomas testifying to the know-how of the southern workers and there is an impressive old chest of drawers.

PESCI
Piazza della Fontana di Trevi, 89
Tel: 06–6792210
Located on one of the most touristy squares in Rome, this pharmacy often goes unnoticed, and yet it is surely

one of the oldest in Europe, as a large bronze mortar on a marble plinth bears the date 1552. About thirty pharmacy pots are all that remain now of a collection that numbered five times that, but they are enough, along with the beautiful eighteenth-century wooden furniture, to create a very evocative atmosphere.

PONTEFICIA
ERBORISTERIA SALLEMI
Via Pozzo delle Cornacchie, 26
Tel: 06–6861201
This establishment is said to be even

older than Antica Erboristeria Romana. Founded in 1780, it has recently been modernized, but some interesting decorative elements have been retained.

SANTA MARIA DELLA SCALA
Piazza Santa Maria della Scala, 21
Tel: 06–5806217
This former pharmacy of the barefoot Carmelites is the forerunner of modern dispensaries.
You can still ask to visit two splendid authentic rooms, complete with their period containers, painted cupboards and utensils for preparing concoctions. .

THE ENVIRONS OF ROME

Ever since antiquity, Romans have enjoyed getting out of their city and every trip to Rome should include at least a glimpse of the surrounding region. It is essential for understanding the roots of the Roman world. Although the Latin culture no longer forms the basis of education, nobody could be indifferent to the view of the plain of Latium—the cradle of one of the most extraordinary human adventures in history—from Monte Cavo. Once outside the city, you can, within the same day, soak up the memories of antiquity, the Middle Ages and the Renaissance, enjoy country cooking or the produce caught by the fishermen of Latium, sample the pleasures of the beach and breathe mountain air.

OSTIA: RUINS AND BEACHES

The excavations of Ostia Antica, a place which is not easy to find, plunge the visitor into the atmosphere of ancient Rome. Given its interest, this site has surprisingly few visitors, but it is a very moving place, particularly in the light of a late afternoon. If you like solitude, wander as far as you can from the entrance, making sure to take a bottle of water with you. It is important to have a good guide book, which should ensure you do not walk past certain vestiges which are particularly revealing about life in ancient Rome. The many remains include those of houses which used to belong to the rich and which were forerunners of the modern garden city.

A visit to Ostia can be combined with a bathe. The local beach, the Lido di Ostia, consists of dark gray sand and has a bad reputation because of pollution. The town of Fiumicino, next to the airport of the same name, was originally a fishing village. Impossibly crowded at weekends, it is much calmer during the week. A few kilometers to the north, Fregene is a seaside town which is not without interest. It is reached by going through a pine forest. To get to the beach itself you have to pass through bathing establishments. To the north of Fregene, the site of Cerveteri provides a striking introduction to Etruscan civilization. This vast necropolis is made up of round tumuli out of which graves were dug. Although they have lost their stucco or painted decoration, they are still intensely evocative, and a walk in this necropolis leaves an indelible memory.

Numerous restaurants on the coast offer seafood, including:

Fiumicino

GINA AL PORTO
Viale Trajano, 141
Tel: 06–6522422
Particularly worth trying are the stuffed squid and the spaghetti with seafood.

LA PERLA
Via Torre Clementina, 214
Tel: 06–6505038
A traditional restaurant, well situated in the port, the excellence of which has been recognized by the Italian academy of cuisine. Particularly worth trying is the cream of lentil soup with seafood.

Fregene

LA CONCHIGLIA
Lungomare di Ponente, 4
Tel: 06–6685385
Probably the best in this part of the seafront. The *spaghetti ai calamaretti* is particularly delightful.

MASTINO
Via Silvi Marina, 19
Tel: 06–66560700

This is the best-known restaurant in this old fishing village, as well as the smartest.

TIVOLI: THE DREAMS OF AN EMPEROR AND A CARDINAL

Some 20 kilometers from the capital, Tivoli, formerly Tibur, was one of the favorite resorts of ancient Romans. Its hillside location and waterfalls have inspired nearly every artist who has stayed in Rome or visited Italy, particularly Fragonard and Hubert Robert. Below the town stands the villa that Hadrian had built at the beginning of the second century C.E. In fact, the term villa does not do justice to the place, which was a veritable city where the philosopher emperor reconstituted his favorite places, souvenirs of his trips to Greece, Egypt and Asia Minor. The vestiges were stripped of their riches long ago, but remain considerable. A walk among these immense poetic ruins gives a good idea of the grandeur of the Roman Empire and makes it easier to understand the fascination it has exerted over the centuries.

The little town of Tivoli, in addition to its remarkable location, is also known for the Villa d'Este, built in the middle of the sixteenth century by the disreputable cardinal Ippolito II d'Este, the son of Lucrezia Borgia. The building is of less interest than the splendid terraced gardens, dotted with a multitude of fountains. Less frequented, the Villa Gregoriana has a beautiful cascade.

Tivoli has a large number of restaurants.

ANTICA TRATTORIA DEL FALCONE
Via del Trevio, 34
Tel: 07–7422358

In Tivoli itself, this restaurant offers cooking which is in the purest regional tradition.

HOTEL RISTORANTE ADRIANO
Via di Villa Adriana, 194
Tel: 07–74382235 ; fax: 07–74535122
Situated next to the Villa Adriana, this hotel does not have many rooms, but its restaurant is well worth visiting, providing tasty family cuisine.

HOTEL SIRENE
Piazza Massimo, 4
Tel: 07–74330605 ; fax: 07–74330608
Housed in a villa dating from 1865, this restaurant has a magnificent view of the Temple of the Sibyl, the waterfalls and the Villa Gregoriana.

CASTELLI ROMANI: VOLCANOES AND VILLAS

The Alban Hills, or Colli Albani, are a volcanic group situated about 15 kilometers from Rome. In antiquity, important people possessed summer residences there. Cicero's country home was in Tusculum, hence the title *Tusculan Disputations* given to one of his works, which is full of anecdotes and philosophical reflections.

During the turbulent centuries of the Middle Ages, villages were fortified by the feudal families of Latium, hence the name Castelli Romani given to them collectively. In the Renaissance, the pope, cardinals and the most important members of the Roman nobility often had sumptuous villas built here. The most beautiful are in Frascati, also famous for its wines, but bombardments during World War II caused considerable damage. Such is the case, for example, with the austere Villa Lancellotti, which the Massimo Lancellotti family is restoring with infinite patience.

On the other hand, the majestic architecture and hillside gardens of the Villa Aldobrandini have remained intact. The small town of Ariccia has for a long time been the stronghold of the Chigis, for whom Bernini created a chateau of elegant sobriety, together with the pretty square in front of it. The summer residence of the pope is at Castel Gandolfo.

The most remarkable natural features of the Castelli Romani have remained unspoilt. These include the Lago di Nemi, which has remained wilder than the Lago Albano. From Frascati and from Monte Cavo, the second highest summit of the Alban Hills, the view of Rome and the surrounding plain (the Campagna di Roma) is impressive. It is best to see it on a day when the heat and the pollution do not obscure the landscape, for example on a beautiful Sunday in winter or when it is very windy. However, growing urbanization has profoundly changed the landscape. Less attractive by day, at night it is magical, when the lights of the city and its suburbs twinkle.

The small towns of the Castelli contain numerous restaurants, which are generally quiet during the week and crowded at weekends.

Ariccia

LA CASINA DEL MINISTRO
Tel: 06–93391022
A good place to savor the beauty of the location.

Frascati

CACCIARI
Via A. Diaz, 13
Tel: 06–9420378
This restaurant has a beautiful panoramic view and its inclusion of old local recipes, such as *abbacchio alla cacciatora*, is most welcome. Dining there at sunset and watching the city light up is a dream come true.

LA TABERNA MAMILIUS
Viale Balilla, 1
Tel: 06–9421559
This establishment also serves typical dishes of Latium, such as braised lamb's tripe.

Castel Gandolfo

ANTICO RISTORANTE PAGNANELLI
Via A. Gramsci, 19
This establishment dating from the nineteenth century has remained faithful to local traditional cuisine. Try the *fettuccine alla papalina*.

Monteporzio Catone

DA FRANCO
Via Duca degli Abruzzi, 19
Tel: 06–9449205
The name of the village calls to mind Cato, the most austere figure of the Roman republic. The decor is simple and the cuisine enjoyable, in particular the delicious beef fillet with cream of boletus mushroom.

Grottaferrata

AL TINELLO
Via Domenichino, 9
Tel: 06–9458395
This family restaurant, which replaced a very old wine merchant, brings a touch of inventiveness to traditional Roman cooking.

LA CAVOLA D'ORO
Via Anagnina, 35
Tel: 06–94315755
This restaurant is near the village of Grottaferrata, known for its very beautiful abbey which was founded in the eleventh century and is occupied by Basilian monks. It offers authentic cooking at modest prices. Particularly fine during the truffle season are the *gnocchetti verdi con tartufo*.

LA TAVERNA DELLA SPUNTINO
Via Cicerone, 20
Tel: 06–9459366

This restaurant offers good country cooking, combining the traditions of Latium and the Marches.

Nemi

LA TRATTORIA DELLA SORA MARIA
Tel: 06–9368020
This *trattoria* offers a magnificent view of the mysteriously beautiful lake, in a village reputed to be the capital of wild strawberries.

Labico

ANTONELLO COLONNA
Via Roma, 89
Tel: 06–9510032
Located near the freeway to Naples, this restaurant lies outside the Castelli Romani, but is well worth visiting for the quality of its cooking. Notable dishes include lamb cutlets with fennel or tagliatelle in rabbit juice with herbs.

VITERBO AND NORTHERN LATIUM: ETRUSCAN AND MEDIEVAL VESTIGES

Often passed through at speed by travelers who are in a hurry, this region is interesting for several reasons. The landscapes and the architecture in gray stone bear the traces of its volcanic past. Indeed, Bracciano and Bolsena are crater lakes. This was one of the centers of the Etruscan civilization, of which there are remarkable vestiges at Tarquinia and Tuscania. The necropolis at Tarquinia, or Tarquinii to give it its Latin name, with its admirable painted tombs, is a good way of rounding off a trip to Cerveteri. The two towns also possess important monuments from the Middle Ages, notably the moving church of Santa Maria Maggiore, which is located on the outskirts of Tuscania.

The larger town of Viterbo is full of remains from the period when the

popes sought refuge here from the upheavals in Rome. Its medieval quarter around Via San Pellegrino is one of the best preserved in Italy. The town is near the Lago di Bolsena, to the north, on the shore of which lies the little town of the same name, also medieval, and the lakes of Vico and Bracciano to the south. The Farnese palace at Caprarola is one of the most important monuments in the region.

The fantastic gardens at the Villa Orsini in Bomarzo, created in the sixteenth century, are a fascinating curiosity. The *sacro bosco* has a multitude of constructions and strange or terrifying figures. The site has become very touristy and its charm is spoilt by the presence of picnic areas. It is best to visit the gardens outside the most popular days or periods, and the same applies to the whole region.
There are several addresses which provide agreeable places to eat:

Bolsena

DA PICCHIETTO
Via Porta Fiorentina, 15
Tel: 0761–799158
Located in the center of town, this family restaurant has a pleasant garden and serves fish from the lake, marinated or grilled.

Bracciano

TRATTORIA DEL CASTELLO
Piazza Mazzini, 1
Tel: 06–99804339
This restaurant is housed in a sixteenth-century building and offers pleasant cooking which includes fish from the lake, but also from the sea.

Tuscania

AL GALLO
Via del Gallo
Tel: 0761–443388
Located in the medieval town, this place offers inventive cooking in a traditional setting.

Viterbo

IL RICHIASTRO
Via della Marrocca, 16
Tel: 0761–223609
Located in a thirteenth-century
building, this place offers typical local
cuisine, sometimes adapting very
old recipes.

TRATTORIA DI PORTA ROMANA
Via della Bontà, 12
Tel: 0761–307118
This little family restaurant also serves
tasty country cooking, such as
the *porchetta* (suckling pig).

GOING SOUTH: SEA AND MOUNTAINS

The coastal plain which extends to
the southeast of Rome was for a
long time an unhealthy place. The
draining and agricultural development
of the famous Pontine Marshes was
one of the biggest undertakings of the
Mussolini regime. Towns like Latina,
with their characteristic urban
planning, are an interesting legacy of
this period.

The coast has vast beaches.
The rocky headland of Monte Circeo
rises as if by magic over a dull and
flat landscape. At its foot stretches
a dense forest of eucalyptus and
a series of small lakes which add to
its mysterious charm. It is easy to
believe that this could have been
the extraordinary site of the
sorceress Circe, who nearly got the
better of Ulysses. Further south,
a good two hours frim Rome, is the
popular seaside resort of Sperlonga,
overlooked by a picturesque perched
village. Nearby is the famous cave of

Tiberius, which the fearsome
emperor had made.

The coastal plain is bordered
by steep hills. A number of perched
villages cluster around a medieval
fortress, a vestige of the time when
insecurity ruled on land and sea.
Not far from Latina, the village of
Sermoneta, above which looms the
large residence of the Caetani, offers
an admirable view of the plain.
It dominates one of the most
extraordinary sites in the region,
created at.the beginning of the
twentieth century by the Caetani in
one of their immemorial domains,
Ninfa. Of the medieval town,
where a pope was crowned and
which was for a long time a key
defensive outpost on the road to
Naples, only a few meager yet poetic
vestiges survive. But in this place
which is abundantly irrigated and
sheltered by a crescent of mountains,
the Caetani had the brilliant idea of
creating a dream garden. The
microclimate has enabled the trees to
grow with remarkable rapidity (some
which look a hundred years old are in
fact younger) and has made it
possible to introduce species which
are normally unknown in Europe. The
foundation which manages the legacy
of the Caetani family, which died out
recently, has set up a series of guided
visits. In the spring and early autumn,
the garden of Ninfa is quite dazzling.
Despite the distance from Rome, it is
a sight well worth visiting.

More inland, the Rome-Naples
freeway takes you through
magnificent mountain landscapes.
At the beginning of the Middle Ages,
this region was one of the centers
of monasticism in Italy.

Near Frosinone, two beautiful

abbeys have survived: Fossanova
and Casamari. These remarkable
examples of Cistercian architecture
are more or less intact. Unfortunately,
this is not the case for the famous
abbey of Monte Cassino, visible
from the freeway, which was entirely
destroyed during World War II
and rebuilt exactly as it was.
The memory of Saint Benedict,
the founder of monasticism in
western Europe, has been preserved
not only in Cassino, but also at
Subiaco, which is best reached by
taking the Tivoli freeway. The two
monasteries preserve the memory
of the saint and his sister Saint
Scholastica. The site is superb and
the atmosphere captivating.

Near Subiaco, Monte Livata is the
nearest ski station to Rome, some 60
kilometers away, something which few
non-Romans know. Although the
slopes cannot rival those of the Alps,
it is nonetheless a special delight to
go there on a beautiful winter's day.
The climate is harsh in this part of
Latium.

The following addresses are mostly
concentrated in the coastal areas.

Latina

CASABLANCA
Strada Statale 156 dei Monti Lepini
Tel: 0773–241861
A quite remarkable fish restaurant.
One of the many dishes worth trying is
the *lasagnette di pesce al forno*.

Sabaudia

LA PINETA
Corso Vittorio Emmanuele III
Tel: 0773–515053
More of a family establishment which

offers hundreds of variations on the
sea theme.

San Felice Circeo

The village of San Felice Circeo, which
started spilling out of the original
center on the slopes of Monte Circeo
long ago, also has good facilities.
There are two establishments
providing top-quality cuisine.

LA STIVA DI ULISSE
Lungomare Circe, 32
Tel: 0773–548814
A vast, modern restaurant with
a large park overlooking the sea,
where you can enjoy the *grigliata mista*
with fish freshly fished from the
Tyrrhenian Sea.

LA VERANDA, MAGA CIRCE HOTEL
Via Amm. Bergamini, 1
Tel: 0773–547821
The terrace offers a panoramic view
and the cuisine is quite remarkable,
in particular the mushroom risotto.

Inland, there are good addresses at
Fiuggi, an ancient spa town:

HOTEL VILLA HERNICUS
Corso Nuova Italia, 3
Tel: 0775–55254
The hotel's restaurant offers authentic
local cuisine which is also
imaginative, such as the wholemeal
flour *gnocchetti* with zucchini and
smoked goose.

LA TORRE
Piazza Trento e Trieste, 18
Tel: 0775–515382
This welcoming family restaurant also
offers updated traditional recipes.

FESTIVALS AND SEASONS IN ROME

There is no "bad season" as such in Rome, although in the latter part of autumn and in winter the weather can be cold and wet, with some very gray days, if not weeks. In October, the weather is in general quite warm and the golden light—what the Romans call "ottobratta"—is unforgettable. On sunny winter days, temperatures can be very mild. Neither is there really a "quiet season" in Rome, although the number of visitors goes down between Epiphany and Lent.

RELIGIOUS FESTIVALS

Life in the city is inextricably linked not only to climatic changes but also to the liturgical calendar. Christmas, Holy Week and Easter, Ascension and Pentecost draw an appreciable number of Italian and foreign pilgrims. December 8, the feast of the Immaculate Conception, the pope frequently goes to Piazza di Spagna, the side dominated by the statue of the Virgin Mary on the top of a column. During this period, which is that of Advent, cribs appear in numerous churches. The best known are at Santa Maria Maggiore and Aracoeli on the Capitoline. There is also a very beautiful animated crib on the Spanish Steps. Christmas and Epiphany, February 6, are almost equally important, at least as far as children are concerned. Indeed, the day of Epiphany, Befana, a witch with two faces, rewards the good children and punishes the bad by offering them coal (or black sugar today). In between, Romans celebrate New Year's Day, or Capodanno. April 21 is the anniversary of the birth of Rome in 753 B.C., celebrated among other things by a firework display on the Capitoline.

During Holy Week, the washing of feet on Thursday and the stations of the Cross at the Colosseum on Friday, presided over by the pope, are heavily attended, as is the papal benediction given from the balcony of Saint Peter's. Easter Monday (Pasquetta), many families have picnics in the city's parks or environs. June 29, the festival of the patron saints of Rome, Peter and Paul, is an important event in Rome. Mid-July is when the festival of the Trastevere neighborhood takes place. Known as Noantri, it was depicted in Fellini's movie *Roma*. For Assumption, which Italians call Ferragosto, August 15 and neighboring days, the city is dead. At this time, the pope generally retires to his residence at Castel Gandolfo.

Throughout the year, the Sunday angelus in Piazza San Pietro is a commonplace event for Romans, who go there as New Yorkers go to Central Park for a stroll, while the numerous pilgrims react with great fervor. Frequent Church events, such as beatifications and canonizations, or infrequent ones, such as councils, jubilees or changes of pope, are marked by impressive ceremonies.

The formal services of the great basilicas are obviously beautiful, but the emotion of the occasion is sometimes diluted by the size of the setting. For those seeking greater intensity, it is worth enquiring about services celebrated in monastic communities or shrines assigned to Eastern Churches linked to Rome. The Benedictine monks of Sant'Anselmo, on the Aventine Hill, maintain the tradition of Gregorian chant, but the neo-medieval buildings are sadly lacking in charm. Elsewhere, the beautiful Renaissance church of Sant'Atanasio dei Greci, Via del Babiuno, in the Piazza di Spagna neighborhood, where the congregation is rather sparse, gives an idea of the beauty of the Byzantine liturgy. But the strongest impression will perhaps be made by the astonishing Coptic liturgy, which draws immigrants from the former Italian colonies of Eritrea and Ethiopia (San Tommaso in Parione, Via di Parione, 33). All these examples illustrate better than any international organization the universal vocation of Rome.

CULTURAL EVENTS

Roman cultural life does not have the same richness as that of London, Paris, Berlin or New York. Often, it retains a slightly provincial air which is not without charm. Thus the Teatro dell'Opera, to give just one example, cannot be compared with the San Carlo theater in Naples, no doubt the most beautiful in Europe, or La Scala in Milan. However, considerable efforts are being made to bolster the major cultural institutions and to create modern facilities, notably with the construction of the large auditorium that Rome needs so badly (due to open in 2000). The state and the municipality play a key role in this respect, but private initiatives also play an important part, exemplified by the contribution of film director Nanni Moretti.

The simplest way to find out what is on is to consult the weekly programs, such as *Trova Roma*—the daily supplement of *La Repubblica*—or *Roma c'è*, which gives detailed information and useful advice.

As regards music, of particular interest are the programmes of the Accademia di Santa Cecilia, founded in the sixteenth century, which has its own symphony orchestra and choir. Until the new auditorium opens, concerts will continue to take place in the hall at Via della Conciliazione, 4, and, in summer, in the marvelous setting of the nymphaeum of the Villa Giulia. Similarly, the Accademia Filarmonica Romana, founded in 1821, organizes a season of concerts, in particular at the Teatro Olimpico, Piazza Gentile da Fabriano, 17 (tel: 06–3234890).

For theater, there is the Quirino, Via M. Minghetti, 1 (tel: 06–6794585). For those who would like to discover Roman popular theater, with its dialect, characters, and comedy, which is never coarse, the place to go is the Fiorenzo Fiorentini theater, Sala Petrolini, Via Rubattino, 5 (tel: 06–5757488).

For movies, there is an interesting program at the Nuovo Sacher, the auditorium that Nanni Moretti saved in Trastevere, Largo Ascianghi, 1 (tel: 06–5818116). A bar and a bookshop have been opened inside. Mondays, the shows are in the original language, which is rare in Italy. The recently modernized Alcazar, also in Trastevere, Via Merry del Val, 14 (tel: 06–5880099), is very comfortable and offers, also Mondays, original-language versions.

ESTATE ROMANA

The Estate Romana ("Roman Summer") deserves particular mention. Reinstated a few years ago by the municipality, this big summer festival has been a remarkable tonic for the city. There is no organized program as such, but rather a blossoming of events of all kinds, combining music, cinema, theater, dance and other disciplines.

The most original aspect is the number of open-air movie shows. The "historical" event is Massenzio, which, year in year out, wanders throughout the city with the aim of putting the spotlight on different neighborhoods or sights worth revisiting, such as the Circo Massimo, Piazza del Popolo or the Via Appia Antica. The gardens of the Villa Mercede, Via Tiburtina, 113, serve as the setting for sessions of the Sotto le Stelle di San Lorenzo. Although this neighborhood is becoming fashionable, it remains working class and is therefore not deserted in the summer months. But there are other festivals worth discovering, such as the Notti di Cinema a Piazza Vittorio, which has evenings for children with circus shows, or the Isola del Cinema.

Oriented toward theater, music and dance, the RomaEuropa festival starts in the summer, often at the Villa Medici, and continues until autumn. It organizes, alone or in conjunction with other cultural institutions, a vast range of contemporary shows.

The most venerable institutions, such as the Accademia di Santa Cecilia, often expand their repertoires, and at the Villa Giulia, for example, an evening devoted to Rossini could be sandwiched between a homage to rock musician Jimi Hendrix and the film music of

Ennio Morricone.

Jazz is much in evidence at Testaccio Village, as is pop and rock. Music from around the world is spreading, whether it be at the Villa Ada, Via di Ponte Salario, or the Hippodrome delle Capanelle, Via Appia, 1245.

Open-air opera no longer takes place at the Baths of Caracalla, but rather at the Stadio Olimpico. This is an extraordinary spectacle, on account of the crowd as much as the music.

In the environs of Rome, the Roman theater at Ostia Antica offers a very eclectic program, where plays by

Sophocles or Seneca can alternate with Patti Smith.

Finally, it would be a serious omission not to mention the city's passion for soccer. Rome has two rival teams, Roma, who play in red and gold, and Lazio, who wear blue and white striped jerseys. The city, and even individual families, are divided according to whether they support the one or the other. The supporters, or *tifosi*, noisily express their joy after a victory. And the local derby between the two teams can lead to spectacular scenes of rejoicing or depression.

FILMOGRAPHY

Just after World War II, Rome and Cinecittà formed one of the centers of world cinema. The city itself plays an important part in numerous movies of different kinds. The great movies by Fellini show the depth of his attachment to the city: one never tires of seeing these rich and unique works. Here, put together with the help of Alain Fleischer and Dominique Païni, director of the French cinematheque, is a list of feature films set entirely or largely in Rome.

La Tosca, by Karl Koch and Jean Renoir (1940). With Michel Simon and Imperio Argentina.
Rome, Open City, by Roberto Rossellini (1945). With Anna Magnani.
The Bicycle Thief, by Vittorio de Sica (1948). With Lamberto Maggiorani.
The White Sheik, by Federico Fellini (1951). With Alberto Sordi and Giulietta Masina.
Roman Holiday, by William Wyler (1953). With Gregory Peck and Audrey Hepburn.
Three Coins in the Fountain, by Jean Negulesco (1954). With Clifton Webb, Dorothy McGuire and Louis Jourdan.
The Nights of Cabiria, by Federico Fellini (1957). With Giulietta Masina and François Périer.
La Dolce Vita, by Federico Fellini (1960). With Marcello Mastroianni, Anita Ekberg and Alain Cuny.
Accatone, by Pier Paolo Pasolini (1961). With Franco Citti.
The Roman Spring of Mrs. Stone, by Jose Quintero (1961). With

Vivien Leigh and Warren Beatty.
Mamma Roma, by Pier Paolo Pasolini (1962). With Anna Magnani.
Two Weeks in Another Town, by Vincente Minnelli (1962). With Kirk Douglas, Edward G. Robinson and Cyd Charisse.
Il Sorpasso (The Easy Life), by Dino Risi (1962). With Vittorio Gassman, Jean-Louis Trintignant, Catherine Spaak and Annette Stroyberg.
Rome Adventure, by Delmer Daves (1962). With Angie Dickinson and Troy Donahue.
Il Boom, by Vittorio de Sica (1963). With Alberto Sordi.
Partner, by Bernardo Bertolucci (1968). With Pierre Clementi, Stefania Sandrelli and Tina Aumont.
Othon/Les Yeux ne Veulent pas en Tout Temps se Fermer/ Peut-être qu'un jour Rome se permettra de choisir à son tour, by Jean-Marie Straub and Danièle Huillet (1969).
Fellini's Satyricon, by Federico Fellini (1969).

Fellini's Roma, by Federico Fellini (1972).
Leçons d'Histoire, by Jean-Marie Straub and Danièle Huillet (1972).
A Special Day, by Ettore Scola (1977). With Sophia Loren and Marcello Mastroianni.
Identification of a Woman, by Michelangelo Antonioni (1982). With Thomas Milian, Christine Boisson and Daniela Silverio.
History, by Luigi Comencini (1985). With Claudia Cardinale and Lambert Wilson.
Rome, Romeo, by Alain Fleischer (1989). With John Hargreaves, Danièle Schirman, Yann Collette and Laszlo Szabo.
The Godfather, Part III, by Francis Ford Coppola (1990). With Al Pacino and Diane Keaton.
Night on Earth, by Jim Jarmusch (1991). With Roberto Benigni and Winona Ryder.
Dear Diary, by Nanni Moretti (1994). With Nanni Moretti.

BIBLIOGRAPHY

Aicher, Peter J. *Guide to the Aqueducts of Ancient Rome*. Wauconda, Ill.: Bolchazy Carducci Publishers, 1995.

Barocco, Ambiente, Stefanie Walker, and Frederick Hammond. *Life and the Arts in the Baroque Palaces of Rome*. New Haven: Yale University Press, 1999.

Boccazzi-Varotto, Attilio, and Marco Filaferro. *Rome 360°*. New York: Random House, 1998.

Carcopino, Jerome. *Daily Life in Ancient Rome*. London: Penguin Books, 1991.

Carr-Gomm, Sarah. *Rome*. Art in Focus series. Boston: Bullfinch Press, 1996.

Cary, Max. *A History of Rome Down to the Reign of Constantine*. New York: St. Martin's Press, 1975.

Claridge, Amanda. *Rome*. Oxford Archaeological Guide. Oxford: Oxford University Press, 1998.

Cornell, Tim. *The Beginnings of Rome*. London: Routledge, 1995.

Cornell, Tim, and John Matthews. *Atlas of the Roman World*. New York: Facts on File, Incorporated, 1982.

Friedman, Joe, Frances Venturi, Marella Caracciolo, and Francesco Venturi. *Inside Rome: Discovering Rome's Classic Interiors*. London: Phaidon, 1993.

Gendlin, Frances. *Rome at Your Door*. Portland: Graphic Arts Center Publishing Company, 1997.

Hibbert, Christopher. *Rome: the Biography of a City*. London: Penguin Books, 1987.

Hofer, Hans, and Dorothy Stannard. *Insight Guides Rome*. Maspeth, N.Y.: Langenscheidt Publishers, 1998.

Hofmann, Paul, and Joanne Morgante. *The Seasons of Rome: A Journal*. Boston: Henry Holt and Co., 1997.

Jepson, Tim. *Fodor's Exploring Rome*. 4th edition. New York: Fodor, 1999.

Krautheimer, Richard. *Rome, Profile of a City: 312–1308*. Princeton: Princeton University Press, 1980.

Macadam, Alta. *Rome*. Blue Guide. London: A & C Black, 1998.

Masson, Georgina. *The Companion Guide to Rome*. London: W. M. Collins Sons & Co., 1965.

Novelli, Italo. *Atlas of Rome*. Marsilio Publishers, 1992.

Paoli, Ugo Enrico, and R. D. Macnaughton. *Rome: Its People, Life and Customs*. Bristol Classical Press, 1990.

Payne, Robert. *Rome Triumphant*. Barnes and Noble Books, 1994.

Porter, Darwin, and Danforth Prince. *Frommer's Rome*. Macmillan, 1998.

Rome. Eyewitness Travel Guides. London: Dorling Kindersley, 1999.

Rome. Knopf Guide. New York: A. A. Knopf, 1994.

Rome. Michelin Green Guide. Michelin Travel Publications, 1999.

Shelton, Jo-Ann. *As the Romans Did: A Sourcebook in Roman Social History*. Oxford: Oxford University Press, 1998.

Testa, Judith Anne. *Rome is Love Spelled Backward: Enjoying Art and Architecture in the Eternal City*. Dekalb, Ill.: Northern Illinois University Press, 1998.

Varriano, John. *A Literary Companion to Rome*. New York: St. Martin's Press, 1995.

INDEX

ACKNOWLEDGMENTS

This book would not have been possible without the help and support of my wife, Béatrice, who has accompanied me throughout the project. Danielle Schirman has played an invaluable role for Alain Fleischer. Lovers of Rome since their stay at the Villa Medici, both have provided me with numerous useful suggestions. I would also like to thank all those who, in one way or another, have contributed to this book, either through their advice and support or by generously inviting me into their homes. In alphabetical order, they are: Carla Accardi, a major figure in Italian painting; Prince and Princess Giovanni Aldobrandini; Dottore Antonelli, president of the Caetani Foundation; the late Monsignor Jean-François Arrighi, who, along with René Brouillet, French ambassador to the Holy See from 1963 to 1974, introduced me to the Eternal City; the Baiocco family, whose trade of stucco making is handed down from generation to generation in Trastevere; Jacques Blot, French ambassador in Italy, and his wife Régine, who gave free access to the Palazzo Farnese; Olivier Bonfait, art history officer at the Villa Medici and successor to Michel Hochmann; Delphine Borione, who runs the Futuro association with her husband; Caroline Bruzelius, former director of the American Academy in Rome; Maria Castellino, director of the Spada Gallery, Nicolà Chiatante, eminent representative of the Italian Academy of Cuisine in Rome; Anne Coliva, of the department of art history and culture; Baron and Baroness Coppa Solari, currently refurbishing the Palazzo Pirro; Enzo Crea, historian, writer and publisher; Luigi de Conciliis, enthusiastic collector of ancient and modern art; Christophe Drzydzinski, thanks to whom we gained access to the property belonging to the Order of Malta; Marco Dolcetta, intellectual and film director and producer; Prince Jonathan Doria Pamphili, who were most helpful when showing what is one of the most beautiful palaces in Rome; Vicky and Isabella Ducrot, great travelers and lovers of Rome; Federico Forquet, whose apartment is a synthesis of Rome and Naples; Massimiliano Fuksas, a major figure in modern architecture, simultaneously Roman and international, and his wife Doriana; Joseph Kosuth and his wife Cornelia, who recently settled in Rome (a sign that the city continues to attract artists whose work apparently has little in common with the "classical" tradition); Alexandra Lapierre, a novelist who has managed to re-create the atmosphere of baroque Rome with remarkable success; Fabrizio and Fiammetta Lemme, great collectors and generous donators, notably to the Louvre; Lester Little, director of the American Academy in Rome; Milton Gendel, an American who has had a passion for Rome for fifty years, and his wife Monica Incisa, a talented designer and illustrator; Raniero Gnoli, a remarkable connoisseur of everything relating to marble and the crafts in general; Alvar Gonzalez Palacios, an art historian who enjoys living in Rome, writing in Paris and dreaming in Spain, and whose help has been invaluable; Priscilla Grazioli, who maintains the tradition of great family marble firms; Jean Guéguinou, French ambassador to the Holy See, successor to Pauline Borghese at the Villa Bonaparte, which he kindly let us visit; Renato Laschena, president of the Council of State, thanks to whom we were able to visit the Palazzo Spada; Maurice Lévy, manager of the Hotel Eden; Olimpia Marini Clarelli, for his support and kindness at the Galleria Doria Pamphili; Bertrand and Piera Marret, who are lucky enough to live in a studio once used by Picasso; Marco Cesar Naslausky, Brazilian ambassador to the Holy See, and his wife Sandra, who brought a personal touch to the apartments in the Palazzo Caetani; Princess Maria Massimo Lancellotti, for her advice; Alessandro Merola, plenipotentiary minister, for his support in numerous initiatives; Marisita Notas, for her help at the Museo Barracco, Princess Martini Orsini, for her advice; Princess Pallavicini, who was kind enough to open up the private apartment of her palace to us; her daughter Princess Maria-Camilla Pallavicini, who enabled us to visit the famous Casino dell'Aurora; Emanuele Pantanella, who has gone from running the family businesses to creating objets d'art; the Marchioness Florence Patrizi, for her advice and addresses; Catherine Payling, who is in charge of the Keats-Shelley Memorial; the Dominican fathers of Santa Sabina; Raymond and Janine Petri-Guasco, pillars of the French community in Rome; Mario Pieroni, who worked in Rome with the greatest artists of our day; Ludovico Pratesi, art critic and defender of the younger generation of artists; Elisabetta Rasy, a subtle and passionate novelist; Dominique Reviller, librarian at the French Academy in Rome; Franco Sapio, who opened the gardens of the Quirinal for us; Jacques and Nadine Schneider, lovers of Rome and its gardens; Letizia Signorini, for the generous help she gave me in enriching my knowledge of Rome; Dora Stiefelmeier, who has been working for years with Mario Pieroni in support of contemporary art; Monsignor Terrancle, who helped us in our dealings with religious institutions; Michela Terreri, secretary to successive directors of the Villa Medici, invaluable for her kindness and efficiency; Dino Trappetti, who upholds the reputation of the Tirelli firm; Ambassador Umberto Vattani, general secretary of the Italian Ministry of Foreign Affairs; Roberto Wirth, manager of the Hotel Hassler; Dante Zanon, who continues the tradition of marble craftsmanship.

I would like to thank in particular Ghislaine Bavoillot, head of the Art de Vivre department at Flammarion, for her constant attention, and her assistants, notably Hélène Boulanger and Blandine Serret for her patient rereading, as well as Frédéric Vitoux, the author of *Art de Vivre à Venise*, who suggested I share my passion for Rome.

Bruno Racine

The proposition to collaborate with Bruno Racine on this portrait of Rome—a city we both love—was due to his friendship and trust. Reciprocal feelings prompted me to accept without hesitatation what was for me a new photographic exercise, one for which other were patently better prepared than I. The optimism and convivial hospitality of Béatrice, Bruno's wife, proved precious for our morale. Ghislaine Bavoillot provided constant useful guidance from a distance and kept us on course. Finally, without Danielle Schirman, this adventure would quite simply have been impossible, since Rome has been our adventure and our joint possession for years. I would like to thank friends, old and new, as well as chance acquaintances, who kindly opened their doors so that we could carry out our geometrical tightrope-walking operations. As for Rome and Romans, we owe them more than any homage could express.

Alain Fleischer